THE BRUCE BECKONS

Barrow Bay

After etchings by John Byrne

THE BRUCE
BECKONS

The Story of Lake Huron's Great Peninsula

By WILLIAM SHERWOOD FOX
Former President, University of Western Ontario

DRAWINGS BY CLARE BICE
AND VINCENT ELLIOTT

REVISED AND ENLARGED EDITION

UNIVERSITY OF TORONTO PRESS
TORONTO AND BUFFALO

BY WILLIAM SHERWOOD FOX

THE BRUCE BECKONS

ST. IGNACE: Canadian Altar of Martyrdom

'T AIN'T RUNNIN' NO MORE

THE LETTERS OF WILLIAM DAVIES

THE MYTHOLOGY OF GREECE AND ROME

*To the Men and Women of The Bruce
who accepted the challenges
of a hard land and moody waters
with brave hearts and smiling faces*

ACKNOWLEDGEMENTS

THIS book would never have been written but for the generous help accorded me by many friends. Of all the documents that I have found to be of real service *The History of Bruce County*, published by the late Mr. Norman Robertson of Walkerton in 1906, stands indisputably in the first place. Most of the articles on the Bruce Peninsula that have appeared since then have been based upon passages in that book; few indeed have been derived from other records or from independent observations.

To the *Queen's Quarterly* and to *Inland Seas* (the bulletin of the Great Lakes Historical Society) I am grateful for permission to include as chapters in this book papers of mine that originally were printed in these journals. In retelling stories of nearly a century of shipwrecks I am under obligation to *Saturday Night* of Toronto and to the *Daily Sun-Times* of Owen Sound, in whose columns accounts of some of the wrecks have appeared at sundry times during the last fifty years. To the *Canadian Lumberman* and to Walter M. Newman of Wiarton I am indebted for many of the details recorded in the chapter, "And the Trees Trooped Out."

Much of the material that is published here for the first time has been drawn out of the memories of several of the Peninsula's oldest inhabitants; worthy of special mention are: William Gilchrist (who died in Owen Sound at the age of ninety-two on February 28 of this year); Charles Williams (who died at the age of eighty in Lion's Head on January 15); Robert Lymburner, of Owen Sound, eighty-nine; Canon R. W. James, long Sky Pilot of Lion's Head, who is now enjoying active retirement in Port Burwell, Ontario. To various sources of information already in print I have been guided by Howard Fleming of Owen Sound; J. Stuart Fleming of Niagara Falls, New York, and Owen Sound; Roy F. Fleming of Ottawa; James Baillie Jr. of the Royal Ontario Museum of Zoology, Toronto; Norman Fee of the Public Archives of Canada, Ottawa; Dr. Percy J. Robinson, Toronto; Dr. Fred Landon, London, author of *Lake Huron*; the staff of the Canadian Hydrographic Service, Ottawa. It was Miss Edith L. Marsh of Clarksburg, Grey County, who generously placed at my disposal the late Peter Trout's manuscript, "What I Know of John Muir." Shortly before his lamented death, my old friend, Arthur Stringer, Canadian poet and novelist, gave permission to quote from one of his new poems the lines that fittingly head the chapter, "Lilacs and Log Cabins."

Among my former colleagues of the University of Western Ontario who have unstintingly assisted me in numerous ways are: Professors W. F. Tamblyn, G. H. Reavely, Helen Battle, N. C. Hart; Dr. J. J. Talman, and Miss Lillian Benson of the Library. Through their skilful, interpretative sketches Clare Bice and Vincent Elliott, both former students of mine and among my companions on many a ramble in the Peninsula, have given this book an atmosphere quite beyond my unaided power to create. Another former student, Mr. Archie Stevens of London, has rendered valuable service in making the publication of the book known to the reading public. In writing the text I have found my daughter, Katharine Sherwood Fox, a consistently exacting and stimulating critic and in the reading of proof vision itself. My friend Mr. Donald Campbell of Goderich has graciously given me experienced assistance in ways too various to specify. From the author's point of view his relations with the University of Toronto Press have been of the happiest and in every respect most helpful. No small measure of such qualities as *The Bruce Beckons* may possess is to be credited to the several representatives of the Press with whom I have conferred, notably the Editor, Professor George Brown, and Miss Eleanor Harman, and their associates, Misses Francess Halpenny and M. Jean Houston.

London, Ontario
August 1, 1952

W. SHERWOOD FOX

NOTE TO THE REVISED EDITION

I have taken the opportunity provided by this new printing to add a sketch of Tobermory, Scotland, by Clare Bice, as a companion to that of "Little Tub." I have included also, as an appendix, additional material on the lumbering industry in The Bruce, which rounds out the story of chapter 16, "And the Trees Trooped Out."

W.S.F.

SPONSORS OF *THE BRUCE BECKONS*

Native sons and residents of Bruce County, the Bruce Peninsula and neighbouring places, Councils and Service Clubs of the district, whose gracious sponsorship of this volume is gratefully welcomed by the publishers and the author

THE HONOURABLE LEIGHTON MCCARTHY	*Toronto*
Former Ambassador of Canada to the United States	
SENATOR JAMES A. MACKINNON	*Ottawa*
Former Minister of Trade and Commerce	
J. W. RANSBURY	*Tobermory*
Warden of the County of Bruce	
JAMES EDWARD MCCONNELL	*London*
ALLAN MCLAY	*Stokes Bay*
MR. AND MRS. A. B. SAMELLS	*Sauble Forest*
MR. AND MRS. T. A. SINE	*Hepworth*
WILLIAM H. WOOD	*Lion's Head*
FRED BRUIN	*Lion's Head*
ROY GREIG	*Lion's Head*
MR. AND MRS. CARL WHICHER	*Colpoy's Bay*
HOWARD FLEMING	*Owen Sound*
J. STUART FLEMING	*Niagara Falls, N.Y., and Owen Sound*
DOWSLEY KENNEDY	*Owen Sound*
CUYLER HAUCH, M.D.	*Owen Sound*
E. E. PATERSON	*Wiarton*
A. B. CORDINGLEY	*Wiarton*
ROY F. FLEMING	*Ottawa and Fishing Islands*
CHESTER MCDIARMID	*Port Elgin*
RALPH PEQUEGNAT	*Port Elgin*
MORLEY LYMBURNER	*Port Elgin*
CECIL BOWMAN	*Southampton*
BRUCE PENINSULA RESORT ASSOCIATION	*Wiarton*
TOWN COUNCIL	*Wiarton*
ROTARY CLUB	*Hepworth-Shallow Lake*
ROTARY CLUB	*Southampton*
ROTARY CLUB	*Tara-Allenford*
ROTARY CLUB	*Wiarton*

CONTENTS

PART FIVE: FOREST AND WOODSMAN

PART SIX: SKY PILOT AND SETTLER

APPENDIX

ILLUSTRATIONS

AN INTRODUCTION

AT his first sight of the Bruce Peninsula the visitor cannot but be aware of a land astonishingly unlike any he has seen before. The kind of shock he gets—pleasant or the contrary—depends upon his own particular way of looking upon the world of physical things. The tidy soul who feels no thrill except in cosy landscapes or in fitting every act of life into the pigeonhole marked for it by a community long set in the ways of propriety, will not be apt to warm to The Bruce. But he will never forget what he saw there. If, on the other hand, the visitor delights in rough wild tracts of land and water and is eager to wander long among uncouth scenes, he is ready to fall in love with The Bruce at once. And in this propensity he belongs to the great majority. Happily, it seems to be true that most men, despite the stifling effects of modern life, still keep alive in their souls the race's rare power to perceive in any wilderness—however barren, unfriendly, and unkempt—witcheries that beckon to quest and adventure. In qualifications of that order The Bruce is indeed extraordinarily rich.

But you do not have to see the Peninsula itself to find cause for marvelling about it. Only look intently at its outline on the map of mid–North America. In regard to all Lake Huron it is a sword that has cleaved a body clean in twain: instead of one lake there are two. From another point of view it is a spear piercing the very heart of the Great Lakes; yes, the heart, for the point of the blade lies almost halfway between the east end of Lake Ontario and the west end of Superior, very close indeed to the centre of the lake system's channels of traffic and travel. Again, in the eyes of sailors this same land mass may be just a formidable obstacle dropped most inconveniently across routes which would otherwise be short and easy. Whatever figure of speech you employ, the obstacle forces itself upon your attention.

All the peoples who have lived in the Great Lakes region have,

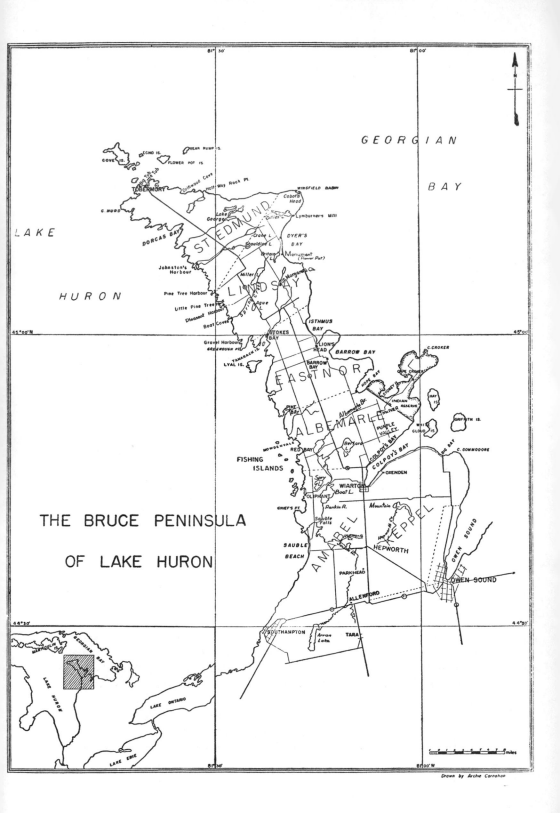

THE BRUCE PENINSULA

OF LAKE HURON

Drawn by Archie Carnahan

with dread, felt the great promontory to be a factor in their lives. Its size, shape, and situation have made it international. It is enough just now to note briefly why: it is international because it puts checks and limits upon the movements of whole peoples. For centuries it was effective among the numerous Indian nations, then, successively, between Indians and French and between French and English. Later, when England-in-America split into two national units the colossal barrier of The Bruce made the Georgian Bay a closed British sea. Even today its dual influence endures. Politically a part of an Ontario county, the Peninsula is a giant causeway on which rests the last reach of a highway for the wheeled traffic of two nations. For many citizens of the United States it affords the best land route to Manitoulin Island, the North Shore of Lake Huron, and the hinterland that fans out beyond. For this service it is Nature we must thank. By leaving the great yawning mouth of Saginaw Bay to break the Michigan shoreline of Lake Huron, she funnels a host of northbound travellers into a direct thoroughfare on the Canadian side of the lake.

. In still another realm Nature has made The Bruce a land of more than one nation. Most appropriately has the tract been called "the great North American rendezvous of plants." Some mysterious complex of influences has drawn plants hither from all points of the compass. One marvellous plant alone, the Hart's Tongue fern, has, by a chain of green fronds, linked the Peninsula with every continent except South America and Australia. Of this bond and others like it the botanists of the world have long known. Through its plants The Bruce is a famous place.

Of such a land one who has long been held captive by its wonders can say many things, even many more than the weird medley the Walrus recited to Alice. Brought together, they might be called a history. But that thought compels me to make my position clear. The text that follows is *not* a history of the Bruce Peninsula; that is altogether too formal, too schoolish a title. I crave a strange privilege: I want to be allowed to call the book just a *holiday*—a holiday between covers—because, for the most part, I have put into it just what I liked. And that is precisely what my readers themselves do with those spells of freedom which the world calls holidays. Of course, as I know with keen regret, lack of time and space has made it necessary to leave out many things of great interest and importance. If the reader really insists upon having before him a detailed, diary-like history of our peninsula I direct him to volumes that merit the name, or bid him go a-digging for dates and events in the ancient dust of township offices and county registries. And if he seeks a hand-book to guide him by day to every vista worth seeing and, at the setting of the sun, to hostelries where he may rest from the fatigue of his wayfarings, I shall disappoint him even more.

One more word must be said. After all, the chief concern of this holiday of mine is not the things of The Bruce; rather is it the people who have lived, who still live, among these things. Always this question stands high above all else in my thoughts: How have these people "reacted" to the divers physical aspects of the Bruce Peninsula, the kindly and lovely things, the harsh and unfriendly things, among which they have chosen to live their lives? Long, intimate knowledge of them enables me to give a cheerful answer. The solid strength of character I know them as a group to possess they have acquired in the only way men can acquire that quality. Over the years they have from day to day, without amazement or dismay, faced each challenge of a hard land just as it came, and, after soberly taking its measure, have accepted it cheerfully and with courage.

PART ONE: THE BRUCE

"Little Tub"

Tobermory, Scotland
After a mural in the Cunard Company's Ivernia

Chapter 1

THE ROAD TO TOBERMORY

TO ramble with most profit in The Bruce we must be
certain of our bearings before leaving the beaten paths.
So let us away, on the winged wheels of fancy, for a quick
survey of this remarkable unit of land. On its small scale our
journey will not be unlike a flight from Land's End to John o'
Groats. There is one difference, as we shall see more clearly
presently: here, we have two Land's Ends from which to start.
One thing both journeys have in common: their destinations are
Scottish, for about three-quarters of a century ago the Tobermory
we seek was given its name by a lonely, homesick Scot.

According to d'Anville's map of 1755 the Peninsula had a name
of its own. In carefully formed letters it stands out clearly before
the eye: OUENDIAGUI. This is how a Frenchman would indicate its pronunciation; a person of English speech would probably
write it WENDIACHY. The word must be very ancient and
doubtless was the one used by Indians of the Huron family of
nations in speaking to Champlain about the rocky foreland that
reminded him of his familiar Brittany. In the opinion of a
Canadian scholar who has long made a close study of the Huron
language the name is highly suitable: he takes it to mean "island
or peninsula cut off." If that is so, the designation would aptly
fit either the Peninsula or the ancient portage route from the
present Wiarton by way of Boat Lake to Lake Huron. Assuredly,
so important a "carry" is a "cut off" *par excellence*. At this point
it is useful to recall that the pure Latin word *peninsula* and its
French counterpart, *presqu'ile*, both mean "near-island." But however appropriate Ouendiagui was as a name it did not stick,
doubtless because there were no longer enough Hurons left in
the region to keep it in circulation.

The Indian name of the Peninsula at the time the white man
began taking a serious interest in its soil and other resources
stems from a different linguistic stock, the Algonquin. When

3

Southampton was settled in 1848, the Peninsula was still an Ojibway hunting ground and bore its inhabitants' tribal name, "Saugink" or "Sauking," as it was first spelled in print, and now "Saugeen." Thanks to a lingering shred of sentiment this highly suitable name has not been wholly lost among the labels that clutter today's map. Some old-timers still speak of the "Saugeen Peninsula," and the greater part of Southampton lies in the Township of Saugeen. That, too, is the name of the comely river which, within the very town limits, pours into the great lake the clear spring waters of the Blue Mountains of Grey County. It is also the name of an area of submarginal sand and wildwood which, in the legal guise of generosity, the Crown has "reserved" for the Saugeen Indian "to have and to hold" forever as his homeland.

From Two Land's Ends to the Tobermory Road

Nature endowed the Bruce Peninsula with two Land's Ends— Owen Sound at the southeastern corner, Southampton at the southwestern. To the most casual eye the topographical cast of the country about each end is quite different. In simple general terms the terrain of the eastern end is elevated and creased with conspicuous hills and valleys, whereas that of the opposite end is relatively low and spread out into plains. This remark is of much more than local application: the type of terrain seen at Owen Sound prevails along the whole eastern flank of the Peninsula; similarly, the type observed at Southampton sets the pattern for the western flank to the very tip of Cape Hurd. Any traveller who seeks a true vision of the Peninsula as a unit of land will do best to start his journey at both Land's Ends; he will thus equip himself with a ready explanation of the varying contours of the territory through which he passes.

The problem of being in two places at once does not exist on such a trip as ours. So we shall set out from Owen Sound, our eastern Land's End, to span the few miles of paved highway to the Road to Tobermory; there we shall await our own return from a second start at our western Land's End, Southampton.

From Owen Sound

Among the cities of the central Great Lakes Owen Sound can boast of a site that is uniquely fascinating in its setting. It lies in a long, deep-sunk notch which, in the shape of a spearhead, jabs southward far into the thick mass of the Niagara Escarpment. This notch is the last reach of the lovely Sydenham River. Indeed, the notch was created partly by the stream itself in its efforts to attain the Georgian Bay and partly by the battering and grinding of successive glaciers. In general the valley floor is comparatively flat and lies but a few feet above the waters of the Sound outside, that is, normally, 581 feet above sea level. As we travel, that figure must be kept in mind.

In striking contrast to the level of the valley are the towering walls of limestone that form the two sides of the spearhead. As

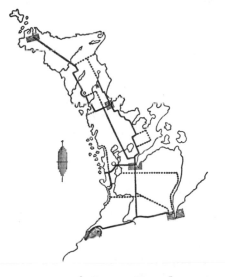

we leave the lower town of Owen Sound on our way west we have no choice but to scale one of these formidable walls. But the roadmakers long ago solved the problem. By a long, steep, but even gradient and a series of loops the highway lifts us to the upper level of an attractive suburb. What is of chief concern here is not the scene, however, but the elevation. Not far south of this point, states the official chart of the region, the land lies 850 feet above sea level. To touch the waters of Lake Huron proper, then, we must drop down 270 feet.

Here in a relatively small area we can see the nature of the land contours as far north as Cabot's Head and even beyond. The summit of the west bluff of that headland is only 40 feet higher than the highland overlooking Owen Sound. A moment of observation is enough to fix a major fact of the Bruce in our minds: like a gigantic stone slab the entire mass of the Peninsula is tilted towards the west. The conspicuous surface-wrinkles of hills and valleys may conceal the slant from the traveller, whether eastbound or westbound, but it is there all the same. The height of land is plainly visible only a furlong or two west of the cliffs that form the Peninsula's eastern wall. Hence nearly all The Bruce's watercourses flow into Lake Huron. The few that seek the Georgian Bay are of meagre volume, short, rapid, and noisy. So, then, as we move west from the elevated outskirts of Owen Sound we are going down hill. At the hamlet of Jackson we have already descended 60 feet and when we halt at the foot of the main road leading to our John o' Groats we shall have descended several more.

From Southampton

Resorting to the magic of fancy, we start now at our western Land's End. As we wheel off the town bridge to the north side of the Saugeen River at Southampton we find ourselves on a solid provincial thoroughfare that almost coincides with the east-west road allowance surveyed by Rankin in 1846 to link the Georgian Bay with Lake Huron. That line, we must observe, is virtually the base of the Peninsula. The highway—No. 21—leads us into the Saugeen Reserve and carries us through it for two or three miles. The unpleasant sight of slovenly tillage on either hand raises the question, Where shall one lay the blame for this sorry condition? Upon the unkind soil? Upon the folk for whom it was reserved in the name of kindness? Or—is it dangerous thinking even to play with the idea?—upon the mock philanthropy of the giver?

At our left a couple of roads cut north through the Reserve into an enticing tangle of woodland and promise to land us on the sands of the famous Sauble Beach. We ignore the temptation now in order to approach the place more profitably later by another route. So we carry on past the cluster of habitations embellished with the romantic name of Elsinore and thence, a couple of miles farther on, over the bridge spanning the Sauble River. For a quarter of a mile the highway swings in graceful curves that conform to the windings of the green-fringed stream that flows close to the very edge of the pavement. So smooth is our course that we are quite unaware we are going up hill; a few rods away from the river flats and within the limits of the village of Allenford, we are 750 feet above the sea, and before we end this present brief jaunt will have added a few feet to that figure.

As settlements go in these parts Allenford is among the oldest, and in its century of random growth it has gathered round it a certain rural aura that is akin to charm. What a pity, though, that our modern craze for standardization has stripped it of the finest adornment of its antiquity—its Indian name. At the shallows of the river recurring floods used to heap up into huge jams the broken branches and uprooted trunks carried downstream from the forests up-country. Over these uncouth bridges wayfaring Indians passed dryshod. So the place was called Driftwood Crossing. Even if retained only in translation the name would have given the community distinction.

Two miles east of Allenford we rejoin ourselves at our appointed rendezvous at the foot of the Road to Tobermory. Here a three-armed signpost carries the terse message: 14 miles from Southampton; 9 from Owen Sound; and, of major concern to us, 65 from Tobermory via Provincial Highway No. 6.

Up the "Spine" to Wiarton

No. 6, one should realize at the outset, is much more than a highway: it is a spinal column, the traffic backbone of the whole Peninsula. Along it flow, now up, now down, the vital impulses upon which all settled parts of this body of land depend for their normal activities and even for their very existence. True, this backbone is afflicted with a number of curvatures rather than with the easy curves one would expect, but it is nevertheless a backbone. The sideroads project from it on either hand and at various angles—right, acute, obtuse. What are these but ribs, true and false, or, as the anatomist would have us say, "sternal and floating." It is along these "rib-roads" that we shall find most of the scenes in which later on we shall linger.

Five minutes' drive brings us to Parkhead Junction and the tracks of the Canadian National Railway which here begin to descend eastward to Owen Sound. The cluster of homes not far to our left is of historical importance; near here in 1856 William Simpson became the first settler on the peninsular lands recently conveyed to the Crown by the Saugeen Indians.

Three miles past the railway we glide over a level tract into the straggling village of Hepworth. In the popular mind, which is apt to find a major amusement in slips of speech or plays upon words, this community has one distinction only: its name is encumbered with a superfluous letter. In the early days of the

settlement, it seems, the minister of the local Methodist cause, a
Reverend Mr. Green, a native of England, was asked to bestow
a name upon the place. At once, loyalty to his church brought to
mind John Wesley's birthplace—Epworth. His fellow-villagers,
ignorant of Methodist history, accepted the designation just as
they heard it pronounced, and "Hepworth," in print and on the
tongue, it is to this day.

At the crossroads in mid-village the traveller can quickly get
his bearings in reference to the surrounding territory. The road
to the left leads to Sauble Beach a few miles distant; the road
to the right is the paved short route to Owen Sound. As we halt
here we see a place that seems utterly barren of material interest;
the terrain is deadly flat and the whole scene drab. But we are
quite wrong: both above ground and below, Hepworth offers
the unusual.

This village whose situation seems to be depressingly low is
actually reposing on a broad plateau with an elevation of 710
feet. The ridge of sterile blow-sand that bounds the plateau on
the east, just a quarter of a mile away, is really a geological
monument, a precious relic of prehistoric antiquity—the shoreline of long-vanished Lake Algonquin, the predecessor of Lake
Huron.

Hepworth's other wonder is hidden from the eye. Deep down
under the village, through channels that pierce the limestone
foundations of the Peninsula, flows a watercourse. Sometimes,
especially in periods of flood and in the quiet watches of the
night, villagers hear, below the foundations of their homes, the
clamour of rushing water. Its source is Mountain Lake a few
miles to the northeast. A mile west of Hepworth the stream
bursts into the open as if fetched from the rock by Moses' rod,
and, with the volume of a river, flows, in a course of modest
length, through fields and woodland into the Sauble and thence
into Lake Huron. Under the name of Spring Creek it has long
been the most famous natural trout water in this part of Ontario.

As we drive northward out of Hepworth the puffing of a loco-
motive reminds us that we are running parallel to the railway.
Shortly, the rails cut obliquely across our path from west to east
and then begin to slip down the long gradient to the level of the
Wiarton docks. A mile south of the town limits two signs point,
one west to Boat Lake, the other east towards Kemble.

In the light of our present errand these pointers merit our

notice. Boat Lake, as has already been said, was the vital link in the age-old portage route between the Georgian Bay and Lake Huron. The lift from the end of Colpoy's Bay, the site of Wiarton, to the marshy reed-fringed lake is about four miles. From Boat Lake the traveller had a choice between two courses: either to paddle down the Rankin River and from there by way of the Sauble into Huron, or to make two short portages, first into Spry Lake and from there over a narrow neck into the big water. It is possible that in the early summer of 1701 the first company of Cadillac's settlers[1] used this portage route across the Peninsula on their way to the Detroit River. We know that they came by way of the Ottawa and the French; to resort to this short-cut between the Georgian Bay and Lake Huron would be the normal choice of guides acquainted with the distances and perils of these waters.

The sign pointing toward Kemble rouses the plant-lover within us. But as keeper of treasured rarities it behoves me to speak guardedly. In widely separated places, all hidden deep within the shaded clefts and cliffs of a heavy hardwood forest, are three colonies of the rare Hart's Tongue fern. That is all I may say: find them if you can, for the quest is, in itself, well worth while.

The view that greets us as we near Wiarton and the sparkling blue expanse of Colpoy's Bay is one of the most beautiful in the Canadian landscape. Around the shore is a frame of bold shining grey cliffs in a continuous, sharply drawn line. Far down the long bay to the northeast is the perfect background: three large wooded islands—Hay, White Cloud, and Griffith. Reluctantly we turn away as the highway drops smoothly over the edge of the Escarpment into Wiarton.

The site of this busy town, like the site of Oliphant, was laid out in the original survey of Amabel Township. Favoured by Nature and by founders of energy and vision the place was soon well on the way to good fortune. It seems to have received its first settler in 1866, but its lots were not put up for sale until 1868. The town lies both in and around a spacious half-bowl formed by a recession of the cliffs landward, that is, toward the west. Residences are scattered over high levels and low levels alike, but stores, offices, and factories are kept, literally, *down* town. Early, Wiarton became an active centre of the lumber industry, the story of whose heyday and decline we tell elsewhere.

1. Cadillac himself, for special reasons, took the longer route via Mackinac.

Today the place has two chief interests: on a large scale it serves the needs of numerous tourists, summer campers, and the permanent residents of an extensive countryside; if we have regard for trade only and shut our eyes to geography, it is truly "The Gateway to the Bruce Peninsula."

For us Wiarton is of special concern at this time in its role of a major vertebra in the spinal highway to Tobermory. From it branch off, one to the left, one to the right, two important "rib-roads." If we explore these in that order we shall go far towards understanding the geographical anatomy of the Peninsula.

West "Rib-road" to Oliphant and Sauble Beach

The west "rib-road" out of Wiarton is not unlike certain ribs of the human frame: its extremity does not lie at a right angle to the column from which the member springs. The extremity of the course we are pursuing is the mouth of the Sauble River, nine air-miles southwest of Wiarton.

Our road leaves Wiarton close to the summit of the height of land that guards the town on the west as with a vertical defensive wall of stone. For a mile or two the pavement runs, with minor ups and downs and bends, at an elevation above the sea varying between 725 and 750 feet. Beyond that it begins to drop gradually but consistently. As we proceed we are interested by the number of excellent farms of considerable acreage and plainly bearing the marks of long settlement. Their substantial, tidy buildings testify to the quality of the soil and of the character of those who till it. On both sides of the road appear an increasing number of moisture-loving trees—soft maples, cedars, and tamaracs. Warned by these signs and by the perceptible descent in the grade, we are not surprised to find ourselves presently passing through a broad expanse of marsh. This is cut in two by the placid course of the Rankin River, which bears the waters of Isaac Lake southward into Boat Lake, the chief link, we recall, in the ancient portage route across the isthmus between Colpoy's Bay and Lake Huron.

For us, the significance of the Rankin River rests upon its place in the geography of this part of the Peninsula. The quiet marshland stream belongs to a drainage system that has its source on the cliff-bounded highlands hard by the Georgian Bay. We shall see that source later on our way to Hope Bay. The outlet of the system is the mouth of the Sauble River. Here have been deposited through the "sequent centuries" the sands and other soils filched from the slopes of the Peninsula's high eastern flank. These the winds and waves of Lake Huron have ironed out and moulded into Sauble Beach and its long-flung dunes. In this single small system of springs, brooks, and lakelets we can see in miniature the structure of a great continental watershed.

Three miles beyond the Rankin River bridge the highway sets us on the Lake Huron shore at Oliphant. This modest hamlet holds a less lowly place in regional history than its situation on the coastal flats would suggest. It was named after Laurence Oliphant who, in 1854, conducted the dealings with the Saugeen Indians that persuaded them to transfer their peninsular lands to the Crown. In the first survey of Amabel Township the place was given a plot generous enough to accommodate a small city. Since it lay on the mainland opposite the nearby Fishing Islands whose fishing industry, though past its prime, was still flourishing, no one doubted that Oliphant would quickly attain the status of a business centre. Soon, however, the lake became more and more niggardly in its yields and the villagers began to realize what they should have seen at the outset: that the coastal waters hereabouts, varying in depth from year to year with the cyclic levels of the lakes, were not such as would make a real port. So Oliphant never got past the stage of being a dream in blueprint. After thirty years of deferred hope a new generation of surveyors juggled the once hopeful townlots into the farmlands that spread along the waterfront today. Oliphant's present role is that of a humble little port of embarkation for anglers, tourists, and campers who seek sport, rest, health and a unique type of scenery among the Fishing Islands or in sundry airy resorts along the rocky shore.

The one-time sandy trail from Oliphant to Sauble Beach is now a good modern thoroughfare. It guides the traveller through a motley but highly interesting scene: sand flats, dunes of various shapes and sizes, mixed stands of conifers and hardwoods, and tantalizing glimpses of swampy recesses that are the natural home of our most gorgeous orchids and other water-loving plants. If we are strong enough in purpose to resist the temptations of these sights, the road will without delay carry us across the bridge by Sauble Falls, past the County Forestry Station, and thence, through a series of loops, to the mouth of the peninsular "River of the Sands."

Here we stand and look into the south. Before us spreads, on either hand, a flat strip of tawny sand several hundred yards wide. Furlong by furlong, the strip draws away from our vision southward, rapidly losing breadth in the narrowing perspective until at last, miles away, it blends with the white of the breaking surf into a blurred line that loses itself in the haze of the horizon. This spacious sandy border of Lake Huron, far from being a vacant, solitary tract, is filled with life. It is at once a roomy playground eminently safe and inviting for bathing, and a highway for wheeled traffic. In summer it is virtually a metropolitan street.

On the landward side Sauble Beach is bounded by a sand dune as long as the Beach itself. Its long, continuous summit is crowned by a monotonous procession of summer residences ranging from near-mansions to the crudest of makeshift shelters. East of the frontal dune and parallel to it is still another dune and behind that still another. But more interesting than the dunes themselves are the spaces between them—the long, narrow, swampy troughs of sand enriched with the wealth of age-old humus. Not many years ago they were golden streets of a botanist's Elysium, paved with rare orchids and gay bladderworts. Thanks to neglect and the hand of the vandal little of their splendour remains. Here again, as in many another lovely corner of earth, man in his blindness has laid upon Nature's body wounds now long past healing.

In making our way back along the "rib-road" to Wiarton we could with pleasure and profit essay a hasty jaunt upshore. We could run on, for instance, to Red Bay and Howdenvale, resorts graced by charms all their own. We could even cross the appalling coastal flats as far north as Big Pike Bay and in so doing learn what a "limestone pavement" really is. But moderation counsels us to return to our main road, lest in a multitude of things seen we miss the very thing we desire most—a comprehensive vision of The Bruce as a clear-cut unit of land.

East "Rib-road" from Wiarton to Lion's Head and St. Margaret's

The junction of No. 6—which, by the way, is also Wiarton's Main Street—and of the right-hand "rib-road" lies two miles north of town. It is now easily reached, thanks to the modern road-builder, who has literally sliced through a lofty cliff a long, steep, tunnel-like passage. At the first glance eastward along our new road we are apt to be deceived: it is not going to give us the simple direct course it seems to promise at the junction. The fact is that it abounds in angles rather than the gentle curves one would expect in a rib. Yet in spite of its deformities it is an indispensable member of the body of The Bruce. Indeed, in every sense it is the chief support of its long eastern flank.

In a few minutes we drop down close to the north shore of Colpoy's Bay and into the substantial village of the same name. This settlement, the first we meet in Albemarle Township, is a few years older than Wiarton. Here the right-of-way swings sharply to the north and inland and, except for two right-angled bends, maintains that direction for eight miles.

Not far beyond Colpoy's is a guidepost we should not miss. It beckons eastward to a place with an intriguing name—Purple Valley; unfortunately, just now we can do no more than muse upon it. Yet how welcome is even a verbal hint of a splash of brightness in a land dominated everywhere by a brooding background of gray. What there is about this modest crossroads hamlet to merit so royal a title is one of the mysteries of local history. Nevertheless, the place has a certain distinction, a distinction it shares with McIver, a village a mile or two to the north. Both lie close to a wild, rocky tract of dense forest in whose deep shadows lurk many a clump of that much-sought fern, the Hart's Tongue. Plant-lovers almost reverence this corner of the Peninsula. That Nature here keeps a safe guard over her treasure I know too well; it cost me many years of search to find my first frond of this lowly, timid herb.

Beyond Purple Valley there reaches toward the northeast and far into the Georgian Bay a mass of land of considerable area: it is actually a peninsula projecting from a peninsula, and in shape, when viewed on the map, reminds one of an oversized spur attached to an enormous heel. This territory, long set aside by the Crown as the Cape Croker Indian Reserve, is little known except in name. It deserves better recognition than is given it, for those who know regard it as an outstanding example of the kind of provision we can make to enable the Indians to develop strong, healthy communities of their own. This reserve is well worth a visit; it is rich in history and abounds in scenes of natural beauty. It merits what cannot, of course, be given here—a whole book.

We can only muse on Purple Valley, we must pass the signpost and go on our way northward. At the second elbow in the road let us pause for a basic lesson in geography. A few rods from the roadside, amid clumps of red osier dogwood and dwarf willow,

is the fountainhead of the natural drainage system to which we
have already referred, a system that conveys its waters across
the Peninsula, first into Isaac Lake and thence, through the
Rankin and Sauble rivers, ultimately into Lake Huron. Here in
its first reach it is known as Albemarle Brook. A couple of miles
north of its springs is a ridge from which in one sweep we can
view the broad expanse of Hope Bay. Down a short side-road and
around a veritable devil's elbow we twist to the shore.

No other indentation on the east coast can show an unbroken
wall of perpendicular cliffs of equal grandeur. Indeed, Hope Bay
reminds us of a colossal stadium floored with blue, its broad, open
end affording an unsurpassed view of the Georgian Bay. But the
place has other claims upon our attention as well as those of
scenery. Like Oliphant, Hope Bay is the locale of an unhappy
venture of enthusiastic pioneers into the treacherous field of real
estate. Doubtless it was from such ill-spent hope that the place
got its name. The 2000-acre tract of forest that sloped upward and
westward from the end of the bay was early plotted into a grid-
iron of town lots and adorned with a pleasing designation—Adair.
But Adair never emerged from the realm of bright expectations.
For lots put up at auction in 1880 there were no buyers. Adair
now exists only as a mirage lingering among other odds-and-ends
in the memory of the antiquarian and as a forgotten item on the
pages of Albemarle's registry.

In a course that loops like a serpent and rolls like the sea the
road sways and rocks us pleasantly through scenes of alternating
forest and farm from Hope Bay to Barrow Bay. Here, on the very
edge of a lofty plateau, Judge's Creek (one of the few streams to
wear its way eastward through the height of land) bisects the
village perched on the naked rock and cascades noisily into a deep
craggy gorge. Thence it slips into a lakelet sheltered, on all sides
except the east, by precipitous cliffs. To the fern-fancier I com-
mend a visit to the chaos of immense angular limestone boulders
gathered at the base of the cliffs. On their shaded, mossy sides
thrive many kinds of the daintiest rock-loving ferns that grow. A
patient quest will be well repaid. The seeker can hardly fail to
come upon the strangest fern of all—the Walking Fern, the
Daddy-long-legs of our native plants, which steps delicately over
the bare face of the limestone on its threadlike fronds.

Our next pause is in the picturesque village of Lion's Head. It
lies on Isthmus Bay, an indentation gouged out of the Escarpment
by the last glacier. Its picturesque name comes from the profile of

a lion's head that overhangs the Georgian Bay from the shaggy brow of a nearby cliff. The place though small in area and population has always been of great regional importance. On its own modest scale it is a port with a two-way traffic; it is what business would call an *entrepôt*. In its time it has played a changeful role in the very changeful industry of fishing. In this day of better roads and swifter motor cars it is a popular rendezvous in summer for tourists and campers, and all the year round for the inhabitants of a large territory.

Still looking into the north we climb out of Lion's Head to the summit of a high ridge from the far side of which we presently slip down, with a pleasure that increases with each rod we advance, into one of Ontario's most impressive natural scenes. For two miles the road hugs the very brink of a lofty limestone bench. From this point of vantage we can see far below us on our right almost every foot of the wave-washed shoreline of Isthmus Bay.

At the north end of this straight course the road, at first to our regret, turns us inland. Soon we discover it is leading us into a veritable labyrinth, or rather plunging us into a heaving sea of soil and rock; we are among the Forty Hills. Here a driver needs to keep a tight rein on his nerve, ever alert to cars suddenly dashing towards him as out of nowhere, or to the still greater peril of local horse-drawn vehicles overtaken from behind. Now we understand what our friends have told us of the east side of the Peninsula. The hills are indeed high and abrupt and, by the same token, the valleys deep and sudden. Did ever a road bend in more awkward places? But we can take comfort from the thought that every Sunday in all weathers, fair or foul, in winter as in summer, many people safely pass this way to church. If we boldly essay every corkscrew twist and let no declivity however startling daunt us, we too shall reach that same destination.

There it stands before us on the crown of one of the Forty Hills—St. Margaret's of Cape Chin. To many it is the Stone Church of the Wildwood. Let us halt beside it; the scenes to which the road would lead us farther on—Dyer's Bay and Gillies Lake—can best be reached by another and less tortuous route. Just now it is of greater profit to our souls and more restful to our bodies to pause and ponder here a little while. The story of how the walls and tower and roof of this little House of God raised themselves stage by stage out of the rocks of the hills, out of the trees of the forest, will be told at length elsewhere in this book.

FROM WIARTON TO JOURNEY'S END

Back again at the crossroad two miles out of Wiarton we resume our course toward Tobermory. To the natives this highway, smooth surfaced at least in summer over most of its length, is appropriately known as the Centre Road. The cost of building it so solidly in the early twenties must have been greater than the assessment of the entire Peninsula at the time. Nevertheless, this generous gift of a short-lived "Farmers' Government" has been for nearly three decades a channel carrying a steadily increasing inflow of prosperity into the Peninsula.

After a straight westward reach of two miles we come to the first marked "curvature" in the "spine." Rounding this to the right we find ourselves facing northwest on a highway that holds tight to that quarter for a score of miles. Ever on the lookout for crossways we soon spot the first one: the west arm leads to Isaac Lake and the east to Berford Lake. Just beyond, Albemarle Brook hurries across our course on its way to Lake Huron. Then for a considerable distance we pass through haylands, sparse pastures, and stands of mixed hardwood. Here and there we espy on the left trails promising to guide us to places on the Huron shore that we have already noticed—Red Bay, Howdenvale, and Big Pike Bay.

But of a sudden the landscape changes: over the brow of a barren gray ridge we fairly dive into a spread of lush green, a broad flat tract of cedar and tamarac—the Eastnor Swamp. The road shoots through it straight as an arrow. Then, rod by rod, the trees thin out, stricken down over the years by fire and axe, and in their place stretches a wide expanse of well-drained grasslands, tilled fields, and tidy homesteads. It is plain even to a greenhorn that this was once the bed of a prehistoric lake; from its rich store of silt many families now draw goodly livings. Through this comfortable pastoral scene we continue until we come to a junction conspicuously labelled Ferndale. To the right a mile or two distant lies Lion's Head; this we shall not attempt to revisit, but, leaving the main thoroughfare for a time, we swerve to the left. In so doing we are not adding to the length of our journey: we are but choosing two sides of a large rectangle in preference to the other two, because they add variety to our knowledge of The Bruce.

We head towards Lake Huron till an arrow pointing to Stokes

Bay—and Tobermory—turns us north. The road we are now on is at once important and interesting. It is important in that it serves in a year many thousands of people—hordes of cottagers and campers as well as the inhabitants of the region. It is interesting because it is the last reasonably good relic of the Road to Tobermory of forty years ago. Though "improved," it retains in no small measure its original, primitive features.

A six-mile sample of trail-breaking for wheeled traffic through a rough terrain of rock and dense stands of mixed forest, it is a veritable museum piece among roads. Like the road through the Forty Hills on the east side, it is a natural roller-coaster, but its hills are lower and shorter and follow each other in closer succession. Locally they are known by a less formidable, kindlier name—Seven Sisters. But are they not really seventy? One of the "sisters" will suddenly throw you backward and in a moment, before you can steady yourself, will toss you forward against the windshield. The next of the Seven, on the very crest of a sharp rise, will fling you to the left, and, before you can straighten your course, jerk you back to the right. One after another this family of hills makes the car a bucking bronco on wheels. Unable to see ahead through rock ridges and around corners you drive on in fear and trembling. Can we wonder now at the tales of the first motorists who ventured this way, at the bouts they had with sea-sickness before they got to Tobermory? It is with relief to body and mind that we bid the Seven Sisters farewell as we ride smoothly into the village of Stokes Bay.

From this typical Lake Huron fishing settlement we bounce northward over a short series of ridges which, in their treatment of travellers, are akin to the Seven Sisters. Soon we cross the township line from Eastnor into Lindsay and then rejoin No. 6. The junction marks the beginning of a genuine curvature in the "spine"—a semi-circle that swings around the west end of little Lake Ira. This uncomely expanse of mud, rushes, and water is an object lesson in the transient character of lakes. Plainly, Lake Ira, like several others in the Peninsula, is well on its way to becoming an open flatland of deep, rich soil. Nature is slowly filling its basin. Each year's rains and melting snows wash into it more earth from its sloping banks. Into this fertile bed Nature plants the thick, fleshy roots of pickerel weed, cat-tails, and water lilies. The coarse network catches and holds the humus of the

annual decay of leaf and stem and twig. Some day the floor of
Lake Ira will be green and orderly with gardens. On a grand scale
of space and time Lake St. Clair offers the same lesson.

As we press on to The Tub haste must not be allowed to hide
from us another little body of water—Ague Lake. An opening
through second-growth hardwood on our left leads to it. Here, in
the low water of late summer, lies a broad sheet of smooth limestone on which the last glacier has written the record of its
passage. In deeply incised parallel lines (which geologists call
striae) it tells us plainly it came from the northeast and moved
on into the southwest.

Half a mile beyond Ague Lake a bridge carries us across Spring
Creek, better known as Rattlesnake Creek, a trout brook of note
meandering westward through a tangle of alder thickets to Boat
Coves. Soon on our left we see signposts directing wayfarers to
such well-known coastal inlets as Pleasant Harbour, Little Pine,
and Big Pine, the latter two being perfect landlocked basins for
small craft and for schools of black bass seeking food in shallow
waters.

We now find ourselves in the very heart of the territory of
limestone pavement. It is the scene of an unlucky experiment
with sheep-raising on a grand scale—the Miller Lake Ranch.
Wolves and a growth of grass too stingy even for sheep ended
the enterprise summarily. But the tract, though unkind to live-
stock, is by no means a waste. Thirty years ago it lay stripped by
fire of trees and herbage, its stark gray rock glaring skyward.
Today it is cloaked with a strong stand of jackpine. How un-
quenchable the spark of life! In the midst of this self-revived
patch of forest an important "rib-road" branches off to the east.
Its frayed ends on the Georgian Bay lead to Gillies Lake, Dyer's
Bay, and the only "flowerpot" on the mainland—the Monument,
or, as it is known to some, the Devil's Pulpit.

Putting off to another day a ramble in that quarter we roll on
to the last reach—almost straight as a die—of the spinal highway.
We are now up to the very shoulders of the Peninsula, the thickest
part of its body. Just beyond the township line between Lindsay
and St. Edmund we pass over the bridge that spans the Crane
River. Here a gravelled trail crosses our route. To the west it
winds through a heavy forest of tall spruce and healthy second-
growth pine to Johnston's Harbour; to the east it will take us to
McVicar, the site of the first saw mill to be set up in these
northern parts, and to a revelation of what the will and skill of

man can achieve in his fight against hard lands: the most charming farm home in the Peninsula and mile-long ribbons of haylands sliced out of dense mixed forest.

As we speed along the highway, now graded to a four-lane width, we resist the lures of the byways beckoning the traveller to sand dunes and beaches, to the haunts of the elusive trout, to lakes concealed by heavy stands of red oak. Fields spread out on both sides, houses become more numerous, and in a minute we are slipping past rows of them lining a real street that leads down to the water's edge. Here we find a tidy harbour neatly framed in a border of docks beside which are moored a great variety of craft ranging from rowboats to imposing cruisers. This is Tobermory's inner haven, Little Tub. A short way off we see the big steam ferry beside her wharf. Northwest of us and on the other side of a great rocky projection, lies Big Tub.

A glance at Tobermory itself will give us at least a partial understanding of its life and importance. Some people call the place a harbour, but they fall short of the truth. Tobermory is two harbours, or rather three. Together the three form two havens, an inner haven for smaller craft and an outer haven for ships of deep draft and heavy burthen. The inner haven consists of two marvellous, canal-like channels that lie close to each other —Big Tub and Little Tub—each cut evenly out of the limestone by an ancient glacier as with an instrument of fine precision. Its perpendicular sides are natural wharves. The outer haven is most impressive—a circular basin three or four miles in diameter shielded from violent winds by an arc of lofty islands that stretches from west to east, a basin spacious enough and deep enough to give safe shelter to a whole navy. Tobermory is one of the great havens of the world.

Who among its many settlers of Scottish birth or descent gave it its name? Nobody now knows. But whoever he was he must have been a man of Mull, for no other could at a glance see how like the Tobermory of his native isle was new-found Collins Inlet, at the peak of the Saugeen Peninsula. The manifest resemblance so warmed his heart that he could not resist changing its name to something that kept bright every day the memory of his Scottish island home. So Collins Inlet became Tobermory or, in the homely vernacular of the region, "Tubbermurry," or just plain *"The Tub."* Perhaps in the words that follow we too can perceive some features common to the two harbours, one of the Old World, the other of the New.

We got safely and agreeably into the harbour of Tobermory, before the wind, which for some days has always risen about noon, came onward. Tobermory is really a noble harbour. An island lies before it; and it is surrounded by a hilly theatre. . . . There will be sometimes sixty or seventy sail here. There was [*sic*] today twelve or fourteen vessels. To see such a fleet was the next thing to seeing a town. The vessels were from different places. . . . After having been shut up in Coll, the sight of such an assemblage of moving habitations gave me much gaiety of spirit. Mr. Johnson said, "Boswell is now all alive. He is like Antaeus; he gets new vigour whenever he touches land." I went to the top of a hill fronting the harbour, and took a good view of it.

Boswell wrote those lines on October 14, 1773, during his visit to the Hebrides with Dr. Johnson. With a few changes of detail they can be read as a broadly treated sketch of the Tobermory we know in The Bruce of the Great Lakes of North America.

But not yet have we come to our goal. Veering to the right, we follow the convex edge of the sickle-shaped channel of Little Tub. Suddenly a gaunt limestone ridge lying athwart the right-of-way stops us short. Capping this barrier is a building holding aloft a legend that spells finality: TRAIL'S END. This is North Point, The Bruce's John o' Groats.

From the look-out perched on the ridge we gaze upon a majestic scene. To the northeast, perhaps four or five miles away, a couple of lonely islands rear green-capped heads—Flowerpot and Bear's Rump. Northwest of us an arc of islets and islands, from Doctor to Cove, enfolds a deep-water haven spacious enough to shelter an armada of the largest ships. The generous expanse of waters that reaches out toward the pole star is bounded in the remote background by a solid though faint line that might be either shadow or land. This is Great Manitoulin and its outlying islands.

Can we do other than pause and wonder? Though our reconnaissance has been as summary as the flight of a roving bird, we have seen much. By much I do not mean, of course, merely many things. What we have really seen and, perchance, understood, is a sharply defined, unique unit of land, a veritable country in itself, with a soul of its own. If we have understood this, then we shall also have understood something else of far greater moment—the folk who love to spend leisure days and weeks roaming over the face of this land, and, above all, the folk who have chosen to live their lives, for richer or for poorer, for better or for worse, within its borders.

Chapter 2

A GARDEN NORTHWARD

THE Lord God who planted a garden eastward in Eden did not forget to plant a garden northward as well. It is none other than the great clear-cut promontory of the Great Lakes of which we have just made a cursory survey, the Bruce Peninsula of Ontario, or, simply and crisply, The Bruce. Those who do not at once recognize the name know but little of this corner of the world. But a garden? you protest. This long, steel-grey blade that cleaves a whole lake in two? Yes, truly a garden. I know it well. Moreover, it is a garden which has served as a model for many a rockery designed to brighten the drab corners of cramped city lots. A rock garden is a garden for a' that.

Let the unbeliever go to the Peninsula in May, when the lowly Bird's Eye Primula drapes the gravels and shingles of the lake shore as with scarves of pale voile; when the Dwarf Iris, native only to the north part of Lake Huron, lays strips of green, dotted with the blue and gold of tiny *fleur de lis*, along the beaches above the high-water line. Or go in mid-June when the damp, sandy flats of the lakeside inlets are covered with mile-long rugs, more gorgeous than Persia ever dreamed, woven of mingled scarlet Painted Cup, Blue-eyed Grasses, and Golden Ragwort. Or go even in July when the boggy nooks among the tamaracs are lighted by the most colourful of our native orchids, the stately rose-purple and white Queen Lady Slipper. Even a fleeting glimpse of any of these will banish all remnants of the ancient prejudice that where there is rock life is not. Are not the rocks the very stuff that soil is made of? Are not the pockets, both great and small, which catch and hold the soil—the chinks, fissures, gullies, and valleys—carved out of rock?

Yes, The Bruce is a garden, a garden fostering many orders of the race of plants—herbs, grasses, sedges, mosses, lichens, ferns, shrubs, and trees. It abounds, too, in beasts and in fowls of the air. Even that "humblest beast of the field," the serpent, is there,

21

and, as in the garden planted eastward, has its part to play in the northern gardener's life.[1]

Altogether, The Bruce has within its narrow bounds a host of those things that have always roused wonder in the souls of men—those that fly, those that move upon the land, those that swim in the waters. The author of the Book of Proverbs could have written of The Bruce: "There are three things which are too wonderful for me . . . the way of an eagle in the air; the way of a serpent upon a rock; the way of a ship in the midst of the sea." All these may be seen by one who goes about The Bruce with open eyes.

But this land is above all a garden of trees; so the story of the garden is in no small part a story of how the trees have been tended by the keepers of the garden. In a most spectacular way they gave a defiant answer to Macbeth's indignant question:

> Who can impress the forest, bid the tree
> Unfix his earth-bound root?

For the keepers allowed the forest to be impressed, and the trees to march out in unending columns along the ruthless ways of commerce. But to understand all this we must know something of the making of the garden.

In essaying to describe so great a natural phenomenon as the Bruce Peninsula I find myself in a dilemma. The words of a professional scientist will give us facts, but perhaps clouded by a haze of technical terms and untouched by wonder. On the other hand, the zealous nature-lover, apt to view the world in the rosy hues of his own feelings, may paint a picture which though pleasing can be misleading. But, happily, the dilemma is quickly resolved: a sequence of passages can be found that will set forth the facts and yet stir the imagination. In a book[2] of great charm their author leads his readers into the Bruce in such a way as to kindle in them the expectation of finding it to be a land abounding in wonders.

"Great geological formations have an uncanny habit of writhing up in unexpected spots," writes Professor Pease. ". . . The Niagara Escarpment has a way of disclosing itself in unforeseen places, sometimes in the form of high and often weirdly shaped cliffs,

---

1. See chapter XI, "The Serpent."
2. *Sequestered Vales of Life*, by Arthur Stanley Pease, Pope Professor of Latin Language and Literature, Harvard University, and formerly President of Amherst College; Harvard University Press, 1946, pp. 58–9. Permission to quote has been given by both author and publishers.

elsewhere in curious flat pavements of limestone. One is prepared for it at Niagara Falls, but less so in the woods south of
Syracuse; you cannot escape it as your train in Ontario climbs
laboriously westward." Were Professor Pease a resident of Ontario
he would surely have cited two other similar ascents of the Escarpment—the lumbering journey of the Canadian National to Guelph
and thence north to Wiarton; and the corkscrew climb of the
Canadian Pacific up the Caledon Mountain and over the height
of land, Ontario's Blue Mountains, which at Dundalk are 1700
feet above the sea.

"The old acquaintance," continues the author, "crops out in the
Bruce Peninsula, on Manitoulin Island, and in curiously sculptured
precipices near St. Ignace, only to sweep around to the west across
Michigan to northeastern Wisconsin. . . . The limestone 'pavements' may be seen at their best in the Bruce Peninsula and on
the neighboring Manitoulin Island, where it appears as though
the country were artificially paved with sterile flat slabs of limestone, separated at intervals of four or five feet by vertical cracks
a few inches in width, of considerable depth, and with little or
no trace of vegetation. When one looks into these cracks, however,
he discovers a strange but undeveloped flora of ferns and tiny
flowering plants, protected from the parching rays of the sun
and nourished by the richness of the limestone."

There is The Bruce in a nutshell. The sketch prods me to add
a touch or two to bring out my personal feelings however whim-
sical they be. Many years ago, long before steamers began to
carry motor cars between The Tub and South Baymouth on the
Manitoulin, I used to brood, in mild though futile resentment,
upon the hardship inflicted on man by the interposition of a broad
gaping strait between these two ports. I found that the old-
timers felt as I did. Nowhere does the ancient phrase, "so near
and yet so far," apply more aptly than here. The traveller who
wants to go to Manitoulin can stand on the cliffs by The Tub
and through the haze descry his destination as it were just over
the way. In horse-and-buggy days and when the automobile was
a novelty, anyone who desired to go on wheels from one of these
ports to the other had to make a veritable grand tour of several
hundred miles, in fact, the complete circuit of the Georgian Bay
clockwise or counter-clockwise, by way of Owen Sound, Barrie,
Gravenhurst, North Bay, Sudbury, and Little Current. Was the
Bruce Peninsula meant to be a bridge joining the north and south
mainlands of prehistoric Lake Algonquin, Huron's predecessor?

I am yielding, I know, to the false allurements of the great "pathetic" fallacy. Yet I seem to see, untold eras ago, great hands attempting to bridge the expanse of waters between southern Ontario and the North Shore. On the south coast of this span they set on end a colossal slab of grey stone and let it topple toward the north. Alas! the shock of the fall shatters its far extremity into many fragments. These still lie where they crashed, the islands of the strait—Fitzwilliam, Cove, Echo, Flowerpot, Bear's Rump, and many others. So what in my musing might have been a giant causeway now appears, on the map, as a narrow stone jetty that reaches out vainly toward a distant shore.

But fantasies solve no problems. Happily, we are not entirely ignorant of what has taken place. In some early twilight age, we are told, there was no space here to be bridged, for the Peninsula, Manitoulin, and the satellite islands were all one piece of the Escarpment. But what force was great enough to cleave the solid mass apart? The answer is simple: ICE. The ways of ice are wonderful and without number. The same force that breached a channel miles wide through the stone ramparts of the Escarpment also wrought upon them with a daintiness of touch that passes human marvel. Out of their hard faces it produced rock-flours of amazing fineness to become an ingredient of soil, and then carved out countless minute receptacles in which to hold it.

Whence did the ice-fields come and whither did they move? They have left behind them the records of their course. The most legible of these are delicately engraved on rock. Look for them on the broad sheet of dolomite that forms the east shore of shallow Ague Lake. They appear as fine parallel grooves scored into the shoreline as if by a gigantic harrow. All these scorings, undeviating as the rays of the sun, run straight into the southwest. Into that quarter, then, once rolled the ruthless juggernaut of the ice-sheet. Another record tells us from where the ice came: the hosts of "drift" boulders left behind it as it retreated reveal that the far-off northeastern land of its origin was none other than upper Labrador, the mother lode of such rocks as those of which the boulders are composed.

If we wish to know how the ice-masses do their work we do not have to go out of Canada; the ice-field of the Columbia River is a perfect object-lesson. The famous Agassiz once gave an impressive answer to our question: "The glacier is God's great plow." The comparison is as near to perfection as it could be. One day last summer I thought I had found a better one. A few miles south

The Glacier's Record of Its Path (Stokes Bay)[1]

of Tobermory we were forced to halt our car while a fleet of
ponderous modern bulldozers crashed through a limestone ridge
and a range of small gravel hills to open a new reach of Highway
No. 6. A parody of Agassiz's words slipped off my tongue: "The
glacier is God's bulldozer." But in a moment I humbly gave the
palm back to Agassiz. No, the glacier does not push dislodged
material in front of it as does the bulldozer. On the contrary, like
the plow it cuts and scores its way over the surface leaving its
debris along its edges. So each glacier that passed this way
plowed across the original Escarpment. Thousands of feet thick
it was driven forward by the thrust of the snow and ice ceaselessly piling up behind it. As each mass in its turn pressed on it
planed off one stratum of limestone after another. Much of this,
milled into powder, mixed with the flours of the various "drift"
rocks from Labrador. Each time the process went on for thousands
of years. Then came a period of indecision, full stop, and the
start of a long sluggish retreat into the frigid northeast where the
march had begun. When the very last of the ice masses, the
Wisconsin, had withdrawn, it left rich gifts behind it. With the
advent of a warmer climate a plant life of divers forms burst

1. The bridge shown in the above illustration was destroyed by a violent *seiche*
in May 1952 while this book was still in the press.

forth. Each autumn twigs and leaves decayed into precious
humus; this, added to the rock-grist already there, became a
true, balanced soil. Thus did the garden of the Bruce come into
being.

Besides doing the petty work of preparing an infinite variety
of garden plots, the ice shaped the massive contours of the whole
peninsula, giving its surface a gentle tilt to the west—an average
of twenty feet to the mile—from the crest of the Georgian Bay
cliffs all the way to Lake Huron. On the Lake Huron side, in the
form of bare shelves of limestone, it dips beneath the waters again
and again, each time farther out than before in the new guise of
reefs and shoals that are a menace to men and ships. Moreover,
the moving ice shredded all the western coast into the ragged
fringe of indentations that are its most striking feature. Of these
the largest is beautiful Stokes Bay.

But we must not forget the lofty east front of the Escarpment.
In the main, though sorely disfigured by the battering-ram of the
glaciers, this stood firm. Even today its stance is defiant. To realize
its power of resistance one need only glance at the massive cliffs
of the tallest of the Cabot's Head bluffs: 309 feet of solid
perpendicular rock. To gouge harbours out of an obstruction like
that was almost too much even for a glacier. That is why there
is only one thoroughly safe and commodious haven on the east
side of the Peninsula—Colpoy's Bay, the pride of Wiarton.

When the Wisconsin ice departed other agents took over the
task of giving form to the land mass. Slower and more modest
though they were, they did their work well. Among them, the
weather with its own special tools—sunshine, rain, snow, wind and
frost—all the year round wore down and chipped away, grain by
grain, flake by flake, the hard stone surface. In the growing season
plants carried on the heavier work which man now does by means
of explosives: with their cleaving power root and rootlet blasted
great blocks of stone out of hill and cliff. In time the Peninsula
took on the appearance it had on the day the Indian first beheld
it. And little had this changed, in all probability, in that January
of 1616 when Champlain saw it and recognized it as a great
peninsula comparable to Brittany in his native France. But what
a pity, I often think, that this most understanding of observers
did not see the Peninsula in its midsummer glories rather than in
its midwinter mantle! Of what a garden he could then have told
the world!

Chapter 3

AN UNKNOWN LAND

This country is fine and pleasant, for the most part cleared, shaped like Brittany and similarly situated, being almost surrounded and enclosed by la Mer Douce.

THESE words of Samuel Sieur de Champlain are the first we know to have been written concerning the *mainland* of the Bruce Peninsula. They set forth partly what he himself saw of that tract in mid-January of 1616, and partly what he learned about it from its Indian inhabitants. But sixteen years passed before the words appeared in print and were supported by a map. In so long an interval many important details must have faded from even so keen a memory as Champlain's. His statement must therefore be examined with the greatest care. There is another, almost startling, reason for caution; not until 1788—a blank of nearly two centuries after Champlain's visit—is there another reference to the mainland of the great promontory. The silence is mysterious. We know that in the meantime eminent travellers passed that way, but not one of them left even a scribble to tell us what the Peninsula looked like. The reason for such neglect must have been real and final; in 1788 we learn that it was.

The value of Champlain's observations depends, of course, upon where he was when he made them, and this he virtually tells us. When he states that the country was "fine and pleasant" and "for the most part cleared," he as much as says that he had never gone far into the Peninsula proper. What we know of the density of its virgin forest when the Saugeen Indians ceded the land to the Crown leaves no doubt that the area could never have been "for the most part cleared" at any previous time. Champlain seems to have got at least as far as the site of Owen Sound and to have explored very hastily a section of the Tobacco Nation country lying to the southwest. He probably skirted the northern boundary of the Neutrals' territory. In the patchwork of clearings he saw here he recognized the fields in which the natives raised their

27

crops of "Turkey corn" and tobacco. It was very easy for the
transient visitor to leap to the conclusion that the Peninsula was
likewise dotted with similar open spaces devoted to tillage.

Since, at the best, Champlain's view of the region in the middle
of winter must have been very limited, his statement that the
country was a peninsula could have been based only on what he
had heard from the Indians. Its likeness to Brittany was his own
conception. In the escarpment bounding the waters of Owen
Sound he had seen enough rocky cliffs and crags to be reminded
of the famous *presqu'île* of his native France. At any rate, his
comparison could not be bettered.

The sight of the sorry, tattered remnants of The Bruce forest
today always makes me ask: What was the appearance of this
wild land in Champlain's day? One answer has come from a
most unlikely quarter—the realm of fiction—in a word-picture
drawn by that intriguing creature of Oliver Goldsmith's fancy,
the Chinese philosopher and Citizen of the World. It is a country,
he would say, "where nature sports in primeval rudeness, where
she pours forth her wonders in solitude; . . . from whence the
rigorous climate, the sweeping inundation, the drifted desert, the
howling forest . . . banish the husbandman and spread extensive
desolation; . . . where the brown Tartar wanders for a precarious
subsistence, with a heart that never felt pity, himself more hideous
than the wilderness he makes." For "drifted desert" read "sand
dunes and vast beaches," and for "Tartar," "American Indian";
then behold The Bruce much as it must have looked in that
January of three centuries ago when Champlain and Father Le
Caron tramped through the snows to its borders.

The explorer's sketch of this "fine and pleasant" country, while
cheerful, was not glittering enough to charm his fellow-country-
men into flocking after him. The first to follow his trail were drawn
not by the lure of gaining new lands and glory for France but
by the noble zeal to save pagan souls. On November 1, 1639—
most fittingly for such an errand, All Saints' Day—Fathers Charles
Garnier and Isaac Jogues set out, presumably on foot, for the
country of the Petuns or Tobacco Nation. Upon this region they
bestowed the grandiloquent title, "Mission of the Apostles." Ten
of its villages they took over as stations and gave them the names
of the Twelve Apostles. One of these villages became St. Simon
and St. Jude. This we know from Father Du Creux's map of
1660 to have been in the north part of the Peninsula close to the

Georgian Bay. In the winter of 1640–1 Father Garnier with Father Pierre Pijart made several trips among the stations of the Mission. The missionaries' activities here in two seasons are duly set forth in the official reports of the Huron Mission—the *Relations* of 1640 and 1642—but, mysteriously enough, there is not a syllable about the appearance of the territory in which any station lies.

In 1650, with the destruction of the Jesuit mission in Huronia and the dispersal of the Huron peoples, began a period of complete silence. The Iroquois terror caused the entire Indian population of the Peninsula and Manitoulin Island to flee from their lands to shores and waters in the west. For years even the white man shunned the area as if certain death awaited him there.

But unexpectedly our hopes of ascertaining some facts concerning the great peninsula are encouraged when some one reminds us of Pierre Esprit Radisson, who recorded that in 1654 he made a clockwise circuit of the Georgian Bay. In this account, which was not written till 1669, Radisson claims to have led a party of Frenchmen and Indians southward from the mouth of the French River to the scene of the ill-fated Mission to the Hurons. This he describes as "a delicious place, albeit we could but see it afarre off. . . ." Then in a vague, confused narrative Radisson traces the hard, tedious passage of his flotilla westward along the shore of Nottawasaga Bay, until, after many days, it arrived at a large island where the "wildmen" found their wives and children awaiting them. But what island was this? No one knows for sure. And no wonder, for in recent years exacting critics have found good reasons for believing that this particular story of Radisson's is a fiction; though apparently based on second-hand knowledge of a few facts it is nevertheless an invention, a cunning device of Radisson's to enhance his reputation as successful explorer and thus secure for himself in England a commission to explore Hudson Bay. It is useless, then, to expect from this source authentic news of a peninsula the author had never even glimpsed.

About forty years after the dispersal of the Huron Nation the Baron de Lahontan skirted the Lake Huron side of the forbidding peninsula. Perhaps he has dropped a word or two about it? The loquacious Baron has left us an account of his endeavour to attack the Iroquois from the rear, an enterprise which but for the barrier of the Peninsula Champlain and others would have undertaken many years before. On June 2, 1688, the Baron tells us, he left Sault Ste Marie bound for Lake Erie and the Iroquois country.

With his company of Ottawa and Sauteur warriors he made Manitoulin Island in four days. "We coasted upon that Isle a whole day; and being favour'd by a Calm, crossed from Isle to Isle, till we made the East-side of the Lake. In this passage we cross'd between two Islands that were six Leagues distant the one from the other. . . ." "Between two Islands"! Doubtless Fitzwilliam and Cove. But not a word about a mainland. Once again our hopes of news are shattered.

Manifestly, both leader and company knew little of the lands and water hereabouts. We learn from Lahontan's map, a sketch on which, as he unctuously assures us, he marked only things he had himself seen, that to him the Peninsula was not a long, outstretched arm of land; it was no more than a tiny wart barely visible on the body of a solid land mass and lying in the shadow of imaginary islands. All the way from Cove Island to the River of the Hurons, the Saugeen, the land he saw on his left was actually the west coast of the Peninsula. But he did not know it.

Nevertheless we shall perhaps find maps in general more rewarding than written records. Out of a series of early maps that show the Great Lakes about a dozen yield some positive information.

Boisseau, 1643 (after Champlain, 1632)

What Champlain saw and heard of The Bruce in 1616 was not given to the world in the form of a map until 1632. We now know that the outline he presented was a huge if honest guess. The draughtsman has given the Peninsula an axis lying east and west parallel to the lines of latitude. On the scale employed he has stretched out the already long limb of land to the prodigious length of four or five hundred miles. More, he starts the St. Clair River at Cape Hurd on the Peninsula itself and makes it flow, generally eastward, in a long, sweeping curve to the south that

Sanson, Paris, 1656   Du Creux, Paris, 1660

leaves out Lake Erie, right into Lake St. Louis, that is, Lake
Ontario. Champlain's conception of the lie of the region was
indeed lamentably incorrect.

In 1656 Sanson included in his map of New France an attempt
to depict the outline of the Peninsula. In a tiny space he skilfully
brought out two important points: that this tract was part of the
Petun or Tobacco Indian country; that somewhere in its extreme
north was the Mission of St. Simon and St. Jude. Four years
later the Jesuit, Father Du Creux, in a somewhat better sketch
reaffirms the site of the Mission. As a former member of the
Huron Mission he must have known about where the remote
station was established. So it cannot have been by chance that
to indicate this outpost he placed a little round dot in the hollow
of a certain dent in the upper eastern shoreline of the Peninsula.
This dent seems to be what is now called Dyer's Bay.[1] Somewhere
near here, then, one should search for vestiges of the lost Mission
of St. Simon and St. Jude.

From the records of such keen observers as the Sulpicians,
Galinée and Dollier de Casson, we should expect much. Actually
we learn little from their map of 1670, but the information is at
least positive. They clearly show the long chain of the Fishing
Islands on the west shore of the Peninsula and throw a ray of light
on the mainland opposite: it is too rugged and barren a country,
they note, even for game to live on it. But above all they recognize

1. Near this point de Léry's map of 1725 shows an Indian community named
Papinachois, "Funny Men." It was possible, then, for an Indian settlement to
exist in this area.

Dollier de Casson and
Galinée, Paris, 1670

Father Hennepin, 1683

de Maurepas, Quebec, 1699

Hermann Moll, 1709–20

Mortier, Amsterdam, c. 1710

the relative size of the Peninsula and its true tilt straight into the northwest.

Obviously, the good Father Hennepin had not seen the Sulpicians' sketch when he brought out his map in 1693. He seems to have been so obsessed with the magnitude of Niagara Falls that he left The Bruce out of Lake Huron altogether. In its place he put in a couple of islands that existed only in his fancy.

For the next three-quarters of a century the map-makers of Canada show a strange ignorance of the Peninsula. Their floundering is difficult to understand, for while the Frenchman's and the Englishman's knowledge of the remotest parts of the Great Lakes is growing apace, their knowledge of the great *presqu'île* that obstructs the very centre of the lake system is rapidly fading out. In 1699 Maurepas catches a glimpse of the Peninsula's form and orientation. Ten or fifteen years later Moll, in a British-made

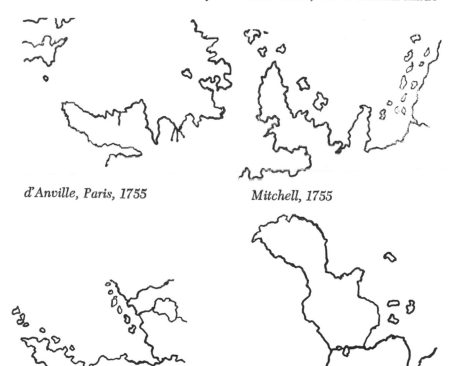

d'Anville, Paris, 1755   *Mitchell, 1755*

Bellin, Paris, 1755   *Gother Mann, Quebec, 1788*

chart, magnifies the area into colossal proportions and squeezes
the Georgian Bay into a mere slit in the coastal wall. About the
same time Mortier, in Amsterdam, with equally ludicrous dis-
tortion of facts, inflates the Bay while shrinking the Peninsula to
a mere bulge of the mainland.

By 1755 one would expect both French and British to be
accurately posted in regard to all Lake Huron. But what do we
find? In three maps of that year—one British and two French—
the Peninsula is presented with three different shapes not one of
which is as near the truth as Sanson's and Du Creux's maps of
1656 and 1660. It is surprising to find that, only four years before
England took over New France, and twenty before the Thirteen
Colonies essayed to become a new nation, there should be so little
accurate information about a prominent geographical feature.

It is a document of three decades later that finally, with a few
authentic words, banishes our wonder. In 1788 a certain Gother
Mann, who had been commissioned by Lord Dorchester to ascer-
tain what parts of the British coasts and waters of Lake Huron
should be chosen as points of defence in the event of war with
the United States, produced a map to show his findings. Only in
a few details was he wrong about the shape of the Peninsula. And
in the blunt, plain words that Mann inscribed across the face of
his map we can discern why he did not venture close enough to
shore to see what the land was really like. "The whole coast of
this projecting Point being a steep rock Cliff without any Camp
Ground or Landing Place is extremely dangerous for Boats or
Canoes to go round and is therefore rarely attempted. Of those
who have ventured several have perished." Here at last is the
explanation for the ignorance of the other explorers who passed
that way.

In 1815 the gist of Mann's warning is echoed by David
Thompson, Astronomer Royal, when assigned a commission like
Mann's. Of Cabot's Head he says: "It is dangerous going round
this head as [at] the least swell of the lake there is no possibility
of landing for which reason the Portage is always taken." Mann's
chart is the first to show the portage (that is, from Colpoy's Bay
to Boat Lake and thence to Lake Huron), though for untold
centuries it must have been the Indians' usual route between the
two big waters. And for many years after Mann and Thompson
it served Indian and white travellers alike. It was by that passage
that in 1848 the two former Hudson's Bay Company men, Captains

John Spence and William Kennedy, made their way by canoe from Owen Sound to the mouth of the Saugeen River to found Southampton.

Before the end of 1815 still more light had been thrown upon the Peninsula. In September of that year Captain W. F. Owen made a survey of its coasts and waters. He took his mission seriously. He allowed no fears of reef or shoal or waves to keep him from digging out the kind of facts he sought. His effort was fruitful: it produced the first safe chart of the region and afforded the

Captain Owen, 1815

first glimpse of the Peninsula's wooded shoreline. On his map Owen wrote: "All the land here represented is covered with stunted Timber, but has no soil whatsoever, being loose Rock and Moss only."

And what land was this? He leaves us in no doubt: the narrow strip of shales and broken limestone that lines the base of the cliffs from Cape Hurd to Cabot's Head and thence winds southward like a ragged green ribbon to Cape Croker and even beyond. What Owen said about that coast in 1815 is true today, except that the ribbon is now cut in many places to make room for summer cottages.

There is a third achievement of Owen's that must be revived in the memory of Canadians: he was the first to give our Peninsula an English name of its own. Keenly conscious of the young country's debt to its early explorers he called the rugged land mass "Little Cabotia." But the name never caught the fancy of government or of the public. It was no sooner coined than it vanished into the limbo of forgotten tags.

John Galt of the Canada Company in his autobiography of 1833 adds an illuminating touch to the picture. After a visit to the "island of the Flower Pots, lofty rocks which rise from the Lake, shaped like such utensils, and bearing a gigantic bouquet of trees" his gunboat, the *Bee,* bore away for Cabot's Head. "With the sight of [this]," he notes, "I was agreeably disappointed, having learned something of its alleged stormy features, and expected to see a lofty promontory; but the descriptions were much exaggerated, we saw only a woody stretch of land not very lofty, lying calm in the sunshine of a still afternoon, and instead of dark clouds and lurid lightnings, beheld only beauty and calm."

A personal experience of fifty years ago helps me understand the fears that kept travellers of the seventeenth century from knowing the Bruce Peninsula. Within one year it was my lot to view, from the decks of large ships, both sides of the Peninsula. Early in October, 1900, I boarded the *City of Collingwood* at Sarnia for Fort William. A heavy northwest gale forced the steamer to sail so close to the Ontario shore that with the captain's glass we could see the seas foaming over the off-shore reefs of the Peninsula. Beyond this unbroken line of white lay a low, flat land as forbidding as Sable Island in an Atlantic storm. But where was Champlain's lofty foreland that reminded him of Brittany? The very next spring I learned.

When one morning in May of 1901 the good ship *Manitoba* rounded Cabot's Head on her way to Owen Sound, there in full view of all on board towered the beetling, forest-crowned cliffs of Champlain's new-world Brittany. The thin gray and green line of craggy heights ran southward, league upon league, parallel to the steamer's course. The continuous, cold, ashen face of that inhospitable rampart of stone fairly shouted over the waters: "No shelter here." I had discovered a master fact of The Bruce: each coast of this rock-bound promontory is in its own way just as un-friendly as the other!

But what I saw of both coasts I saw from the safety of great, staunch ships. Unnerving indeed must have been the terror even of those hardy, daring men who first ventured into these waters in frail cockleshells of bark. When we censure, as we sometimes do, the ignorance and the lagging progress of the pathfinders of our inland seas, we should remind ourselves that we are apt to be unfair judges: we live in a day of easy, swift, and safe power-navigation and of charts little short of perfect.

The Bruce is one of the world's remarkable peninsulas. Like the others it has been cast by Nature as though, by design, to block a main highway of water traffic. What Jutland is to Germany and Denmark; what the Iberian peninsula is to the Mediterranean and western Europe; what stormy Mount Athos was to Greece and to the invading Xerxes, so on its own modest scale the Bruce Peninsula is to Lake Huron and the Georgian Bay. Germany neutralized the obstacle of Jutland by digging the Kiel Canal. Xerxes dodged the perils of Athos by cutting the neck of land behind it. But here comparisons end. The Bruce remains the impediment that Nature made it and there is no reason to change it. Today anyone who has need to traverse the base of the Penin-sula from Lake Huron to Owen Sound, may, within the law, make the journey in less than half an hour.

What, then, shall we do with The Bruce? The answer is not far to seek. Enjoy it, enjoy it, I say, for it abounds in wonderful things.

PART TWO: SHIPWRECK AND FOLKLORE

Wreck of the Severn
After contemporary sketch by E. Tucker

Chapter 4

PERILS OF A FRESHWATER SEA

THE crisp note written by Gother Mann in 1788 beside his outline of The Bruce was more than a warning to the mariners of his own day; it was a solemn omen of events yet to be. What he really said was simply this: one must always expect wrecks to occur off the rock-bound shores of Lake Huron's great promontory. In 1815 David Thompson, the Astronomer Royal, added, as we have seen, a warning of his own.[1]

Though both warnings refer only to canoes and other cockle-shell craft, their mention of the lack of landing-places would make them apply to larger craft as well. Already the clumsy mackinaw boats were avoiding these treacherous waters if they could; they preferred to sneak through the longer route afforded by the long chain of straits between Manitoulin and the North Shore now known as the North Channel. By this time small two-masted schooners had begun to appear here and there on the Georgian Bay; as one by one they cautiously felt their way into the little-known waters beyond, they made sure to give a wide berth to any stretch of The Bruce's coast near which they had to pass. The very mention of the Peninsula put fear into the sailor's heart.

The coming of steam was welcomed as a great boon by those who sailed the Upper Lakes. True, it did not banish all dread of sailing in these perilous waters but it lessened apprehension appreciably. The steamer's greater draft kept it from taking short cuts that small sailing craft could pass through with ease, but the loss was more than made up in its ability to hold to safe, stated courses. As for tempest and high seas, the sailor, on wager, gave the steamboat the odds of outriding all but the very worst. But, above all, steam was a money-maker. In the love of quick gain one may see the real cause of many of the early wrecks. At all costs traffic must not be allowed to lag. So, back to its route

1. See p. 34.

was sent many a patched-up derelict. Others, mysteriously remade in divers ways, were commissioned afresh to ply their trade under new names and, perhaps, under new owners. "Changes in ownership were frequent; indeed, buying and selling vessels seemed to have some of the same charm that has long been associated with horse trading and in all probability there were some deals that rivaled horse trading in their slickness."[1]

The list of ships lost in all parts of Lake Huron in the nineteenth century seems as long as the roll of the martyrs of old. But we can spare ourselves the distress of reading all of it, since our sole concern is with the Bruce Peninsula. But even that record is too long for us. Our present effort, then, must be limited to setting forth what is known of the last hours of only a few of the ill-fated vessels, and the men and women aboard them, that perished off the Peninsula's unfriendly coasts.

In reviving these stories one is always aware of working under restraint, a curb imposed by the nature of the sources at one's command. At one time or another all these stories appeared in the press, either daily or weekly, as records of fact. Only one is less than thirty years old; several belong to the last decades of the nineteenth century; one came out in 1854. The substance of the accounts must be accepted as it stands. Only a few changes, and these superficial, are permissible: shifts in order and emphasis; the use of different words and phrases where desirable; and, to help the reader get and hold his bearings, the insertion of references to points of geography.

THE "BRUCE MINES" FOUNDERS OFF CAPE HURD

For a side-wheeler the *Bruce Mines* was a pretty good ship, though sailors who knew the Upper Lakes thought a propeller better suited to her particular business and to the waters of the North Channel of Lake Huron. She could not have been longer than 125 feet, for otherwise she could not have passed through the locks of the Welland Canal of that time. Owned by the Montreal Mining Company, which in 1847 purchased and began working the copper deposits at Bruce on the North Shore, thirty-odd miles east of Sault Ste Marie, she was the only link between this lonely industrial outpost and the older settlements of Upper and Lower Canada. The Canadian Pacific Railway, a branch of

1. Fred Landon, *Lake Huron* (Indianapolis and New York: Bobbs Merrill Co., 1944), p. 311.

which now serves the North Shore, did not then exist, and the steamer was the miners' lifeline: to them she was tools, machinery, mining supplies of all kinds, food, and news. It was her task to see that the volume of material stores was always equal to the needs of the community. Her most important trip of each year was the last one: before navigation closed early in December she had to convey to the mines enough of everything for the winter.

With this vital errand on her books the *Bruce Mines,* late in November of 1854, took to Toronto a cargo of sorted slag and copper ore. There it was to be loaded on to other vessels for transport to Britain and modern smelters. This long and costly haul had for several years been necessary because the smelter at the Mines—the first copper smelter in Canada—had been burned down soon after its erection in 1848. At Toronto, in the place of the ore the steamer stowed away a large and very valuable mixed cargo: naturally enough, one important item was a great quantity of blasting powder. Clearing from Toronto she crossed Lake Ontario, passed through the Welland Canal, and made good time through Erie, St. Clair, and lower Huron.

On Monday, November 27, the *Bruce Mines* put in at Goderich at the mouth of the Maitland River. There she took on a heavy load of various supplies, probably mostly foodstuffs since these were the only materials which Goderich could produce in volume at that time. In the evening of the same day with twenty-six people on board, four of whom were passengers, she steamed out of the little port and turned her bows straight into the northwest. The point for which she was headed was the entrance into the strait on the east side of Drummond Island. Her competent skipper, Captain Frederick McKenzie Fraser, counted on delivering her cargo at the Bruce dock the next day. At the same time the whole population of the place, keenly conscious that their fate for the winter depended on the coming of the steamer, was in imagination anxiously following her progress step by step to her destination.

Apparently, at the time when Captain Fraser left Goderich there was little wind and no sea; the last leg of the voyage gave promise of being completed without delay. So when near midnight a terrific gale burst out of the west he was as rudely taken by surprise as was any of the passengers. In only a few minutes, it seemed, the waves rose to the height of hills which rolled tumultuously and with unbridled violence against the vessel. Her

high freeboard and shallow draft made her the plaything of such
ruthless power. A great sea suddenly threw her in one direction,
and just as suddenly while she was still in motion another sea
tossed her back. This subjected her relatively light hull to all
manner of uncalculated strains. In no more than a quarter of an
hour the pounding and the twisting had so loosened her frame
that the men on board could feel it give and quiver like a shed
about to fall apart. A number of seams were wrenched open and
through them the water poured like a river into the hold. Already
everybody could see that the steamer was sinking.

If any chance of safety was left it lay in the possibility of pro-
longing the time she could remain afloat. "Overboard with the
cargo!" commanded the Captain. And forthwith into the raging
seas went every article, every packing case that could be reached.
Unfortunately, by this time most of the ship's load was submerged
in the water flooding the hold. In spite of the heroic effort to
lighten ship the water gained. All hands worked frantically at the
pumps in frequent relays. By daylight the fires under the boilers
were put out. The engines stopped dead. The rudder was too
badly broken to be of use even if the ship had still any headway.
The steamer was bobbing about like a helpless cockleshell on the
foaming, wind-blown crests of the waves.

At two o'clock in the afternoon an officer at the mast-head said
he could see land to leeward. Through the haze and spray it
seemed to be about twenty miles away. As far as one could reckon,
the rate of the steamer's drift to the east was about a mile an
hour. The crew's systematic labour at the pumps had enabled
her to keep afloat several hours longer than had at first seemed
possible. The united hope of all was that they might still keep
afloat long enough to let the ship run aground on an offshore
reef; from there they could easily row to land in the boats. But
all hope was suddenly destroyed by the report of the carpenter:
rushing up from below he shouted that the ship would go down
in five minutes, perhaps even in less time than that.

At once there was a concerted dash for the boats. For twenty-
six people there were only two boats, and they were small. Utter
panic and disorder seemed imminent. But on no ship commanded
by Captain Fraser could any such scene prevail. He was a com-
mander of the British marine tradition. He had his wits about
him, and a brace of pistols. Drawing these from their cases he
cocked them and, holding one in each hand, firmly but calmly

declared he would shoot the first man who tried to get into a boat before he, Captain Fraser, gave the order. There was something about the man that left no doubt that he meant what he said. There was perfect order.

To launch two lifeboats and stow twenty-six people in them was a formidable task for an uncertain five minutes. Fraser assigned one boat to the mate, Duncan Lambert of Goderich, and the other to himself. With him he took nine men. This boat was lowered without the slightest difficulty. But with the mate's boat everything seemed to go wrong that could go wrong. The tackle that held it suspended got into a snarl and the ropes would not run through the pulley-blocks. A glance was enough to show the mate that an attempt to adjust the tackle might mean death for himself and all in his care. So with quick strokes of an axe, so close together that they were like a single stroke, he cut the ropes from which the boat was dangling in midair, and the boat, containing the mate and fourteen others, hit the water with a force that seemed to crack the keel.

There was to have been a sixteenth person on board—the ship's carpenter. He, poor fellow, had been left on deck when the boat dropped: he made a wild leap for it but missed it by inches, plummeting into the water like a stone. This was the only fatality of the disaster. When the steamer sank a minute or two later the lives of all twenty-five men in the boats were suddenly threatened. But this tragic doom was averted when her promenade deck parted from the hull and floated between the vortex and the overcrowded lifeboats. Its movement was so prompt that it seemed to be impelled by a power with a purpose: to interpose an effective barrier between a company of human souls and certain destruction in seventy fathoms of water.

Through the story told in the *Globe* of Toronto by one of the *Bruce Mines'* passengers—who did not sign his name to his letter —we know something of the experiences of the men who were saved in the mate's boat. Once afloat in that tiny craft, though still unaware in just what quarter safety lay, they shouted triumphantly in unison. But the chill of cold waters soon calmed their exuberance. Their escape, it was plain, was simply the exchange of one danger for another. At best they were only five miles nearer land than when they had first sighted it. For navigation they had no more than two oars among them, and, by the favour of chance, two ship's buckets. Two men at the oars, how-

ever, were a vital power in the crisis: they were able at least to
hold the boat's bow on land while wind and sea provided headway. And so the lagging hours went on.

As the men pulled away from the sinking wreck Captain Fraser
exclaimed with conviction that neither lifeboat could last ten
minutes. In the case of Mate Lambert's boat it was the buckets
that foiled the fulfilment of that gloomy prophecy: methodical
bailing in the intervals of seconds between wave-crests kept the
water below the fatal level. While two men rowed—the same two
all the time—thirteen went through the dull routine with the
buckets. Nothing but the stark knowledge that upon this effort
alone their lives depended kept them from yielding to the
paralysis of cold and cramp.

About ten o'clock at night they heard breakers on the right,
but in the darkness could not see how close they were. Then they
heard waves crashing on the left and, a minute later, on both
sides at once. Yet in front of them there was no sound but that
of the screaming gale. They seemed to be passing through a
narrow gut between reefs. Tingling with wonder they let the
wind carry them on. In five minutes, which seemed hours, their
boat steadied to an even keel in an expanse of calm water. The
roar of the surf was now behind them. In the utter blackness of
the night they groped about the basin in which they found themselves, feeling their way now on this side, now on that. At last
they touched a point of rock and dragged themselves ashore.
When day broke they saw they were on a small island lying in
the lee of Cape Hurd, the northwestern tip of the Saugeen, now
the Bruce, Peninsula. The eyewitness of the scene writes of the
experience as of a miracle. "If we had touched even one hundred
yards farther down than we did we should have been dashed
against the rocks and all inevitably lost. That dangerous coast
extended about one hundred miles, but it was the will of the
Almighty that we should land on the only spot of all that coast
where we could possibly save ourselves, and that in the dark."

To get a fire going was everybody's first thought—a fire big
enough to warm the fifteen shivering survivors at one time. Driftwood in many forms—brush, branches, sticks, and logs both large
and small—lay all about in abundance. A huge fire was soon blazing.
The two men, a deckhand and the passenger who later gave this
story to the world, who without relief had worked the oars from the
scene of the wreck to the barren island, labouring continuously

from three o'clock in the afternoon to eleven at night, were dragged by their companions from the boat. Their muscles were so stiff and cramped that they could not move an inch. They were carried to places beside the fire. Not until their clothes steamed like boilers did the rigidity of their bodies begin to disappear. They were conscious of thawing out as it were inch by inch and only after an hour or more of this process were they able to walk freely. The passenger later noted, with amazement, that the ordeal had left him no ill effects.

Daylight enabled the party to appraise the lie of the land and waters. There they were, fifteen weary but doughty men, shipwrecked without an ounce of food on a desolate islet. Of them all only one—the mate, Duncan Lambert—knew anything of the Georgian Bay at whose rugged portal they lay stranded, and not even he knew in detail the course to the nearest inhabited port. That, by his rough reckoning, was probably Owen Sound. In his ignorance, for which he could be forgiven, he magnified its distance to 130 miles, a figure that fairly stunned his companions. The gap that yawned between their first meal and themselves could be traversed only by water; the mainland of the Peninsula was pathless. But just when their spirits had sagged to their lowest depths they were cheered by the sight of a column of smoke rising over a nearby island. Captain Fraser had also made his way to land.

By means of smoke signals Lambert caught the attention of the other party and summoned them to join him and his men. In the general parley that ensued a clear decision was reached: the only way promising even the faintest hope of safety was to row to Owen Sound. Not a man dared utter aloud the question that disturbed them all: Could they, without food, hold out long enough to keep the oars going? One fact, however, gave them cheer: Captain Fraser knew every mile of the route. On the other hand, he took care not to mislead the men. In all honesty he could not assure them that the distance would be shorter than they feared it would be; if, in order to take advantage of the lee afforded by the high cliffs on the east side of the Peninsula, the boats were to hug the shore all the way down to the Sound, the distance might prove to be all that the mate had estimated.

Early in the morning of Wednesday, November 29, the two lifeboats set out for Owen Sound, the Captain leading. Eastward they pressed, scudding at a brisk clip before the gale which was

even stronger than when the steamer went down. Before long
both boats passed the entrance to Collins Inlet, which a few years
later was called by some homesick man of Mull, Tobermory. No
lighthouse was to be seen on Cove Island, for none was placed
there until 1859. During the trying voyage nobody, even the
passenger who later wrote about it, attempted to keep a record
of the day-by-day progress of the mate's boat. In each all too
brief spell of daylight all eyes dwelt intently upon every outstanding landmark as the boat slowly drew towards it and just
as slowly let it blend into the hazy distance behind. Cabot's Head,
Cape Chin, Lion's Head, Cape Croker, Hay Island, all were
names still unknown to the mate and those with him.

During the first night the two boats lost touch with each other.
Somehow, the mate's boat pulled ahead and kept the lead to the
very end. At eight in the evening of Saturday, December 2, the
last relay-pair of exhausted oarsmen rowed their craft into Owen
Sound, four days and five hours after the *Bruce Mines* went
down. At three next morning, Sunday, they were joined by
Captain Fraser and his crew.

At Owen Sound fortune still smiled on the passengers of the
lost steamer. As if by prearrangement, a schooner, soon to set sail
for the Mines, lay at the dock at which they landed. After rest
and food they boarded the vessel and in a day or two reached
their destination. Uppermost in their thoughts was the gallant
mate. Through stormy, strange waters he had guided safely to a
distant haven a small, ill-equipped lifeboat, laden with a precious
burden of human lives. By his calm poise he had held their spirits
high above despair; by his courage he had given them strength.
To at least one of the passengers it seemed that merely to feel
gratitude to such a man was not enough; here was one of whom
the whole country should hear. So without delay he sent a letter
to the Toronto *Globe*. It appeared in print on December 16, 1854.
In his zeal to pay the full meed of tribute due to a true hero, the
writer of the letter failed to sign his own name. However, he had
gained his end: henceforth, Duncan Lambert, mate of the *Bruce
Mines*, could never be entirely forgotten.

Chapter 5

THE EIGHTIES TAKE THEIR TOLL

WITHIN the span of a single day, September 11, 1881, there took place two wrecks of vessels engaged in the Lake Huron trade. The almost simultaneous occurrence of these events brought into relief a fact of great importance to navigation, an obvious fact and one as ancient as ships and the art of sailing, but one all too often ignored: the nature of a cargo and the way in which it has been stowed away can create conditions in which even a very moderate gale may with amazing swiftness send a vessel to the bottom.

On this fateful day in September, 1881, the propeller[1] *Columbia*, which sailed on the Chicago–Collingwood run, was, in fifteen minutes, sunk in Lake Michigan through the shifting of her cargo of grain, although at the time the wind was blowing no more than thirty-six miles an hour. In the same unlucky twenty-four hours the Canadian schooner *Regina* was dragged down to her doom by the leaden mass of a water-logged load of salt, and that when she was only a few minutes away from the safe, soft cushion of a sandbar.

THE "REGINA" WRECKED ON COVE ISLAND

In 1881 William Foster of Owen Sound had two small schooners, the *Annie E. Foster* and the *Regina*, which plied a busy though tramplike trade among the various ports of the Georgian Bay and Lake Huron. And a very profitable trade it was, for, though the cargoes were small and of a motley character, there were comparatively few keels for the available business. Naturally, then, it paid an owner to keep a ship in service just as long as she would remain afloat, and the waters of the Lake and the great Bay seemed to teem with ships in the last stages of old age. If a census of sail and steam of this region were available

1. That is, driven by a screw rather than by paddlewheels.

now it would probably shock even the greenest seafaring man of
our day. The owner of the *Annie E. Foster* and the *Regina* adroitly
concealed their age but the appearance of the two vessels was
such as to leave no doubt that they were very old. Indeed, in the
gossip of the Bay ports they were frankly spoken of as "coffin-
ships." "She ought to have been laid up on the shore to rot out
her last years," was solemnly written of the *Regina* thirty years
ago.

The *Regina* was in the command of Captain Amos Trip, a
sailor well and favourably known in all parts of Lake Huron, and
was manned by a crew of four. That Trip was not unaware of the
rumours about his ship was revealed casually a short time before
her last voyage. While she was loading lumber at Parry Sound a
friend gingerly sounded the captain's opinion of her. "Aren't you
a bit leary, Amos, about sailing the old tub in the fall? It's going
to blow hard any day now." "No, no, man," jovially replied the
skipper; "no, the old tub's all right: so long as she's carrying
lumber she'll float ashore somewhere."

But in treating a serious matter so jocularly Amos Trip overlooked for the moment the miscellaneous character of the *Regina*'s
cargoes; in no two voyages in succession could he be sure she
would carry the same kind of load. On the eleventh day of
September, 1881, she was carrying not lumber but a full load of
salt from Goderich, the "salt town" at the mouth of the Maitland
on the Ontario side of Lake Huron, and was bound for some port
on the Bay. She had safely passed the lights of Kincardine,
Southampton, and Stokes Bay in order, had rounded Cape Hurd,
and was nearing Cove Island, when she was suddenly struck by
a violent squall. In an amazingly brief time the seas rose like small
mountains and beat upon her furiously. She was in grave trouble
almost at once. Vicious strains on her hull caused by the sheer
weight of her inert cargo quickly opened many seams in her
planking. Through the multitude of tiny gaps thus created water
began to trickle into the hold. In a few minutes the many trickles
became a strong stream that could not be slowed down, much less
stopped. The salt drank it up, as a blotter imbibes ink, until it
could hold no more.

Everyone on board peered into the hold with an anxiety that
kept mounting with the minutes. How much more water would
the old tub take in and stay on top? At what moment would her

limit be reached? It differs among ships: the fatal climax is one thing for one ship and something else for another. What was it for the *Regina*? The captain's answer was one of cheer and hope: the crucial moment had not yet come. "With the help of all hands I can soon beach the *Regina* on a sandbar just off the shore of Cove Island; I know exactly where we are." But the crew were in no mood for cheer and hope. With one accord they shouted: "She's going down right now." They shoved the ship's one boat overboard and all dropped into it and rowed ashore. Captain Trip refused to leave his ship.

Afterwards the crew had a story to tell—*their* story—and they told it. They made mention, of course, of such pertinent matters as the direction of the wind during the last phase of the fatal voyage, the combination of conditions that forced the men to desert their ship, the time at which she went under. Of these and other like details they had a lot to say. Somehow the way in which they said them left their hearers with a feeling that a great deal had been left unsaid. The truth is that the tale fell upon uneasy ears, ears that became still more uneasy as the days went by.

Facts about the storm soon began to come in from all parts of Lake Huron; no one could help noticing that much of what the crew had said did not fit these facts. For instance, the wind was *not* blowing from the quarter the crew said it was. Later, the *Regina's* clock was found; it had stopped *long after* the time the crew claimed the ship had foundered. As the vessel lay on the bottom not far from the shore of Cove Island the top of a mast stood out above the water. It was manifest she had drawn so close to land that had she been kept afloat a few minutes longer she could have been safely beached on soft sand without the loss of a single life. Captain Trip had been right, and, honourable seaman that he was, he stuck to his conviction to the very end—which was death itself.

The gale that sent the *Regina* to her doom also blew on the waters off Red Rock lighthouse outside of Parry Sound. There her sister ship, the *Annie E. Foster*, found herself in grave difficulties. But her crew were of a different fibre: with courage and patience they brought their vessel through the storm and sailed her into the long, sheltered channel that leads to the town of Parry Sound. Of the crew of the *Regina* many hard things were said. Of these the hardest were that their cowardice needlessly caused the sacrifice of a seaman of great skill and bravery, Amos Trip, a ship's captain with a supremely high sense of duty.

The "Jane Miller" Vanishes

The fate of the little steamer *Jane Miller* is one of the riddles of the Georgian Bay. One day near the close of navigation in 1881 she left Owen Sound for Meaford with a heavy load. Here she took on thirty tons more, and, as some one said later, "staggered" out into the Georgian Bay on her way to Wiarton. At half-past eight in the evening of the same day she tied up for a few minutes at Big Bay near the entrance of Colpoy's Bay. After stowing away some fuel there she slipped out quietly into the night.

It so happened that a certain Mr. Cameron, who lived a short distance west of Big Bay near what is now known as Cameron's Point, was watching that night for the arrival of the *Wiarton Belle* from Owen Sound. Since snow had begun to fall it was hard for him to see clearly over the water. But about nine o'clock, during a lull between snow flurries, he distinctly saw the lights of a westbound vessel pass by. A couple of miles farther on, close to Spencer's Landing where the *Jane Miller* was to take on more cordwood, another observer on shore saw the lights of a steamer go by toward the west. That was the last that was ever seen of the *Jane Miller*.

In June of 1880, soon after she came off the stocks at Little Current on Manitoulin Island, the *Jane Miller* was purchased by Captain Andrew Port. He put her at once on a route that ran from Owen Sound to Wiarton, northward up the east side of the Bruce Peninsula to Tobermory, and from there along the south shore of Manitoulin Island. Somehow ships have a way of acquiring reputations from their skippers; very soon the *Jane Miller* had acquired a reputation—favourable, one is glad to record—from her skipper. But Captain Port, though known on the Upper Lakes as a skilful and experienced sailor, was nevertheless regarded as impulsive and rather prone to take chances. There was solid enough ground for this opinion. One trip that he made in the winter of 1880 became the theme of a story told again and again for many years in Georgian Bay ports.

One day after the intense cold had set in for good Port took the risk of attempting to convey a party on the steam tug, *Prince Albert*, from The Tub to Michael's Bay which lies two or three miles west of South Baymouth on Manitoulin. The distance involved was not more than twenty miles. But the heavy seas and baffling currents of the straits forced him to put back to The Tub. Here in the still water of a narrow, landlocked harbour the tug was frozen in. After a month's stubborn struggle Captain Port fought her free and headed her for Wiarton. Again she was trapped and again the captain freed her. Once she floated in the open waters of the Sound, Port, to his bitter chagrin, discovered that her rudder had been wrenched off by the ice. Yet of such stuff was he made that he brought her through a fortnight of helpless drifting safe into her home port.

The night of November 25, 1881, when Roderick Cameron saw the last sign of the *Jane Miller*, was exceptionally stormy. A wild gale was blowing and carrying with it blinding snow squalls. So furious were the blasts that many ships, as was learned afterward, were on the alert and ready to take extreme measures to make sure of safety. One of them, a staunch screw steamer, *City of Owen Sound*, while making a run into Owen Sound that night had all her anchors set to be let go at a moment's notice. Later, her captain declared that the storm was the worst he had ever fought his way through in a whole lifetime of sailing the Great Lakes.

Next morning it was clear to those at Spencer's Landing who had expected the little steamer to touch there, that she had not come in, for the wood she was to have taken on was still piled on the dock. Nor did she reach Wiarton. An anxious day went by without a word of her and by evening fears of the worst spurred every town and hamlet on Colpoy's Bay to vigorous action. Scarcely a habitation was there along its shores that was not vitally concerned, for here were the homes of most of the *Jane Miller*'s passengers and crew.

Distress and uncertainty filled the minds of the searchers. Had the *Jane Miller* gone to the bottom? If so, it was not high seas that sent her there, for the wind, being from the southeast, was off shore and could not possibly have raised waves of dangerous height over the narrow span of water between the shore and the line of the steamer's course. Only a Pacific typhoon could heap up really threatening seas in so narrow a space as that. Had the steamer's engines been crippled? In that case she would be adrift in sight of land. Had she run aground and held there? Then her mast and some part of her upper works would show above the water. Or had she crashed on a reef, smashed a hole in her

hull, and plunged to her doom in deep water? If that were true
bits of wreckage would already have been cast up somewhere on
shore, or perhaps on the north side of Colpoy's Bay or even on
one of the islands that lie athwart the mouth of the Bay—on Hay,
or Griffith, or White Cloud. One aspect of the situation was
especially disturbing: at the time she left port the *Jane Miller*
carried no ballast; by far the greater part of her load was on the
main deck; she lacked in her hold the additional weight of the
wood she was to have taken on at Spencer's Landing. Only one
conclusion seemed possible. Everyone shrunk fearfully from drawing it.

On the first Sunday after the tragic disappearance, a pleasant
calm day, a Mr. McGregor and his son put out in a rowboat from
Spencer's Landing to make a search of nearby shores and waters.
They headed for a little bay on White Cloud Island. But before
they got there their attention was drawn to a strange agitation of
the surface of the water in a certain spot—the steady rising and
gentle bursting of bubbles. At the same time they noticed that in
a small area roundabout the water was slightly though uniformly
discoloured. The men took their bearings from landmarks on
shore and went on into the bay. There on the beach before them
were some of the very things they sought: a broken flagstaff, four
oars, and a few small packages of freight. Something more convincing still was found close by: five cloth caps. Later, they were
identified as belonging to members of the *Jane Miller's* crew.

The McGregors' report at once roused Wiarton to organized
action; here at last was some positive clue on which to work.
Already Wiarton had seen her duty clearly, for both Captain Port
and the ship belonged to the town. Because of the loss of a week
in enforced waiting a systematic search for the lost vessel was
more arduous than it would have been at first, since by now the
bitter cold and the distressing uncertainties of December weather
had to be faced. But though every citizen realized keenly the
difficulties and dangers there was no hesitation. A volunteer party
under the leadership of an old settler, William Bull, put out on
the tug *Tommy Wright*. Every man on board knew well all the
bays, inlets, islands, and reefs of Colpoy's Bay. Equipped with
every device needed in their quest—grappling hooks, sounding
lines, ropes—they made straight east for Spencer's Landing.

Starting from the Landing they dragged for several long,
tedious hours without finding a trace of a ship. Many depth

soundings were taken. Everywhere the water was deep; only a few hundred yards off the Landing the lead showed thirty fathoms. At White Cloud Island the elder McGregor joined Bull's party and guided them to the spot where he and his son had seen the bubbles, a spot just half a mile northeast of Spencer's, and, it was now manifest, exactly southeast of the cove on White Cloud Island where the McGregors came upon the sailors' caps and the fragments of wreckage. Of greatest significance, however, was this crucial fact: the line drawn between the tract of seething water and the cove coincided precisely with the southeast-north-west path of the gale on the night on which the *Jane Miller* disappeared into the darkness. If the bubbles marked her resting place, then any relics of her that might chance to float free could not escape being thrown up in the tiny island cove.

The logic of it all was simple; so was William Bull's report. "The *Jane Miller*," he concluded, "lay on the bottom in two hundred feet of water, within the radius of a quarter of a mile of the place indicated by McGregor as the probable scene of the disaster. This is about the place where Mr. Cameron would have seen her on her way up the Bay." It may be that the *Jane Miller* sank in the very next "twinkling of an eye" after Mr. Cameron's last glimpse of her! Even a calamity severe enough to shake the world may take place in the fraction of a second.

The unflagging search went on. Again and again the Wiarton men dragged their grappling irons over the bed of Colpoy's Bay. Here, too, diver after diver went down to peer into the dark abysses. None of these endeavours had any result.

In a community torn by the sorrow of calamity a base trait of human nature often shows itself. While many citizens were putting every effort into the labour of search, others were spreading evil rumour. "The *Jane Miller* was not wrecked," they hinted. "Could she not easily have sneaked into some obscure harbour on the other side? It would be no trick to sell her cargo secretly in such a place. There are plenty of ways for disguising vessels—changing their names and colour, remodelling their upper works, registering them in another country, and so on. Many a Canadian vessel has ended her sailing days doing a profitable trade under the American flag and a new name." But the crafty minds that contrived such innuendoes overlooked one thing: the lack of a convincing motive. Indeed, they stupidly ignored two facts: the insurance on the *Jane Miller* was only $6,000, and the owner himself was aboard her when she vanished. The very absurdity of the rumour soon killed it, though not before it had wounded the hearts of many who had lost close kin in the disaster. Not one of the twenty-seven souls who were aboard the steamer on her last voyage—captain, passengers, crew—was ever seen again. Not the slightest taint of dishonour now sullies their names.

Around the coasts of Lake Huron people still talk about the mysterious fate of the *Jane Miller*. In the morning paper of the day in which these words were written a whole column was devoted to the tragic story. She passed out of the world of Great Lakes ships and sailors as if some great magician had waved her out of sight with the stroke of a wand. But though the wonder about her will doubtless never cease, there does seem to be a sound explanation of her sudden disappearance. That was inherent in the report William Bull made to his fellow-citizens of Wiarton a fortnight after the sad event.

The *Jane Miller* was both overloaded and top-heavy when she set out on her last voyage. At a crucial moment an exceptionally violent blast struck her high, wall-like freeboard with such force as to roll her clean over as though she were a floating cylinder. Wind and driving snow between them had probably sent every person on board to take shelter inside behind locked doors or below battened hatches. When the ship sank, Captain Port, crewmen, and passengers were all penned in like animals in a trap; not one of them had a chance to fight for life. Why, then, if the McGregors really found the spot where she lay, did no grapnel ever bring up any sign of having touched the wreck? Nobody who knows the variety of cavernous depths and abysmal hollows that are found in the world's great limestone areas can fail to guess the answer. The *Jane Miller* must have slipped into an extraordinarily profound underwater chasm that divides that part of the Niagara Escarpment in which lies the basin that holds the blue waters of Colpoy's Bay.

THE BENTLEY GALE

Very often, strange indeed are the ways in which names are given to ships. But much more strange is it, at least to a landsman, that a ship should give a name to a wind. Yet in the latter decades of the nineteenth century such instances were far from being unknown in the Georgian Bay. The fierce wind of November, 1879, which destroyed the decrepit old *Waubuno* became known as

the Waubuno Gale. Similarly, the wind which three Novembers later sent the steamer *Asia* to the bottom and took the lives of all but two of her crew and passengers was for years afterward referred to as the Asia Gale. So there was sound precedent for the *Bentley* to pass on her name to an exceptional wind in which her experience had stood out above the experiences of all other ships on the same waters at the time. What was strange about this case is that so modest a craft as a mere sailing barge should gain such great distinction.

The Bentley Gale began in the daylight hours of October 15, 1886. From the first it was a stiff blow, as much as twenty-five miles an hour, but because it came overland from the east its real strength was not sensed along the Parry Sound waterfront nor for a considerable distance out in the Georgian Bay. For several hours its gain in speed was so gradual as to seem to be under mechanical control. By ten o'clock "it was blowing great guns" and without abating its force started veering to the south. On it swung past the line of north and south, and point by point inched its way into the west. At midnight it had pushed the official wind gauge at Parry Sound up to the figure of sixty-six miles an hour. Occasional spurts shot the gauge up to a peak of seventy-five or eighty. Then of a sudden, as if weary and ashamed of causing so much fear, it settled back for a few hours to a monotonous though still menacing fifty.

The next morning between four and five the storm's line of direction moved on into the northwest. The attainment of this point marked the peak of the wind's strength. Then it began to abate, as if some unseen remote control was inverting the order of the increase in strength the day before. First it sagged back to a moderate thirty-five miles an hour, held at this stage for a while, shifted into due north, and from that quarter leisurely petered out in a gentle breeze. The Bentley Gale did not last as long as the Asia Gale, but what it lacked in duration it made up in rampant fury. An Owen Sound citizen once claimed for it this unique distinction: "This gale lives in the memory of the old residents of the Georgian Bay as a storm without precedent or parallel."

The havoc wrought by the "Bentley" in and around Parry Sound alone serves as a yardstick to measure its stupendous force. It is common knowledge, even among landsmen, that a strong wind blowing steadily across a body of water will raise appreci-

ably the level on the shore upon which the wind beats. But
the "Bentley" was in a class of its own: it broke all records known
for the region up to that time. At Parry Sound the water was
seven feet above the high water mark. Apparently, this extreme
height was attained because nature happened just then to be in
the mood to add to the powers of the wind the unpredictable
powers of the so-called lake tide, the *seiche*.[1] The flooding of the
eastern shores of the Sound covered the docks, put out the fires
under sawmill boilers, ripped apart wharves and breakwaters, and
wrecked numerous pleasure craft anchored in "absolutely safe"
bays and channels.

The sailing barge *Bentley* was owned by Captain W. B. Hall
of Toronto. She was taking on lumber at the Parry Sound Lumber
Company's dock when the blow from the east began, and the
loading had come to an end before the wind reached the pitch of
a storm. On her deck and in her hold the vessel carried half a
million feet of lumber. From her point of view the wind while
strong was "fair"; to make the most of his luck the captain sailed
her out into the Sound without delay. Under the shelter of the
high land behind the dock he was unable to perceive just how
violent the off-shore wind was. Not till he had passed the Red
Rock lighthouse at the mouth of the Sound—and then too late—
did the grim reality burst upon him. The huge following seas,
travelling faster than the ship, lifted her stern aloft and rolled
her hull from side to side as if it had been an empty barrel. The
movement gained momentum, each roll swinging a bit farther
than the one before, until the ship seemed like a pendulum without control. The arc through which she was now swaying was so
great that captain and crew feared the additional push of a
particularly big wave might turn the ship right over. And the
fear was far from being groundless. At last a veritable mountain
of a wave tilted the *Bentley* beyond the angle of safety and gave
her deck the slope of a toboggan slide. In an instant into the
water slithered the whole deckload, an avalanche of timbers,
planks, and boards.

However, the mishap was a boon as well as a loss: it lowered
the vessel's centre of gravity and gave her a welcome period of
respite. Taking in sail to a point that would still leave some steering power, the captain laid the *Bentley*'s bow plumb on Cabot's
Head fifty miles due west on the Bruce Peninsula. What was his

1. See chap. VIII, "The Tides o' Bruce."

idea? is a question still asked by those who know that forbidding
part of the coast. Although today a storm-caught ship drawing
as much as fifteen feet can slip through the channel into tranquil
Wingfield Basin, in those days it was yet as Nature had made it,
a passage no more than five feet deep at the bar. But the captain
laid a wager with chance: that the wind would stay in the east
and let the *Bentley* sail into the quiet lee behind the lofty North
Bluff of Cabot's Head. He won.

In the relative calm of the lee all on board mused gratefully as
well as a bit proudly upon the experience they had just passed
through. Never before had a craft of the *Bentley's* type raced at
such a speed across the full breadth of the Georgian Bay. With a
few yards of sail the old barge had put steam to shame! But no
one wanted to repeat the passage. Their leisurely musing lasted
only as long as the wind remained where it was, however. In an
hour or two it edged over, as though by stealth, from the east
into the south, into the southwest, into the west and, at last,
squarely into the northwest. Then trouble, real trouble, began
again. The nor'wester was beating upon the very waters where
the *Bentley* had hoped to ride out the storm.

With no sea room and no power but that of sail the captain saw
only one course of action open: to try to hold the barge where
she was. He had all the anchors cast out to windward. The hold
they offered was shaky indeed, but there was nothing better.
Little by little they began to give way. First one anchor dragged,
the line of another parted, and soon nothing was left even to
slow down the drift. Sideways, like a log shifted by a canthook,
the *Bentley* rolled up on the sharp rocks and coarse shingle of the
shore.

Since this is the story of a wind and not of a ship, its end is not
yet. True, the Bentley Gale proper came to an end, but it carried
on into a sequel of other winds which in their turn caused a new
chain of untoward events. Who has not heard of good money
being thrown after bad? Some men do it with the lawful tokens of
exchange; some do it with ships. The *Bentley's* owner, learning
of the ship's sorry fate, sent his namesake, the steam barge *W. B.
Hall*, to the scene of the disaster, with the schooner *Lady Dufferin*
in tow. To the latter ship was to be transferred what was left of
the *Bentley's* underdeck cargo. Thus lightened, it was thought,
the barge might be floated and towed out to deep water. But she
turned out to be a total wreck—the mangled skeleton of a ship—

and could not be moved. The remnant of her load was shifted to
the *Lady Dufferin*, which was taken in tow by the *Hall* in an
attempt to reach the quiet haven of Tobermory. Again hopes were
shattered. By the time the ships had made ten miles and were off
Halfway Rock Point the wind had risen to a gale and had churned
up huge seas in the broad channel. The struggle against wind and
wave could not last long—it was spun out just long enough for the
two vessels to make four miles more. When they came opposite
Driftwood Cove the towline snapped. The *Hall* steamed off alone
to seek safety while the schooner with all hands was left to the
mercy of the tempest. Without means of navigation she bobbed
about like a chip in a swirling eddy. The crew could do nothing
but get ready to act the instant their ship grounded. Then one
brave fellow among them swam ashore with a rope by means of
which all his comrades were drawn to safety.

The steam barge *W. B. Hall* had not yet come under the
"hoodoo" that seemed to pursue her latter years. She managed to
live through the minor gale that dashed the *Lady Dufferin* on
the rocks and for several seasons went about her business on her
old familiar runs. In time, length of days and the ills to which
busy ships are heir began to weigh heavily on her. Seeing some
sparks of usefulness still lingering in her James Playfair of Mid-
land bought her, put her in the shipyard at Owen Sound, and
had her rebuilt. About the turn of the century the newspaper
press told the world that a steamer, the *St. Andrew*, had gone
down somewhere in the Great Lakes. That report was in fact, as
we now know, the public obituary of the steam barge *W. B. Hall*,
one of the last reminders then afloat of the great Bentley Gale.

Anxiety gripped hundreds of Georgian Bay homes throughout
the long hours of this great storm. Reports of wrecked craft of all
sorts and sizes (two vessels, now nameless, went ashore not far
from the *Bentley*), of battered wharves and waterside buildings,
streamed over the wires from all parts of the Georgian Bay. But
there was no word of loss of life. For days families and friends
dared not believe that they had been told the full truth. But at
the end of the week it became certain that they had every reason
for rejoicing: with all its extraordinary violence and madness the
great wind had indeed not taken a single human life. Can one
wonder that the Bentley Gale is famous?

Chapter 6

WEST SIDE, EAST SIDE

IN 1895 the steam barge *Africa* was not what she used to be;
in the social scale of lake steamers of that day she had lost
caste. Well built in a good shipyard in 1872 as a propeller she
plied the Lower Lakes with the worthy rank of a carrier of
passengers. Her length was designed to permit her to pass through
the St. Lawrence and Welland canals. In the early eighties, along
with the side-wheelers *Magnet* and *Spartan* (the latter of which
the writer knew on Lake Ontario and the St. Lawrence), she was
transferred to Upper Lake routes radiating from Owen Sound.
One unlucky day while reposing at her dock in this port she was
swept by a fire that left her little more than a floating trough.

Courageously the owners refused to count her a total loss. In
a few months they crowned her scorched remains with bright new
upperworks, refitted her engines, and sent the remade vessel out
on the Great Lakes with the lowly status of "steam barge."
Though now down in the world of shipping she was still useful.
But few folk in those times were really aware that a patched ship
is like a patched garment, old, worn, and weak at the seams, and the
service into which the patched *Africa* was put was as heavy as any
that she had undertaken when she was still new. There was one
difference, however: she now carried goods instead of passengers.
Long before the nineties it was manifest to many a lake sailor
that she belonged in the growing class of "coffin-ships."

The Tow-Barge "Severn" Grounds off Boat Coves

The three-masted tow-barge *Severn* was, like the *Africa*, also
of the vintage of the seventies. In 1881 she was one of a line of
vessels sailing the Georgian Bay and Lake Huron, a line consisting
of three barges of her own type and their towing ship, the steam
barge *Isaac May*, which bore the name of the fleet's owner. All
four bottoms were engaged in carrying lumber, then the most
active trade of the Upper Lakes. Upon Captain May's death the

fleet was sold. Like many other owners the purchasers failed to realize that the *Severn* had gone the way of all busy ships and had become decrepit and unseaworthy. Fittingly did the chronicler of her wreck write not long after that sad event: she "ought to have been laid peacefully on the bottom of some harbour, after having served her day and generation, instead of sailing the lakes with valuable cargoes and precious lives."

The fourth of October, 1895, was a fateful day for the ancient *Africa* and *Severn*: it marked the beginning of their last voyage. Some time during that day the two ships, fully laden with coal, left Ashtabula, Ohio (a busy port not many miles west of Erie), bound for Owen Sound. It was understood that upon delivery of their cargoes there they were to go on to Parry Sound and take on lumber. With the *Africa* towing the *Severn* the 200-mile trip up Lake Erie, the tedious ascent of the Detroit and the Saint Clair, and the first stage of the passage up Lake Huron were completed uneventfully. Not until the morning of October 7 did anything out of the ordinary occur. Some time after the two ships had passed the broad mouth of Saginaw Bay and were standing off Au Sable Point, which lies about opposite Southampton on the Ontario side, a heavy gale from the south suddenly caught them astern. In view of the direction in which the ships were headed a wind from that quarter was not unwelcome. It did not seem to be too strong to make resort to sail unsafe. So the *Severn* hoisted her canvas and the pair scudded northward.

All went well till the middle of the afternoon when the wind freshened and began to shift little by little from the south to the southwest and then into the west where the crews prayed it would stay. But all wishes were vain, for the wind swung on into the northwest. By four o'clock it had settled down in that quarter and was raising seas of an alarming height. Both ships were now beamwise to the gale, but though floundering heavily in the trough of the waves managed to maintain some steering-way. No time this for even the slightest mishap! But a mishap did occur, and no slight one either: the *Severn's* foresail was blown out of the bolt. Half an hour later the main gaff was broken and in a single instant away went the mainsail. But despite the dreadful drag not all headway was lost. For two hours longer tow-boat and tow ploughed on with their bows pointed on the opening to the straits between Cove Island and Manitoulin. The former was now not far off. If only the strength of men and of ships would hold out a little longer, in the lee of Cove Island they could count on safety.

But about half-past six all hopeful reckoning ended abruptly when the captain of the *Africa* became convinced of the futility of trying to keep two vessels moving in such seas. So regretfully he cast the towline over the stern and left the unpowered *Severn* to her own devices. Through the irony of a fate that often pursues seafarers, the barge's captain, James Silversides, was now forced to repeat a harrowing experience that had been seared on his memory not so long since—a long, perilous drift in the helpless barge, *Victor*, over the raging waters of the open lake. Now again, against all prospects of coming through alive, he had to shift for himself and battle for his own life and the lives of his crew.

In reading the story now one's first impulse is to blame Captain Larsen of the *Africa* for losing his head and for reckless action that exposed others to certain death. But in such a case a fireside reader has little right to judge. The very person who was most gravely affected by the action took a kindlier view. Later, in giving his account of the disaster, Captain Silversides freed his colleague from censure on this and other minor points. The *Africa*'s hull, he maintained, had become so weakened under the excessive strain of many hours that it was making water fast and was in extreme danger of foundering at any moment. It was criminal folly for a vessel almost a wreck herself to attempt to tow to safety another vessel in like condition. To cut the *Severn* adrift was a proof of Larsen's seamanship. Since it was just at dusk that the two ships parted company the crew of the barge were perforce too busy with their own imperative duties to be free to give more than an occasional thought to the *Africa*. Their last blurred glimpses of her were to them proof enough that Captain Larsen was sparing no effort to force his ship forward to shelter. After these few fitful views the *Africa* was never seen again. Where did she go down? How long did she ride the gale? Did she carry her crew down with her? Or did they take to the lifeboats and perish in them? No one knows. Of the crew of twelve not one escaped to tell the tale. Only two relics of the *Africa* ever came to light: a lifeboat and a bundle of letters belonging to the stewardess-cook were picked up on the shore of Manitoulin Island.

One concern possessed the captain and crew of the *Severn*— the dual one of saving their lives and then, if possible, their ship.

With the utmost thrift of time and energy they aimed every effort toward that end. To give the ship at least a little headway Silversides had the crew set the staysail and mizzensail. Only two possible shelters were open, and both of these to the east: the well-charted channel into Stokes Bay, a passage lying off the big lighthouse on the north end of Lyal Island; or, six miles up lake, one or other of the narrow, reef-bounded channels leading into the shallow, dubious haven of Boat Coves. Officially known in the *Great Lakes Pilot* as Bradley's Harbour, it is described as a "foul bay fit only for small tugs and boats." Its entrance is hedged about by jagged rocks and half-submerged reefs. Captain Silversides knew that in normal weather he could easily hit the opening squarely and that the *Severn's* draft would carry her through the passage. Of the two possibilities Boat Coves was the nearer. Thus the Captain's mind was made up for him, and the barge was headed forthwith for Boat Coves.

By now her hull was filling very fast. Hope of escape from foundering rested solely upon the strength of the steam pump; this was worked without an instant's lull. But merely to remain afloat was not enough. The greatest reason for alarm was that the ship was now barely steering, since her spread of canvas was too scant to drive her ahead at more than a snail's pace. At last she lost all forward motion. By now not a soul on board had any doubts as to the gravity of the situation; the end was near if not right at hand. In the last hope that by slowing down the vessel's drift she might hold together till daybreak, the crew cast out all the anchors. But one by one their lines parted, and the *Severn* soon afterward, almost on the stroke of ten, crashed on a reef half a mile from shore. At once the seas mounting to great heights on the shoals that lie roundabout washed right over the ship, and, pouring into the hold, put out the fires beneath the boilers of the pump and the hoist engine. To avoid being swept overboard the crew fled to the rigging.

Aloft, in the lashing wind, the men nearly perished from the bitter cold. Since the *Severn* had ridden the reef bow on, it was her stern that had to take the brunt of the waves' pounding as they rushed in from the open lake. In a few minutes it was broken into fragments. Soon the water, dashing in cataracts down the sloping deck, ripped off the hatches. The crew, chilled to the marrow, each watching his chances, one by one slipped into the hold. There with bits of wood from the cabin they kindled a fire on the coal of the cargo and prepared a small meal of sodden bread and hot coffee.

But still more welcome was dawn. Soon after seven o'clock the crew were seen from shore by Steve Bradley and a companion. At the risk of their lives the two launched a rowboat and after valiant efforts finally brought to land all twelve men of the doomed *Severn*. They gave them shelter in a log shanty until seas and skies made it possible to sail them into Stokes Bay village. The distance inland from the shore to the north-south road was only four miles but that was too great for utterly exhausted men to attempt to traverse on foot. Besides, the intervening area, lying in the broad, swampy valley of Spring Creek (locally known, for the best of reasons, as Rattlesnake Creek) was then pathless for the first two miles.

For Bradley and his companion a writer of fifty years ago had high praise: "The act of these two men was a daring one," he said, "and worthy of the Royal Humane Society's medal." Since this eulogy was written facts have come out that were unknown to its author. There is grave reason to believe that Bradley just missed being a hero. For the food and drink consumed by the rescued band he demanded payment. Worse still, to make sure that he got it he forced Captain Silversides to give up his watch as security. That was the story the good captain told John MacKay, the keeper of the lighthouse on Lyal Island at the entrance to Stokes Bay; not very long ago MacKay's son, Neil, told it to me.

Steve Bradley,[1] though long since dead, is not forgotten. While the scene of the rescue is commonly called Boat Coves, yet in the Canadian government's volume, *Great Lakes Pilot*, for Lake Huron and the Georgian Bay, it has for years borne the name of Bradley's Harbour. Did this designation just happen? If so, chance was not wholly mistaken.

Farewell, "Macassa"

"The *Manitoulin* on her way to the scrap heap." Crisp as a headline this dispatch, fresh from a well-known port of the Upper Lakes, appeared recently in the daily press. In the minds of men who have been conversant with Great Lakes ships and shipping of the last sixty years it wakened many memories. What these memories actually were will come as a surprise to many. They

1. See chap. XI, "The Serpent in the Garden."

related not to the long line of *Manitoulins* that reaches back to
the first of the name in 1880, but rather to the name originally
borne long ago by this the last *Manitoulin.* It is as the *Modjeska*
that she will more readily be recognized, the stately *Modjeska*
which with her somewhat older sister-ship, the *Macassa,* for many
years sailed the day route between Toronto and Hamilton on
Lake Ontario.

When the horn of the motor car sounded the knell of steamer
traffic over this short run, both ships, still apparently sound of
hull and fully seaworthy, were taken to Owen Sound to work
out of that port in the Georgian Bay and the northern part of
Lake Huron. Naturally enough, they were christened afresh, not
to cloak sinister reputations but to bedeck them with names that
helped blend them into their new scene of service in the ancient
Indian country and its waters. In that change the *Macassa* became
Manasoo. Into the space afforded by her length of 160 feet and a
rather narrow beam her owners managed to squeeze enough
cabins and staterooms for seventy passengers. She was equipped
to handle freight also. In April of 1928 she became an active
member of the fleet operated by the Owen Sound Transportation
Company on the route serving Owen Sound, Manitoulin Island,
Sault Ste Marie, and Mackinac.

Early in September of this same year the *Manasoo* had already
concluded her regular schedule for the season, which had been
a very profitable one. Thus left free to take special commissions
she made a trip to West Bay—a village on a deep indentation in
the north shore of Manitoulin Island west of Little Current—to
take on a load of cattle. On September 14 with her live cargo she
left the Island bound for Owen Sound. In the early hours of the
next morning she ran into very heavy weather while making her
way southward across Georgian Bay. Nevertheless she was making
positive headway, and nobody saw the slightest reason for apprehension. Sailing through the kind of gale that was blowing was
a mere commonplace for the captain and his experienced crew.
From the lights on the Peninsula they knew that they had passed
Cape Croker and probably Hay Island as well. Soon they would
be off Griffith Island, the outermost of the three islands lying
athwart the entrance into Colpoy's Bay, and would then be no
more than twenty miles from port.

But when the *Manasoo* came abreast of the big island and was riding about a mile off its shore a strange, violent tremor shook her whole frame. In all their days afloat neither master nor crew had ever felt its like before. Unsuspecting confidence in an instant gave way to acute alarm. The decks seemed to sag underfoot. Captain John McKay thrust away the thought that the ship might be sinking and sent Mate Oswald Long below to see what was wrong. Before Long could descend far he saw that the *Manasoo* was doomed. A veritable river was streaming into the hull, a deluge that no human power could halt. Long's report was never made, for already the ship was dropping like a sounding lead toward the bottom of the Bay.

All hope was now pinned upon the lifeboats and the raft. So brief was the moment when the main deck was level with the water, that it was scarcely perceptible. Yet in that flash of time the crew succeeded in pushing off into the waves two boats and the raft. As these floated off only a couple of the men were able to scramble aboard; all the others had to leap into the raging waters and take chances on joining their comrades on either raft or boats.

Day broke three hours after the *Manasoo* went down. The survivors on the raft scanned the waters all about them. They were filled with dismay: they were adrift on the broad, open expanse of the great Bay and were being rapidly carried eastward by the powerful westerly gale. In the offing, and drifting in the same direction, an overturned lifeboat was bobbing on the heaving seas; two men were clinging desperately to it. For a few moments the boat would be lost to sight as it sank into a trough; then for the same brief interval it would reappear riding on the foam of a breaking crest. When the men on the raft saw it for the last time only one man was left on the upturned keel.

The *Manasoo* sank in the early hours of a Saturday morning. Not until the afternoon of the following Monday was the raft sighted. By that time only six human forms were aboard it, and one of these was a corpse: Chief Engineer Thomas McCutcheon had died from exposure. Among the five who were still alive were Captain John McKay and Arthur Middlebro, of Owen Sound. When sighted by Captain Davis of the Canadian Pacific steamship *Manitoba,* the raft was in the middle of the broadest tract of the Georgian Bay, about halfway between Vail's Point, about twenty miles north of Meaford, and Hope Island which lies north of

Christian Island. Through sheer good luck the wind had borne it
almost squarely across the course of the *Manitoba* outbound from
Port McNicoll.

The delay of an hour or two in the *Manasoo's* arrival at Owen
Sound caused little comment, for it was clear to everybody that
the strong blow outside would slow down navigation. But when
all Saturday went by and no word had come in about the belated
vessel, anxiety gripped her owners and the people of the town.
With the silence of all Sunday and the greater part of Monday,
anxiety became despair. About three o'clock on the Monday afternoon the first syllable of news was flashed in by radio: Captain
Davis of the *Manitoba* reported that he had rescued Captain
McKay and four others from the raft and would land them in
Owen Sound in three hours. He also relayed Captain McKay's
request that a search be started at once for the two lifeboats and
any members of the crew who might have been able to make
shore.

The response to the appeal was prompt and generous. Many
square miles of waters and coast were scrutinized by the sharp
eyes of sailors and airmen. Tugs and launches from Owen Sound,
Wiarton, and other places scoured the shores, while the task of
scanning the open waters was left to aeroplanes from Camp
Borden and to the *Manitoulin.* No quest devoted to the saving of
human lives was in these parts ever carried out more unselfishly
and more faithfully. To the deep regret of all who were engaged
in it not another survivor of the disaster was found.

Of course, a public inquiry into the sad affair was held in due
time. Every scrap of fact, every promising hint that might satis-
factorily account for the accident, was examined. Of the host of
possible causes considered three seemed to be better supported
by probability than all the others. Either a steel plate of the
Manasoo's hull had suddenly given way before the ceaseless
pounding of the seas; or the stern windward gangway had been
instantly crushed in by a wave carrying the momentum of a
battering ram; or a violent lurch of the vessel to leeward had
hurled the cattle on board out of their stalls in a solid mass and
thus given the craft a terrific list far beyond the margin of safety.
Of the three possibilities it was agreed that the third was the most
valid. But whatever the truth, even the most judicious minds felt
certain that the cause could not have been foreseen: it struck
with the suddenness of a bolt of lightning, and in a fraction of a

second released a flood into the hull which an army, posted for that specific emergency, would have been powerless to dam back.

It was with the obituary not of the *Manasoo* but of her sister, the *Manitoulin*, that we began this story. Yet as we mused upon it our thoughts were really upon the *Manasoo*. No, the *Macassa*. Never could we get used to the new name. In the waters that still ripple and sparkle in our memory the *Macassa* is even yet afloat, an industrious, graceful craft which made it possible for countless city-dwellers to enjoy the tonic of fresh air and sunlight that brood over the open lake.

From the relish of this pleasant memory we must turn with regret to the grimness of a tragic reality. It is indeed cause for sorrow that the ship whose chief service long had been to give wholesome pleasure ended her career in an experience that also meant the end of nearly a score of her faithful sailors. Dramatically the *Macassa* disappeared to join the *Jane Miller*, the *Waubuno*, and a veritable fleet of other unlucky ships that had gone before.

> And there, unmarked of any chart,
> In unrecorded deeps they lie,
> Empearled within the purple heart
> Of the great sea for aye and aye.[1]
> —DUNCAN CAMPBELL SCOTT

1. From "The Piper of Arll," in *Selected Poems of Duncan Campbell Scott*, ed. E. K. Brown (Toronto: The Ryerson Press, 1951), p. 50.

Chapter 7

FOLKLORE OF THE FISHING ISLANDS

THAT the Fishing Islands, on the west of the Peninsula, like White Cloud and others on the east, have mysteries of their own is the most natural thing under the sun. Their very fabric, the perils of dubious shoals and channels that beset them, give manifold reasons for wonder. It is hard to find a likelier place for the brooding and hatching of folklore. Long before the white man came these islands were the scene of wreck and death to Indian wayfarers in the great Freshwater Sea. It was with fear and trembling that even the boldest of the early white adventurers paddled or sailed in these waters. Gother Mann noted that even before 1788 several of those who had essayed to round the Peninsula had lost their lives. Undoubtedly some of them perished among the Fishing Islands, adding the unsightly remains of their bodies and craft to those already scattered along the rocky shores.

When the first permanent settlers came in the 1850's, they found there enough of the grim and the gruesome to provoke fancy to begin weaving a tissue of ghastly tales. Again and again these were retold around driftwood fires on summer beaches as ghost stories are told before the flames of winter hearths. But their telling was more than merely a way of passing the time: it was a manner of reminding fisherman, sailor, and camper that this rugged chain of islands and the nearby mainland bristled with perils. Over the years it has trained a succession of careful navigators.

When Alexander McGregor made Main Station Island his headquarters, he found skeletons strewn here and there on its shores, the remains of Indians bleached by the suns and surf of centuries. His frequent comment upon this experience was passed on by word of mouth from man to man until, embroidered by the imagination of each successive *raconteur*, it became a sort of local saga.

In the fifties something happened that added another chapter

70

to the Island's docket of creepy tales. Whatever it was in fact it was akin to that nebulous order of unverified events which fire the uncritical fancy of lonely frontier folk into a frenzy of surmises that fly from cabin to cabin across the wilderness like sparks over the summer-dry forest. Nothing can check the spread of this flame of gossip; in a few weeks it is accepted as gospel truth. In this particular tale there seems to have been at least one kernel of fact. Apparently, some of the colony of fishermen on Main Station Island had been unfair in their dealings with the Ojibway Indians on the mainland. Not unnaturally, the Indians seem to have given vent to their anger in the form of hasty though futile threats to get even. Here was a theme ready-made for the mind that revels in inventing startling fables out of drab commonplaces. The romancer in this case—he or she, I refrain from saying, though there is reason for suspecting some definite person—declared with the positiveness of a news broadcaster that the Indians carried out their threats in their race's ancient way of wreaking vengeance, by raiding the habitations of those who had wronged them. The affair, says the fable, was like the bloody massacres on the frontiers of New France and New England; all the whites, except two, were killed; these, both children—Hiram Cole and his sister —saved themselves by hiding in a cave at the north end of the Island. To this day a certain hollow under a limestone ledge is known as the Children's Cave.

The way of the "debunker" is hard; yet I cannot but take it. The germ of reality in this thrilling camp-fire story is very small and is far from clear; in the fifties some rather violent domestic upheaval, affecting several families, took place in the fishing colony on Main Station Island; whatever it was it suddenly and mysteriously made orphans of two children of one family, children who grew up to be citizens of the Bruce Peninsula and later were known to a number of people of the region. But that event, one must state as positively as one can, was not an Indian massacre: the Ojibways of the Saugeen Peninsula have always shown themselves to be lovers of peace and respecters of human life.

A score of years after the mythical massacre Main Station Island came back into the news. This time it was one of the scenes of action in the Mercer murder case, a case which gained a great deal of notoriety at the time. Even the passage of three-quarters of a century has not wholly blotted out the memory of this tragedy.

The power exerted on the mind of man by tales of mystery, violence, and death is brought out most vividly by the fact that they can quickly erase long-established names and bestow new ones. Early in the white man's association with the Fishing Islands the presence of a group of tall basswood trees on one island fixed on that area of rock the name Basswood Island. But fifty years later that designation disappeared from popular use and was retained only in the written records. Shortly after the turn of the century a party of campers found the body of a man jammed into a gaping fissure on the island's shelving shore: Deadman's Island it has been ever since.

A few years later the corpse of an unknown was washed ashore one spring on Beament's Island. We say "unknown" despite the fact that several persons maintained they knew it to be the remains of a Southampton fisherman who had been drowned the summer before. But, since they could not prove they were right, a veil of mystery fell upon Beament's that time has not yet lifted.

At no time in its history has this cluster of islands been wholly clear of the disquieting shadow of uncertainties and unsolved problems. Those who reside among them or near them never know when a sudden deluge of trouble may break before their eyes. The memorable cyclonic storm of Sunday, November 9, 1913, brought them one of the most harrowing sights of all. It must have been in the open lake right opposite the islands that two of the many lost ships went down. And great ships these were: the *Isaac M. Scott,* of 9000 tons and 524 feet in length, and the *Hydrus,* of 7000 tons and 436 feet. Ghastly relics of these steamers and their crews were found scattered along the coasts of the islands and the mainland from French Bay north to Pike Bay. Main Station Island alone was given more than its share: the body of a Swedish deck-hand, a life preserver and a lifeboat of the *Isaac Scott,* as well as the engines of the *Hydrus.* At French Bay the body of the *Isaac Scott's* captain was thrown up on the sand, and on Chief's Point was found the body of an unknown. Red Bay yielded two bodies. At Preacher's Point was found the corpse of a deck-hand the content of whose pockets mutely told a story of a wasted life: fifty cents in coin, a packet of obscene cards, a letter from a mother in Cleveland whose heart was being broken by wondering why her son was not writing home.

Even so substantial a ruin as the stone-built headquarters of

McGregor's fishery on Main Station Island[1] is the subject of pure guessing so spun out as to merit being called a legend. The ordinary wayfarer in the district, unversed in the few known facts of its history, and with the common man's blind reverence for the remote past, accepts as the real truth about the old building the story that pushes its origin farthest back in time. Today the ruin is commonly called "The Fort"— a term that smacks richly of antiquity. In support of the view that the nucleus of the building may be of French origin some old-timers point to Baron de Lahontan's general map of Canada. Across the northwest corner of the space representing all Huronia and the Bruce Peninsula are written the words "Fort Supose" (*sic*). What the label means the chatty Baron himself tells us in his book. Fort Supposé, as the name should be written, is the purely imaginary fortified outpost, or "little Castle," which about 1690–1 the Baron recommended to Frontenac should be set up on "the South side of the Bay of *Toronto* [Georgian Bay]" and "at the Mouth" of that bay. Probably he had in mind a defensible site somewhere near the present Tobermory. Even if this "little Castle" had been built Main Station Island as the scene of it must, for a very obvious reason, be ruled out: it is too far south, down open Lake Huron, of the "Mouth of the Bay of *Toronto*." But folklore is a stubborn thing; certain minds forced to give up their belief that "The Fort" was originally French hold it to be a relic of the early days of the Hudson's Bay Company. But when all this wishful surmising is over, one fact stands out, at least for me: Captain Murray McGregor long ago told Norman Robertson, the author of the *History of the County of Bruce,* that his father, Alexander McGregor, began and finished the building; and that word Norman Robertson reported to me in his own home thirty years ago.

And in no niggardly mood did McGregor and his men build. With a quarry hard by they gave their walls the generous thickness one sees in frontier fortresses. Nor did they spare human touches either within or without the walls. In recognition of the body's need of comfort they gave an open hearth to each of the building's two rooms. Nearby, outside, one can still see shaggy, straggling vestiges of their garden of bush-fruits. Still farther off is the sad, untidy relic of the resting place they set aside for their dead. As one looks upon it, one cannot suppress an uneasy wonder.

1. See chap. X, "The Great Draughts of Fishes," pp. 112–13.

Can the few who were laid away here long ago really rest in peace amid all this loneliness? Do their spirits and the spirits of the nameless unburied whom wind and surf idly tossed upon the island, do these ceaselessly roam about the ruin and the bold encroachments of the returning forest? Some minds given to toying with such questions are inclined to attribute to disembodied souls the eerie atmosphere that enwraps the whole tract.

But nothing so quickly hurries the wild flower of fancy to full bloom as the uncanny behaviour of a living man who by choice has made the wilderness his home. Of such persons the worst is always suspected. One instance of the kind I myself knew in the mid-nineties. An unkempt hermit lived in a crumbling log cabin in a small clearing on the portage between Lake Muskoka and Lake Joseph in the District of Muskoka. He had no neighbours nearer than those living at the two ends of the portage trail, and these he avoided, as he did portagers also, as much as he possibly could. One day a comrade and I, frantic with thirst on the heavy three-mile carry from lake to lake, invaded his hovel in search of a drink of water. The old man chanced to be in a mood to talk— just a little. We got this out of him: his name was Thompson and he had studied in Oxford with Gladstone. His neighbours, we learned afterward, knew no more than we did. But out of this tiny shred of knowledge their ingenuity manufactured an astounding character for the old fellow. Nothing but a terrible crime could have driven a schoolman of his social standing out of England into the Canadian wilds. Murder, arson, embezzlement are only a few of the offences of which he was guilty. But, of course, of all these vain imaginings old Thompson knew nothing. When he died a kinsman came from England to settle the petty backwoods estate. In one casual word he cleared a name sullied by years of idle gossip. Thompson's only crime was that of being jilted at the very steps of the altar: a sensitive wounded spirit had gone queer, that's all.

Like Muskoka the Fishing Islands have had their hermit too. Here is his story, just as Roy Fleming told it in 1912.[1]

"Wildman's Island is situated to the south of Bowes' Island. It is a small quaint-looking spot having a few tall trees rising out of short bushes and undergrowth and three small buildings which serve as a protection for fishermen in the fall of the year. Two of

1. Roy F. Fleming, *Oliphant and Its Islands* (Toronto, privately printed, 1912); the tale is retold here with Mr. Fleming's permission.

the houses, one of them a landing place for boats, belonged to old Larry Bellmore, after whom the island was formerly called, and the other one to 'the Wildman' who lived here years ago, and whose story is perhaps worthy of being related.

"Many years ago a man belonging to a Lake Huron hamlet was disappointed in love by the woman he had hoped to make his wife. And so, deep in sorrow, he fled far away from civilization to the Saugeen Islands. There he chose the outermost island of the whole group as his home, and found whatever solace he might in the roar of the breakers of Lake Huron. He built for himself a strange little house of logs and driftwood picked up on the beach, and in this he lived for several years protected against storm and cold. He had a dugout canoe and an old fishnet he had found, and with them he went about amongst the islands, fishing, hunting game, and gathering wild fruits.

"He lived a lonely life, seldom showing himself to anyone, not even to the fishermen who sometimes came to fish the waters roundabout. His face was sad and careworn, as though he carried with him a burden almost too great to bear. When approached he would speed away with powerful strokes in his primitive boat, and at times when returning in the evening from the pursuit of game would give vent to loud weird calls, which would sometimes be heard on the mainland. So they called him the Wildman.

"It happened that in the fall one year at this time, some fishermen were staying on Main Station Island engaged in their regular fall fishing. A storm had blown for several days, and one night when it had about reached its height, from amidst the sound of the breakers and the sighing trees the fishermen thought they heard far-off calls for help. They listened, but heard only the storm.

"In the morning, however, when going through Main Station channel, the fishermen found the empty canoe of the Wildman swept up on shore; they knew then that what they had heard in the storm was the call of the Wildman in distress. No trace of the man was ever found, and whether in the storm he had met with accident, or, having found his life's burden too heavy to bear longer, he had committed himself forever to the sea, can never be told. Sometimes, however, in our fancy, in the dusk of evening or when the storm rages high, we still hear the call of the Wildman, and see him hurry away in his canoe to his island by the sea."

PART THREE : NATURAL WONDERS AND
       RESOURCES

Massasauga and Chipmunk

Chapter 8

THE TIDES O' BRUCE

*"There is a tide in Pleasant Harbour, which,
taken at the flood, leads on to fortune."*

*"Hold her there a while; she'll float out on
the next tide."*

MANIFESTLY, this is salt water language! And yet here we are listening to it on a little bay of a great freshwater sea. But the parody of Shakespeare is not just a joke. In Pleasant Harbour—one of the loveliest inlets of Lake Huron—you will really find a very marked ebb-and-flow of the waters. And that is the same phenomenon that forced the anglers, whose skipper's voice we overheard, to tarry a few minutes at the mouth of the lagoon in North Boat Cove. It was their ill luck that they had tried to make the open lake at slack low "tide," that brief span in the ebb-and-flow when the water in the narrow passage was not deep enough to float their craft. This rise and fall, though real, is not a true tide like that of the oceans. But though the scale of its operation is insignificant compared with the height and sweep and volume of the tides of Fundy and the English Channel, nevertheless it is a great natural phenomenon that is characteristic of all the world's large bodies of fresh water. The very fact that all who frequent The Bruce, residents and visitors alike, dignify this movement of Lake Huron with the name of "tide," shows that they regard it as an occurrence of exceptional interest.

This tide is distinctive enough to be given a name all its own, *seiche* (pronounced saysh), a French word chosen in French-speaking Switzerland in 1730 to designate the tidelike action of Lake Geneva. One cannot believe that the strange but obvious seesaw movements in large freshwater lakes elsewhere in the world escaped the notice even of the most primitive peoples. However, to the Swiss must go the credit of being the first to make an orderly study of them.

So far as I know the first European to note the phenomenon in

79

our American Great Lakes was that puzzling though alert person-
age, the Baron de Lahontan. The powerful shuttling of the
currents he himself saw in the Straits of Mackinac—and which
may of course be seen there still today—he sets forth clearly in a
letter written on May 26, 1688, on the Island of Mackinac.[1] What
the Baron saw was, manifestly, the action of the primary rather
than the secondary *seiche*.

> You can scarcely believe, Sir, what vast sholes of white Fish are catch'd
> about the middle of the Channel, between the Continent and the Isle of
> *Missilimackinac*. The *Outaouas* and the Hurons could never subsist here,
> without that Fishery. . . . In the Channel I now speak of the Currents are
> so strong, that they sometimes suck in the Nets, though they are two or
> three Leagues off. In some seasons, it so falls out that the Currents run
> three days Eastward, two days to the West, one to the South, and four
> Northward; sometimes more and sometimes less. The cause of this diversity
> of Currents could never be fathom'd, for in a calm, they'd run in the space
> of one day to all points of the Compass, i.e. sometimes one way, sometimes
> another, without any limitation of time; so that the decision of this matter
> must be left to the Disciples of Copernicus. . . .

To avoid becoming entangled in a mesh of scientific terms let
us at once view the *seiche* itself. Sail with me into Pleasant
Harbour. When we have gone about two hundred yards up its
straight canal-like entrance, let us cast anchor off the rushes at
our left, and allow our boat to swing freely on her anchor rope.
Shortly she swings into a position of poise that seems to be a
balance struck between wind and currents in the water. There
she hovers for a while and then begins to yield slowly to a power
that gently pushes her back towards the point from which she
started. The arc she has described is virtually that of a semi-circle.
The time elapsed in making it varies somewhat from day to day.
On some days I have noted intervals as short as five minutes and
on others as long as ten. As a rule, however, on any one day,
except when unusual weather conditions obtain, the interval of
ebb and flow holds for that day and for any particular inlet as
faithfully as the pendulum of your clock at home keeps to the
rhythm ordained for it by the clockmaker. Some wonderful thing
is happening here. Moreover, it happens every day and at every
season and in all the countless inlets along that whole shore. The
ice of winter hides these pulsations but they are beating just the
same.

1. Letter XIV; see *Lahontan's Voyages*, ed. Stephen Leacock (Ottawa: Graphic
Publishers, 1932), pp. 66–7.

Every angler who has fished on the Huron side of The Bruce or among the Thirty Thousand Islands of the Georgian Bay knows what I mean. Many a time he has cursed his inability to get his boat to stay close to the pool where he knows the bass are. Though it seems easy enough when the wind blows steadily from one quarter, the boat in a mulish way persists in swinging back and forth, back and forth, in that monotonous half-circle. When the boat points lakeward the fishing lines slant inland; when she points inland the lines slant lakeward, in either case just where the fish are not. It maddens even the most patient of anglers to realize at last that the inexorable oscillations go on for hours and hours on end. If, however, he has any curiosity and will open up his mind just a bit, he will see an interesting instance of cause and effect. A strong current of water pressing landward from the immense expanse of Lake Huron is opposed by a powerful current hastening to return to the lake. First one current prevails and then the other, and so on in an endless and uniform seesaw. For any fisherman who knows the ways of the ocean it is second nature to call this everlasting inflow and outflow, this ceaseless surge and ebb, a tide.

Do you still doubt that what you have just been witnessing is one of Nature's wonders? If so, I can show something more spectacular near at hand. Let us pole the boat to the very head of the channel in Pleasant Harbour, another two hundred yards, perhaps. Straight over the bow we see the channel sharply narrow to a width of a few feet and become very shallow—not more than a foot in depth. Beyond this neck it broadens into a pool a hundred feet long and several feet in depth. Observe the neck closely: a strong stream of water is flowing through it landwards with the rush and stir of a small river. Even as we gaze at it, the current little by little slows down and weakens, comes to a dead standstill, and gradually starts running out toward the lake until at length it is as swift and boisterous as it was when it was coursing in. Here, as at our first anchorage, the flow has reversed itself and would go on thus, it seems, forever. In this little strait the action is more pronounced than in the broader waters farther out because the volume piles up in the narrow passage faster than it can get through to the pool beyond. On its own minute scale is it not another Fundy?

But what has all this to do with our parody? In his own facetious way its author was stating a fact. Any fly-fisherman who

reads this will, through a sixth sense that comes from casting in
many waters, guess at once what it is. In early summer the part
of the pool that lies just above the foaming narrows abounds in
bass. They gather here to refresh themselves in the well-aerated
waters of the reversing rapids. As the current surges in or out they
are keenly alert and will seize a wet fly with a fury that gives fly-
fishing its superior zest and fascination. But at dead slack of low
seiche or high *seiche* the bass are as inert as the stones among
which they lurk. So in that charming corner of Pleasant Harbour
there is really a tide which taken at the flood leads the angler on
to the good fortune of a well-filled creel.

Now that we have seen the *seiche* at work it is easy to understand what the scientists have to say about it. The first Swiss
observers noticed that in Lake Geneva there were temporary but
rhythmical changes of level that were different from waves. In
fact, there were two of these, a primary one with a long rhythm
running parallel to the long axis of the lake, and a secondary one
of shorter rhythm running across the lake. The water rose and fell
alternately, leaving on the shore a ribbon of moisture—perhaps
two or three inches wide—which marked the difference between
the high level and the low level of the surface pulsations. In my
student days at the University of Geneva nearly fifty years ago I
frequently watched the *seiche* at work. Its obvious regularity both
fascinated and mystified me. When *la bise,* the raw northeast
wind of winter, blew down the lake towards its outlet in the city
of Geneva, it hoisted the level of the water at that end. Con-
versely, the southwest wind driving up the deep, narrow gorge
of the Rhone forced the water up lake toward the castle of Chillon.
But in wind and calm alike the surface of the lake kept on rising
and falling in a leisurely but steady rhythm of its own. Meanwhile
a transverse oscillation of much shorter intervals was also working,
swinging southward from the Swiss shore and then back again to
the north. The movement is ceaseless and ever will be until the
contours of the Alps are utterly changed or the winds of central
Europe are funnelled into new courses.

What can be seen on a small scale in Geneva may be seen on
a large scale in Lake Huron. It is very easy there to sense the
force of the primary *seiche,* the powerful current that operates
north and south between Point Edward and the islands of the
North Shore. Anchor a boat a quarter of a mile off Kettle Point,
or Grand Bend, or Goderich, or Southampton, it matters not

which, and throw out a line with a heavy lead. The power that immediately drags line and weight up lake or down lake, as the case may be, is the primary *seiche* whose rhythm is long, slow, and ponderous. Hours may elapse before it reverses its direction —even days. You will have the same experience in the open waters of the Georgian Bay off Pointe au Baril, or in Lake Erie anywhere off shore.

All the time you have been watching the effects of the primary *seiche* in the open expanse of Lake Huron, the secondary *seiche*, or "tide," with its short, quick vibrations has been playing like a tireless shuttle along the deeply indented shoreline, now westward, now eastward. Out in the lake the movements are too slight for the eye to catch, but when they reach the mouths of the rivers or the many shallow basins amongst the coastal shoals they thrust themselves upon the notice. At Goderich they make the Maitland actually flow backward periodically. When once this *seiche* has pierced the gaps in the rocky coast of The Bruce the waters fork out in every direction and like a hundred hydras each with a hundred heads grope amid the maze of tiny channels to find which of them offer passage inland. Such was, and is, the "tide" at Pleasant Harbour and in myriad other narrow coves like it. The water from the lake chokes the constricted openings and, mounting up outside, from its higher level spills inward with all the stir and gurgling of a river dashing down a slope.

Who does not know that moving waters anywhere, either salt or fresh, profoundly affect the fortunes of men who go a-fishing whether for play or for a living? Ocean liners, battleships, yachts, cargo boats, barges, dinghies, gas-boats, dories, canoes, all alike, great or small, on the scale suited to each, move as the waters will that they shall. The majestic *Queen Elizabeth* either casts or weighs anchor at the behest of a modest tide. Our Lake Huron *seiche* is also a bit of a despot. At times, she says when and whither an angler may or may not go with his craft for his daily fishing; and when the wind is in league with her she speaks with an even sharper finality. Some angler may recall Gravel Harbour during the lowest stage of the low-water cycle in the Great Lakes —Gravel Harbour, the best bass pool between Stokes Bay and Cape Hurd. Do you remember how rarely during those impatient years you could get a large gas-boat into its sheltered basin? For that keen disappointment you must in part blame the *seiche* as well as the cycle of low levels.

An insignificant, tiny, harmless thing, this *seiche*, it would seem
—a motion as slight as the swaying of grass in the wind or the
twitching of an aspen leaf. But again and again has the world
suffered sorely from being blind to powers hidden in small
things. If the *seiche* is harmless why do those who sail the Great
Lakes or dwell upon their shores fear it? Why do governments
make it their business to know its ways? The plain truth is that
the *seiche* is as formidable a menace on the water to life and
property as is forest fire on the land. Read what a department of
government[1] has to say: in its very nature such a statement must
be a model of sobriety, no fiction of an amateur. First it describes
the character of the *seiche* and then presents a striking illustration
of the phenomenon still vivid in the memory of many Lake Huron
residents.

The lake surface is never at rest, even during the calmest of weather, and
large scale sensitive recording gauges register continuous irregular oscillations referred to as "seiches." The barometric pressure may be constant in
the vicinity of a recording station, while an area or areas of lower or higher
pressure may be passing or prevailing over distant sections and thus affecting
the whole surface of the lake. The range and time interval of the seiches
vary, being governed by the configuration of the shoreline and offshore
depths; thus at the apex of a bay, with a wide mouth, the seiche range will
be greater than at the entrance, the reverse being observed in large bays
with restricted entrances, the seiche range then being greater at the nar-
rowest section. Generally speaking, a pronounced increase in the normal
seiche range precedes a storm approaching from offshore. The wind con-
tributes a second irregular action by forcing the surface water to pile onto
the lee shore faster than the undercurrents can return the volume to windward. . . .
    On July 16, 1931, starting at 4.30 a.m., a major seiche, or oscillation, of
the water level was recorded by the self-registering gauge located at the
downstream end of the Northern Navigation Company's wharves, in the
St. Clair river at Point Edward, Ontario. The seiches were without doubt
due to areas of sharp variation in barometric pressure, over the lower end
of Lake Huron, preceding a violent wind and electric storm which passed
over the vicinity of the St. Clair river during the following night. The water
level first rose 18½ inches in thirty minutes then receded 46 inches in one
hour and forty-five minutes, followed by a rise of 36 inches in forty-two
minutes. The main seiche was followed by three undulations of 18-inch
average range at intervals of about three hours from crest to crest or from
trough to trough. The oscillations then reduced to a range of about 6
inches, with intervals of two to three hours between crests, until 8 p.m.
July 17. The range then again increased to an average of 12 inches till

1. Canadian Hydrographic Service, *Great Lakes Pilot*, vol. II: *Lake Huron and
Georgian Bay* (1948 ed.), pp. xxviii–xxix.

about 8 a.m. July 18, after which the actions gradually reduced to the normal irregular range of a few inches, peculiar to this location. During the two days of July 16 and 17, the wind at Point Edward and Goderich was reported as light south, and at Port Lambton, twenty-five miles downstream, the weather was reported as calm on both days. The rise and fall of water level carried down the St. Clair river taking approximately one hour and six minutes for each high or low seiche to cover the twenty-five miles to Port Lambton. During the period of travel the range of the major seiche was reduced from the 46 inches to 16 inches, or a ratio of approximately 3 to 1.

A very violent *seiche* took place on Lake Erie on September 25, 1764. A certain Captain Thomas Morris, of His Majesty's 17th Regiment of Infantry, recorded the event in his journal.[1] Captain Morris, it seems, was instrumental in causing General Bradstreet's army to retreat in haste down the Sandusky River where unfriendly Indians had laid an ambush for the troops. "This army suffered extremely afterwards," he notes, "and great numbers were lost in traversing the desert, many of their boats having in the night been dashed to pieces against the shore, while the soldiers were in their tents. The boats were unfortunately too large to be drawn out of the water. The sentinels gave the alarm on finding the sudden swell of the lake, but after infinite labour, from the loss of boats, a large body of men were obliged to attempt to reach Fort Niagara by land, many of whom perished. It is worthy of remark, that, during this violent swell of the waters, soldiers stood on the shore with lighted candles, not a breath of wind being perceived. . . ." The remark concerning the stillness of the air makes it clear that the destruction of the boats was wrought by a *seiche*.

The *seiche* sometimes plays unexpected tricks. In Buffalo, New York, in 1904, a second *seiche* in a most curious way completely reversed the action of the exceptionally high, strong *seiche* that had preceded it.

A lumberman named Fritz Riebenach of Alpena, Michigan, bought the old steamship *Arabia* which had been out of commission for some time in Buffalo. He looked the boat over very carefully and . . . made a contract to buy her "afloat in Buffalo harbor." He came to Cleveland that night where he obtained funds to make the final payment for the ship, after which he took the night boat back to Buffalo and on his arrival there was amazed

1. For the text of the entry in the journal and for comment upon it we are indebted to a note by Dr. E. M. Kindle in the *Canadian Field Naturalist*, vol. XLIV, 1930, pp. 196–7. In vol. XLV, 1931, p. 67, there is additional information on the occurrence of *seiches* in several large bodies of water.

to find his boat not "afloat in Buffalo harbor" but *upon* the dock, about six feet above the lake level, and several feet from the edge of the dock.

This situation was very serious, so Mr. Riebenach took the next train to Cleveland and sought the advice and aid of his attorney, Frank Masten. . . . After a long conference Mr. Riebenach and Mr. Masten went to Buffalo by train. On arrival there they took a cab to the *Arabia's* position, atop the dock, intending to get facts to support legal action for a breach of contract in making delivery of the ship. To their surprise they learned that during the night another seiche had lifted the ship from her new position *on* the dock, and had set her down in her normal position in the water *beside* the dock, which satisfied the contract terms that she be delivered "afloat in Buffalo harbor."

This was a very happy solution of a complicated situation, caused, and later corrected, by the forces of nature. . . .[1]

The setting of the stirring action I am now about to describe is Tamarac Island in Stokes Bay, site of the Tamarac Club.[2] The island is a narrow ridge of limestone rising thirty feet above the surrounding water and has a length of half a mile. An excellent example of the carving power of ice, it lies with its long axis pointing straight into the southwest along the path of the glaciers themselves. On its western side and parallel to it extends a shallow glacial trough which at its south end broadens out into a spacious beaver meadow. Trough and meadow together hold enough water to form a large lagoon which, were it not for the regular churning of the "tide," would be hopelessly stagnant. Not far from the north end of the island the channel that divides it from the mainland contracts to a neck of water about fifty feet wide. Here, back in the eighties, lumbermen threw across the little strait two long, stout pine trunks as stringers to carry the planked floor of a bridge strong enough to bear the weight of the most heavily laden wagons. In the process of providing each end of the structure with an abutment of rough stone the builders narrowed the passage to twenty feet. This had the unforeseen effect of amplifying several times the force of the *seiche* as it rushed back and forth between the lagoon and the bay. Since the channel at this neck is at least ten feet deep the volume of water passing through it is very great and is as sensitive to the slightest variations of pressure as is a thermostat to fine changes in temperature. Its quickness to register them is clear to any one who looks into the water from

1. Benjamin L. Jenks, "Tale of Two *Seiches*," *Inland Seas*, vol. I, 1945, pp. 55–6.
2. The Club was originally a sawmill, and is now unique among the old mills of these parts in that, unlike all the others, it has been salvaged from neglect and decay and put to salutary human uses. See chap. XVIII, "The Mill at Stokes Bay."

the bridge. Nowhere else in the Great Lakes have I ever found a spot where one can view so convincingly the reality, the constancy, and the irresistible power of the secondary *seiche* of a freshwater sea.

Now our scrutiny of this eternal flux and reflux is more than an academic pastime. It is of practical import to angler and navigator. Long has the little strait by Tamarac Island been famous in this region as a gathering place of the black bass. The constant agitation of the current charges the water with oxygen and the fish throng there for a breathing spree. The stories of fabulous catches made in the narrows by loggers and sawyers of threescore years ago are not just reports of actual fact magnified by the memories of what might have been. For that, I have the word of one who, in later life a bishop, was in those early days a member of the timber gangs who cast their angles from the bridge when the day's work was over. In his late teens he was in the employ of his father, a master lumberman, on Tamarac Island. Many a leisure evening did the young man pleasantly spend in whipping the reversing waters. At times so richly were his efforts rewarded that the good bishop still fears to cite the true figures lest he be regarded as just an ordinary fisherman—just one of the common guild who suffer from chronic inflation of the faculty of calculation. Not a word more would he say than this—with a convincing smile: "The rosiest of the tales of fishing here in the old days are all true." He smiled again when I told him that even in these lean days of angling the bass still congregate by the bridge.[1]

The day of the Great Tide! And many there are who remember it. Two aspects of it stand out in their memory above all others: their amazement that a scene of such violence as one usually associates with a tempestuous ocean could take place on an inland lake; their fears at the thought of the stupendous damage that this strange phenomenon, suddenly bursting from the blue, might produce. The exact year I cannot recall: it seems to have been about fifteen years ago. This at least is clear: it happened in one of those few summers when the reef in mid-channel between Tamarac and Garden Islands projected above the surface like a sharp-peaked cairn. So distinct was it that it was its own danger sign to warn strange navigators to give it a wide berth.

Dawn that day in mid-July brought with it an unwonted languor

1. Bishop John Kidd of the Roman Catholic Diocese of London died in 1950 soon after this account was written.

that became perceptibly heavier as the hours shuffled on. Its weight pressed down upon man and beast alike. The clubmen's inveterate passion for going a-fishing yielded to a leaden listlessness: no hampers were packed that morning for shore-dinners at Pleasant Harbour or Little Pine. Even the lonely club cow and a neighbour's horses grazing by the lagoon and the beaver meadow showed no zest for the lush marsh grasses. Perhaps the peculiar atmosphere drugged our fancy into working overtime, but at the time it really did seem that there was less snap in the hop of the grasshoppers and in the leap of the frogs in the grassy fringes of the lagoon. The barn swallows as they swooped and darted and dodged over the water did not seem so sure of themselves as they usually were, and the gulls, which generally spent their mornings cruising over the bay, seemed chained in a long line to the peaked roof-ridge of the old mill.

The water in the channel at the bridge was out of tune with the prevailing mood. The "tide" was busy shuttling back and forth with more than ordinary vigour: the timing between ebb and flow was that common to most days in summer, but each successive pulsation bore with it a greater volume of water. Moreover, whether flowing in or flowing out the stream was rushing with greater speed and vehemence and was making itself heard in a crescendo of splashing and gurgling like a mountain burn in spate. The normally docile minor *seiche* we saw in Pleasant Harbour had become here at Tamarac a turbulent reversing river. But in contrast to this agitation of waters we were sharply aware that the stifling air and the broad expanse of Stokes Bay were still as death. A feeling of apprehension almost made us shiver. Everything around us, animate and inanimate, seemed to share it with us. It was manifest that in the vast cauldron of the elements some extraordinary brew was being mixed.

We were not left long to our guessing. Over the air came a voice giving out a loud, curt warning to mariners. I recall its substance though not its words. "Storm signals out for eastern Superior and northern Huron. All ships of deep draft in lower St. Mary's River anchor at once. Pleasure craft make for shelter without delay. Expect northwest winds sixty miles followed by torrential rain. Clearing later. Tomorrow clear and cooler."

Now we knew what brew of weather to look for. Nor was there much delay in the serving of it. The blanket of light grey which from noon onwards had been almost stealthily drawn over the

sky had by this time become stained with vast patches of an
intensely dark grey. For several minutes it retained this shade
and this formation, and then, as by an unseen hand, the fabric
was rent apart into long parallel strips between which shone rays
of a weird, coppery half-light dyed as with diluted blue-black
ink. Far to the west we could faintly hear what might be the
beating of surf on reefs or on shore, or even the sustained lashing
of the tops of many trees. Even as we listened the air began to
move slightly toward the southeast; its gentle fanning was welcome indeed.

During this interval of wondering and waiting we became
aware that the little strait at the bridge was beginning to boil
and foam in an unusual manner. Each incoming *seiche* was rising
higher and with more commotion than the one before, and each
ebb sank lower and more noisily than the ebb that had just preceded it. The span between high water and low water was now
at least a foot and was increasing with each reversal of the current,
which had now the volume of a stream after a thaw. Though we
were standing on the summit of the island two hundred yards
from the turmoil the roar of it tingled in our ears. The whole
scene touched every nerve within us. Even the birds were be-
having oddly. In the eerie twilight, like that of an eclipse of the
sun I once saw at Rondeau on Lake Erie, the swallows ceased
their skimming over the bay and retired to the rafters of the old
mill as if for the night. In separate flocks the gulls and the crows
set out, each flock in its own direction, with the singleness of
purpose that marks a homeward flight. The only living thing
within our ken that remained unmoved was a lone great blue
heron. There he stood like a tall grey stick lodged in the muddy
bottom of the lagoon. He had the air of waiting for something
worth waiting for. He was right. Doubtless having lived all his
summers in this region of inlets he had known such a scene before.

At last, as though bursting through the rents in the sombre pall
above, a tempest tore upon us. The release of all the winds of
heaven in one moment from Aeolus' bag could not have struck
with greater violence. The winds we had been hearing in the
offing now seemed to take on visible substance. Yielding to their
thrust the forest bowed as one tree and stayed thus fixed for
many moments. Unable to stand longer before the blast we fled
to the shelter of the old mill. Was this a tornado? Surely not in
this corner of the globe! Our anxiety was not allayed by the

Lagoon at Tamarac Island—normal level before a seiche

casual remark of a villager born and reared in Stokes Bay: "Well, in July—1892, I think it was—a twister blowed nearly all Wiarton down"!

No sooner had we dashed into the mill by the front door than we were summoned to the back door by the roaring of the water at the narrows. From the high landing outside we could see the whole lagoon and the bridge. The lagoon was as empty as a drained bath tub! The *seiche* driving in the same direction as the wind had drawn off all the water whose last dregs, churned into mud and strewn with a litter of dead herbage and brush, were pouring madly through the channel under the bridge. On the bare oozy bed of the lagoon stood out some unfamiliar objects— two wooden logging cribs weighted down with a filling of stones; in the lumbering days long past these had served as end-anchors to booms of logs. Round about them flopped helplessly a dozen or more huge carp and a host of small fry such as perch, sunfish, rock bass, and large shiners. And on these the heron, standing drunkenly a-totter in the gale, was lustily banqueting. As each fish descended to its gastric doom we could plainly follow its progress by watching the lump that passed down the long serpentine neck. It's an ill wind indeed that blows nobody good!

But the enterprising bird was not left long to his feasting. In

Lagoon at Tamarac Island—twenty minutes later, after a seiche

a few minutes the water sank to its lowest point, stood still a while, and then began to flow back, at first gently, but soon at a speed that lifted the level of the lagoon eighteen inches above the average height for that summer. And thus the portentous ebb and flow went on for another quarter hour, a rhythmic seesaw of waters on an immense scale. What was the stupendous force that endowed one of Nature's most placid aspects with a capacity for violence?

For an answer hark back to the warning from the air. This force was as it were a fortuitous conspiracy of barometer, wind, and *seiche* to work in unison—a pooling of their powers. The light pressure in the east allowed the waters to rise appreciably along the deeply indented shore of The Bruce. The high pressure on the Michigan side weighed down the level there and by the same action propelled the water eastward. This double push, reinforced by the drive of a near-hurricane, threw up a veritable flood upon the Bruce coast. But this is not yet the sum total of the elemental forces at work here: one has still to reckon with a "tide," the secondary *seiche*, a normally unimpressive little movement but nevertheless a dynamic one which is in action night and day, in sunshine and under cloud, in summer and in winter, forever swinging to and fro in accord with the beating of some cosmic metronome. No skill of man can wholly calm it or nullify its hidden power. When Nature happens to be in the mood to add this force to that of the other conjoint elements, she holds in her hand an engine whose possibilities of destruction defy computation.

From all this tumult on the mainland side of Tamarac Island man was entirely absent except as a helpless onlooker. But on the Stokes Bay side it was different. Heeding the warning from the air, lesser water craft of every pattern, from punts with humming outboard motors to sixty-foot luxurious gas-cruisers, were speeding from the open lake in a long broken column to find shelter or mooring at the government dock near the village of Stokes Bay. Most of the larger vessels were manifestly unfamiliar with these waters. On they hastened toward the dangerous shoal in mid-channel, innocents abroad in strange waters, unaware of the risk they were courting. The heap of jagged rocks was completely buried beneath a flood tide. By sheer luck most of the skippers safely passed by to one side or the other. But to the dismay of our watching group the finest and largest cruiser of the column was headed straight for the hidden peril. We were helpless to aid: the rush of the wind drowned our voices even shouting in concert, and the untimely twilight and the shifting curtain of spray concealed all signals. Now we knew why "it boots not to resist both wind and tide." Before our anxious gaze the graceful craft rode straight on to the lurking shoal. Her bow rose abruptly and her stern dropped. In that position she came to a sharp stop and stood as though impaled on an unseen spike.

But we were not the sole witnesses of this scene. From the government dock a rowboat struck out for the stranded cruiser. Even as the oarsmen sped toward her a strong ebb of the *seiche* set in and the water began to subside. By the time the rowboat reached its goal the peak of the shoal was standing a foot above the water. Upon it was perched the handsome vessel like a streamlined Noah's Ark come to rest on the summit of a miniature Ararat.

But while the two crews conferred the dark blanket of cloud overhead was ripped again and again by jagged strokes of lightning. In a moment large solitary blobs of rain began driving through the air at a rakish slant. After that came the deluge. How long the cataract descended I cannot recall; it seemed to promise no end. In its falling it quickly beat down to a dead level the foaming crests of the breaking swells and ironed out the wrinkles of the wavelets. By the time the clouds had vented themselves of their burden the rain seemed to have subdued even the fury of the gale to the pace of a normal midsummer afternoon breeze.

Not till then could the true plight of the cruiser be observed. By the veriest good fortune, it turned out, she had slid on an even keel upon the only smooth flat slab of dolomite in the whole reef. Had she veered a hand's breadth from her course her hull would have been slit open on the points of limestone that bristled all about. A few hours later the lovely craft was gently eased off the detaining rock into the water, unscathed though not unmarred.

While the cruiser was being set free, the sun, now nigh to setting, was beginning to stain the sky over Lake Huron; the dry, cool northwest breeze of evening was already calming nerves that had been taut and touchy all day long; the swallows were dipping and curvetting as usual over the lagoon; the nighthawks were swooping and screeching overhead, and the minor *seiche*, having spent all her reserves of power in the violent orgy of the daylight hours, was once more in her wonted mood guilelessly and quietly swinging back and forth, back and forth, in the narrows by the old log bridge.

Chapter 9

IN THE DAY OF THE WILD PIGEON

OF the many gifts that Nature bestowed upon The Bruce one in particular will never be seen there again. Indeed, it has vanished from the face of the earth. It is known now only in museums, in slim dockets of old records, and in the memories of a very few men of exceedingly great age. All too soon there will be not a single one of these left who can say: "With my own eyes I have seen this once marvellous gift—the vast armies of the wild passenger pigeon." Among my elderly friends there is only one who saw this bird in the days of what seemed to be its unimpaired abundance. But it was not in The Bruce that he was acquainted with the creature; he knew it in the southern parts of Ontario and in Michigan. The person who first told me of its vast numbers and its habits in the Peninsula was my own father; during my boyhood in the middle eighties he spoke to me again and again of the great flights he saw there. His memory of them was still so vivid that he could never talk of them without considerable excitement.

So far as I can figure out now it was in the latter half of April, 1872, that my father went to the Bruce Peninsula. About the middle of that month he would have completed his freshman year in Toronto and so been free to take up some kind of summer work. As a candidate for the Baptist ministry he was charged with the duty of establishing a mission station on the north shore of Colpoy's Bay in a settlement of the same name. This place—an attractive village today—was ten years older than Wiarton, having been settled in 1856. Though only three miles from Wiarton it is in a different township—Albemarle instead of Amabel—a fact of some significance in regard to our present subject.

My father came to the Bay from Owen Sound by the steamer *Champion* which was then giving a daily service to a number of small places in this corner of the Georgian Bay. He boarded during the summer in the log home of a farmer who had hewed a good-sized farm out of the forest. A picture of his entry into this frontier household was vividly stamped on his memory by two events of the first day: as he stepped from the steamer to the shore and walked to his summer quarters a vast flock of pigeons were flying from the east to their nesting area on the Peninsula and were casting a dark, swiftly moving cloud over the land. At his very first meal, supper, he was served adult wild pigeon. At breakfast the next morning this was the main dish, and for dinner too and then again for supper; indeed, it was the only *pièce de résistance* —and a tough one at that—of each meal for the next five weeks. Moreover, each meal was opened with the same appropriate twofold preface: the head of the family, with no trace of irony in his voice, devoutly thanked the Almighty for the bounty of his tender mercies, and with his first breath after the "Amen" offered the guest an apology for the bounty over-extended in the form of stringy parent pigeons. Somewhere in each grace the host never failed to cite the Lord's goodness to his chosen people in sending them flocks of quail to feed them in the wilderness. Nor in reciting his apology did the good man forget to hold before the stranger within his gates (like Moses portraying his vision of the Promised Land) the prospect of that delectable day soon to come when the butterball squabs would be ready to melt in the settlers' mouths.

The people of the region took pride in believing that the Peninsula was ideal country for the pigeons. It was common opinion around Colpoy's—an opinion based solely on rumour—that the nesting and roosting colonies were so numerous as to form virtually an unbroken chain running northward to a point not far short of Tobermory. Of course, that was not quite true, but to express doubts about it was counted in the new settlement as disloyalty to the wonderful greatness of the Peninsula. However, the only colony that Father himself saw was very long indeed: it began near Chief's Point on Lake Huron just north of the mouth of the Sauble River and extended in a broad sinuous line north to within a couple of miles of Lake Berford. That is, it ran from the west side of Amabel Township to a point two or three miles within Albemarle and slightly less than that distance north of Wiarton. What more natural than for the wild fowl of the air to ignore the boundary lines of a man-made survey! Somehow Father gained a distinct impression as to the direction in which the chain of rookeries ran: it seemed to follow inland and northward the

winding course of a chain of shallow lakes—Boat, Isaac, and Sky—
and their connecting streams and bordering marshlands, almost to
the head of the chain, Berford Lake.

That the colony covered several square miles was all too
obvious, but how many one could only guess without making a
special expedition to determine the exact figure. The area appeared
to offer everything the pigeon needed to thrive—suitable nesting
sites on a huge scale; ample and varied food supply from early
spring to early autumn; swampy tracts and stream beds that
occasionally dried up in midsummer to satisfy a curious craving
for mud and gravel. Nine or ten miles east of Berford Lake was
another large colony of pigeons, but it was closed to the white
settlers because it was within the bounds of the Indian reserve of
Cape Croker. Observation of the colony nearer to his lodgings,
together with the prime bass-fishing in Lake Berford, absorbed all
the scant leisure he had left after completing his pastoral rounds
over the slow trails of a pioneer territory.

The sound and sight of the pigeons as they took wing on their
morning flights and returned to their roosts in the late afternoon
never ceased to impress, no matter how often one had seen or
heard such flights before. The noise evoked as many comparisons
as there were persons who heard it. It reminded Father of the
deep booming basso of the Canadian Falls at Niagara as heard
by one standing on the footway behind the heavy curtain of
falling water. To others it seemed like the deep tones of thunder
as its echoes roll across the sky; to still others it resembled the
roar of an express train rushing past near by. It was astonishing
that such a sustained volume of sound could be produced by such
small creatures. The classic description of the impression made
upon the human mind by the vast flocks of the wild pigeons is
that of the Indian Chief, Simon Pokagon, who gave it to the
world in print in 1895 on the very eve of the bird's extinction; one
can do no better than quote it now. "I have seen them move,"
writes Pokagon, "in one unbroken column for hours across the
sky, like some great river, ever varying in hue; and as the mighty
stream sweeping on at sixty miles an hour, reached some deep
valley, it would pour its living mass headlong down hundreds of
feet, sounding as though a whirlwind was abroad in the land. I
have stood by the grandest waterfall of America and regarded the
descending torrents in wonder and astonishment, yet never have
my astonishment, wonder and admiration been so stirred as when

An Army of Pigeons Invades the Peninsula

I have witnessed these birds drop from their course like meteors from heaven."

The settlers' constant wonder that the pigeons always flew southeastward in the morning across Colpoy's Bay and Owen Sound raised the question of what the birds fed upon. It was surmised, and perhaps correctly, that in Grey, Simcoe, and other easterly counties they found greater areas of land sown to peas and spring wheat where they could easily forage. But what did they eat in April? Of only one thing was anybody really certain: upon alighting after their spring flight the pigeons forthwith addressed themselves in hordes to scratching through the litter of the previous autumn's leaves to pick up the remnant of beechnuts that had escaped the sharp eyes of the red squirrels. In this region it was not acorns they sought, since the white oak did not grow there and red oaks were few, as they still are. The beech, however, was abundant and many specimens are yet to be seen in the area. But when the tasty fare of nuts was gone what did the pigeons eat? None of the oldest inhabitants had an answer to give; I have had to dig it out of books. Undoubtedly, the diet then became a varied one: chiefly the tender leaf and flower buds of such trees as the elm, birch, and aspen; a little later, the winged seeds of the elm (sometimes called elm-nuts) and of the maple. With these green stuffs were mixed several kinds of the previous year's ground berries—wintergreen, partridgeberry, bearberry, and the little red fruit of the lowly Canadian dogwood, the bunchberry. One who knows the prolific plant life that hugs the soil under the screen of the Bruce forest may suspect that the pigeons' spring fare was anything but lean.

What the ravenous fowl ate in summer was never in question, for one could see them as it were at table. In hosts they would drop upon a clearing crimson with wild strawberries and in a few minutes leave it just a patch of rumpled green. By mid July all the Juneberry bushes were stripped of their juicy little fruits, as were also the wild raspberries, currants, and even the prickly gooseberries. Later, the birds pillaged the pin cherries of their tart scarlet bullets. In some parts of the United States the pin cherry was not without reason known as pigeon cherry. In harvest time the pigeons were not a great threat to the newly broken lands of the Peninsula; for them the stooks on the older and broader wheat fields farther south were a greater attraction. But they did annoy the makers of the new clearings for they had a most uncanny way of telling which of these open spaces in the forest were planted to peas. Sometimes the settler had to plant his peas twice in the same season. If the pigeons missed the second planting and allowed it to mature its crop, there was still a chance that they might swoop down upon it and in a mere half hour thresh it clean. In 1872 Father's host, a grower of peas, was one who suffered from this scourge. He who in spring had fervently given thanks before meat for the boon the early pigeons had been to his meagre board, in autumn just as fervently cursed them for robbery.

We can now understand why a certain bishop of New France was driven to lay a curse, like that laid upon the thieving Jackdaw of Rheims, upon the pigeons that plagued the Lake Champlain region. Baron de Lahontan, who was there in September of 1686, tells the story thus: ". . . we eat nothing but Water-fowl for fifteen Days; after which we resolv'd to declare War against the Turtle-Doves, which are so numerous in *Canada*, that the Bishop has been forc'd to excommunicate 'em oftner than once, upon the account of the Damage they do to the Product of the Earth. With that view, we imbarqued and made towards a Meadow, in the Neighbourhood of which, the Trees were cover'd with that sort of Fowl, more than with Leaves: for just then 'twas the season in which they retire from the North Countries, and repair to the Southern

Climates; and one would have thought, that all the Turtle-Doves upon Earth had chose to pass thro' this place. For the eighteen or twenty days that we stay'd there, I firmly believe that a thousand Men might have fed upon 'em heartily, without putting themselves to any trouble."[1]

The wild pigeon, both individually and in its distinctive corporate life, was a creature of rare distinction. From our mourning dove, its closest existing kin, we can recover for ourselves a picture of its extraordinarily graceful lines, and, by a slight amplification of length and breadth, gain an idea of its size. Its habit of congregating in gigantic flocks was unique among the species of the whole pigeon family; the similar instinct of the western variety of the North American mourning dove, as shown in its winter home on the desert of Arizona, is only faintly comparable. All who know our wild pigeon agree that both the male and his somewhat smaller and plainer consort were most beautiful birds: the amazing iridescence of the rosy neck and breast of the male and the rich shaded blue-black of the wings and back of both sexes caught the observer's eye, while their long graceful tails completed the perfect streamlining that made swift, sustained flight possible. Sometimes when the sun's rays fell at a certain angle upon the flying clouds of birds one seemed to be beholding a great trailing streamer of shot-silk billowing across the sky.

In its mass feeding on the ground the wild pigeon had a way of its own: we can see a hint of it on a smaller scale in the orderly foraging march of an army of starlings across an Ontario stubble field. In a cascade the pigeons would fall from high up in the air upon the ground, whether in the forest or in the fields, and then, as if conscious of moving under the orders of a leader, would straightway deploy into a broad front with a relatively shallow depth. The whole body would then rotate forward over the ground like a colossal cylinder with a surface of agitated feathers. While the birds in the van of this animated roller picked the soil and litter clean, those in the rear would flutter overhead and onward to form a new advancing front. And thus this living juggernaut wheeled across tracts of woodland or tilth as ruthlessly as an avalanche tumbles down a mountainside. From all parts of the lower Peninsula men and women thronged to this great open air aviary to watch the pigeons feed. Each sightseer had his own figure of speech to describe the action of the pigeon army in the

1. Letter XI; *Lahontan's Voyages*, ed. Stephen Leacock, p. 46.

field; one of them with a sense of humour and of the picturesque termed it "leapfrog with wings."

In most parts of Ontario frequented by the pigeons, nesting colonies and resting roosts were considerable distances apart, but in the great Amabel-Albemarle rookery they were close together. Hunters of the region found this a great convenience: they could secure their quarry in two kinds of environment without having to travel far. While for nesting the pigeons seemed in the main to prefer deciduous trees, in The Bruce all kinds of conifers—pines, spruces black and white, balsam, cedar, hemlock, and possibly tamarac—were freely occupied. Father had the impression that in this region no species of tree was ignored. In a single tree there might be only one nest or there might be twenty. Each nest was a roughly made affair much like that of the mourning dove. As I write these lines an occupied dove's nest may be seen twenty feet from my study window; made of coarse twigs it reminds me of a random pile of jackstraws pressed down in the middle just enough to form a saucerlike hollow. The nests were placed at different heights above the ground, some as low as eight or ten feet and others in the topmost branches. The birds appeared to have a faint engineering sense, for when they were not crowded for space or pressed for time a pair would lodge their nest in a crotch of a branch close to the trunk of the tree. But when the late-comers found most safe positions of this kind to be already occupied, they built farther and farther out on the limbs until the weight of brooding and roosting birds sometimes snapped the branches off. Down would come a rain of eggs and squab in various stages of development!

To this *pot-pourri* of the living and the decayed was added the offence of the filth that coated the ground beneath the tree. But bad as it was it was not enough to chill the hunters' lust for slaughter. The descriptions of this stench that old hunters once gave me I have been able to appreciate keenly since August of 1931, when I saw Jack Miner's grove of three thousand Scots pines which to the last tree, it seemed, had been killed by the excess of nitrogen dropped on the ground by millions of roosting starlings. The Bruce had its parallel to this forest tragedy: an old-timer of Red Bay used to tell about certain wooded tracts on the edges of the Amabel rookery whose trees, after the pigeons had sojourned in them for two or three seasons, looked as if they had been swept by flames.

A hen pigeon laid one or two eggs at each brooding. Despite the immense total of the pigeons massed in flight the species was not prolific in the sense that the wild duck is prolific. Two factors in particular seemed to account for the enormous size of the pigeon population: the bird's capacity for raising, under favourable conditions, more than one brood in a season and, the almost perfect safety enjoyed by the colonies that nested in the vast unpeopled forests of the Hudson Bay watershed.

The story of the massacre of the wild pigeon of North America is, by reason of its stupendous scale, only a degree less horrible than the story of the long, bloody conflict between white and Indian. However, man was not the pigeon's first foe: long before he came on the scene the larger hawks harried the flocks as they swept across land and water, seizing one by one birds that straggled away from the speeding column. The cold strategy of the attacker and the frantic efforts of the prey to escape were a fascinating spectacle. Plainly, the scheme of the hawks was to scatter the pigeons as much as possible. This they did in several ways. One hawk would hover over the column causing it to dip low; another would tag on the rear, forcing the birds in panic to crowd forward; still another would swoop down on the van and make it veer sharply to one side. Always amid these wild evolutions a few pigeons lost touch with their flock and became easy prey. Here, a successful marauder could be seen in laboured flight bearing away his quarry to devour it in some quiet spot apart; yonder, others were returning singly to repeat their raids. The mad convolutions of the flocks under the shifting pressure on every hand reminded the frontiersman of a dense column of smoke from a forest fire twisting and curling across country before the lashing of cross winds. On a sunny day all the colours of the rainbow glinted from myriads of flashing feathers in splendid play.

The ways of slaughtering the pigeons were many, and varied with the conditions under which the hunter happened to come upon them. In spring their peculiar manner of flying at random all over the country before they decided just when and where to alight made their lives cheap indeed. In this stage of indecision the stupid birds would move in a long trailing line that sped along just above the varying levels of the landscape, rising and falling like waves over the tops of trees, across clearings and woodland roads, and again over shrubs and thickets. When the line barely skimmed the ground bands of men and boys would bat the birds

down with clubs or poles or scoop them out of the air with anglers'
landing nets.

This latter means of capture was suddenly brought back to
my father's mind in 1910. When our family took up residence in
a summer cottage in Muskoka we found a very large colony of
bats lodged in a spacious recess between chimney and rafters.
Prodded by a stick the creatures flew out in a cloud and circled
around the adjacent lamplit room. Father and I both took up a
position, like a batter at the home plate, vigorously swinging
broomsticks and landing nets. At the end of the bout the tally
was forty-four bats. "Just like a pigeon hunt at Colpoy's," gasped
Father, "only the pigeons flew straighter."

The gun was mightier than either club or hand net. But it was
deadly only in the hands of one who knew how to use it. Laugh-
able indeed was the blank amazement of greenhorns who shot
straight into the van of the oncoming birds and failed to drop
even a feather. However, the lesson to hold fire until the birds
had just passed over was soon learned. The echoing reports of
pot-hunters' guns sounded over Amabel as if the township were
the scene of a frontier battle between white man and red man.
What better commentary could one want than this news para-
graph from a Bruce County weekly, the *Paisley Advocate*, of
April 28, 1876: "The immense flocks of pigeons which have been
flying over various parts of the country in an undecided way for
the last week or two have gathered in the township of Amabel
in countless numbers, and have begun building. The nests are in
thousands, and many eggs lie on the ground owing to the breaking
down of branches. The place is visited by scores of persons, and
all the shot in Owen Sound and Southampton seems to have been
fired away as a telegram has been received in Paisley asking for
a supply."[1]

For many reasons there were not as many pigeon hunters in
The Bruce as there were in the older settlements of Ontario and
Michigan frequented by pigeons. The pioneers in The Bruce were
few and could spare but a small part of spring and summer for the
quest of the wild fowl. The remoteness of the Peninsula and the
lack of direct access to it by railway kept down the numbers of
hunters from other areas. The absence of large markets near by
left little incentive for those who would like to become professional

---

1. Norman Robertson, *History of the County of Bruce* (Toronto: William
Briggs, 1906), p. 79.

traffickers in pigeons. Only the Indians of Cape Croker came close to belonging to such a class. However, the few, both white and Indian, in the region who in the summer of 1872 made a trade of the killing, storing, and vending of pigeons gave an account of themselves which in volume would have done credit to an army.

The pigeons were not safe either day or night. When nesting was well under way the birds were taken with the utmost ease. As they sat on their eggs, or perched idly in the trees, or even as they billed and cooed in the ardour of mating, with the stupidity of the spruce grouse they barely moved aside as people came near them. They were clubbed, or shot, or pulled down by ruthless hands, just as they sat. Their captors alertly improvised many ways of killing them quickly so as to lose no time when the stream of slaughter was flowing strong. Some had the knack of giving a bird's neck a deft little twist, some knew the exact spot at the base of the head or behind the eyes to apply the pressure of thumb and finger or even of a pair of pincers—and all was over in a trice. A callous few found their own two jaws as effective as a tool and much more handy. As the butchers worked they threw their victims into bloody heaps, each man to his own.

Revolting as the carnage of adult pigeons was that of the squab was more so. Unable to do more than flutter idly, the young could be picked up like inert lumps of flesh. Being very soft they bled easily. Even children when given the task of wringing necks, without intending to be violent, often pulled the heads right off. The young folk though shrinking at first from the gory work soon became hardened to their part in it by the zest of seeing things done. For several weeks the scene in the forest was almost a continuous shambles day and night: in the daytime twilight of the woods it was ghastly enough to make one look away, but in the fitful red flare of pine knot torches it was so positively ghoulish as to make the flesh creep. But what really stabbed the senses was the sight, illumined by flares, of a tree felled by the hunters' axes crashing its way to the ground through neighbouring trees and carrying with it its helpless population of nests and birds.

There were other ways of reaping this gruesome harvest, notably netting and trapping. Oddly enough, many a hunter whose normal shrinking from cruelty had been numbed by the very excess of it hesitated to resort to these devices on the ground that they were cruel in requiring the use of blinded decoys—"stool pigeons." Whether for this reason or because there

were too few open spaces suited to the spreading of nets, netting
was little used in the Peninsula. Nets varied greatly in size,
ranging from 8 by 30 feet to 40 by 100. I have personally known
only one man who employed this ancient form of "the snare of
the fowler" in The Bruce; he operated in the soggy flat lands
north of Chief's Point on the Lake Huron side. His description of
the nets and how they were worked is too full of details to be
cited here.[1] Apparently, few persons in the region made systematic
use of box traps and liming, that is, smearing branches of trees
with sticky substances to which the pigeons' feet would adhere. It
was thought that the Indians resorted to such objectionable means
in the seclusion of their reserve.

The masses of victims would be taken away on the backs of
men or in wagons (where trails had been opened) or in home-
made boats. None but the sluggard's cabin was entirely without a
supply of pigeons. Market outlets were scant and distant. Inland
towns in south Bruce, north Huron, and in Grey got their birds
from nearby rookeries. The Indians of Cape Croker were by far
the most active purveyors of the whole region. They would muster
all the small craft of the reserve, load them to the gunwhales with
pigeons, and peddle their wares at every shanty and hamlet along
the shores of Colpoy's Bay and the Sound from Wiarton to the
town of Owen Sound itself. In the squab season a little Indian
flotilla plying its coastwise trade was a common sight. One of
these was made up, according to a description I have seen somewhere, of a sailboat laden with birds and behind it in tow a couple
of crude punts one of which was filled with fish and the other
with pigeons. What the peddlers did not sell *en route* was quickly
sold at Owen Sound. This was added to quantities of birds caught
in Grey and then shipped to places even as far away as Toronto.

Many were the ways of preparing pigeon for the table. A list
of the various ways favoured in southern Ontario or in Michigan
held equally well for the settlers of Amabel and Albemarle in the
Peninsula. The adult birds of the early season, though tough with
age and long flights, were a welcome change after a winter's dull
diet of salt pork, beans, and potatoes. Prepared in any way—fried,
stewed, roasted, boiled, or in succulent pot pies—they were ap-
petizing morsels. The last-named dish was favoured above all the
others, but it took time to make. Usually the busy pioneer house-

1. Margaret H. Mitchell, *The Passenger Pigeon in Ontario* (University of
Toronto Press, 1935), p. 124.

wife fried the old birds for the same reason that the modern city matron speeds up the work of the morning by frying bacon. Even now the reading of Mrs. Traill's recipe for pigeon pot pie makes one's mouth water and gives meaning to a popular ditty of a century ago that was patently a parody of a well-known gospel hymn. When I was a small boy my paternal grandmother, re-calling her experiences with the pigeon in the Ottawa valley, used to recite it for me.

> When I can shoot my rifle clear
> At pigeons in the sky,
> I'll say good-bye to pork and beans
> And live on pigeon pie.

In storing squab most people kept only the plump breasts and legs. These were first salted in brine; some were left continuously in the same liquid and others were smoked and dried. In a few homes the numbers of birds packed away were so great that even the dogs were sometimes fed on them. But plenty, like a medal, has two faces—one, contentment, the other, surfeit. With the advent of the spring pigeons the pioneer at his laden table saw only the bright face and never dreamed there was another. How-ever, six weeks of old birds, another six weeks of fresh squab followed by months of both kinds cured and stored, revealed the other face with all its dulness. Those who had feasted were now cloyed. Even the most pious householders were heard to murmur. The young student preacher, himself bored by the excess of a relish, could not consistently chide his flock for their complaining. The situation called back to my father's mind certain events of his boyhood in the fifties. In spring and summer the Atlantic salmon used to run in dense schools up the Châteauguay and other tribu-taries of the St. Lawrence. The rural tables of the district were as heavy with salmon as the tables of The Bruce were with pigeons. At long last Father understood with deep feeling why, before hiring out, farm hands made their employers pledge themselves not to serve salmon oftener than so many times a week. For Father the upshot of the matter was that within himself he prayed that the Lord would not call him to that part of The Bruce the next summer. The prayer was answered. It was not without keen regrets, however, that in 1873 he accepted a charge in another part of Ontario, for he had fallen in love with the Peninsula as a whole, while acquiring a distaste for a daily menu top-heavy with pigeon.

But never again will anyone, in The Bruce or elsewhere in North America, know a surfeit of the passenger pigeon. It has gone forever. In The Bruce its numbers began to dwindle rapidly in the last three years of the seventies; by 1885 the birds were scarce indeed. A resident of Red Bay whom I knew saw his last pigeon near there in 1893. As far as the whole Georgian Bay region is concerned the last word of the race's obituary is this: in May of 1902 three pigeons—a pair and a single bird—were seen near Penetanguishene, Simcoe County.

But who, or what, caused this once uniquely numerous species to disappear, and so quickly? In the light of a bloody record everybody leaps to blame "man, false man, smiling, destructive man." But one must always beware of the obvious. This answer may explain the bison's near extinction, but science in her caution believes it only partly true of the passenger pigeon.

No living person is in a position to tell us, with finality, what the other part of the story is. But several theories put forth by scholars who have studied the problem long and carefully impress one as having the convincing power of truth.[1] All authorities agree that "no one agency was entirely responsible for the disappearance, but . . . it was brought about by a combination of circumstances."[2] All agree too that the basic cause of extermination was in the nature of the pigeon itself. As a species it was a slave of instinctive habit and was supremely lacking in intelligence. When its routine of life was upset it was unable to adjust itself to the resulting changes. It would seem that, like certain other creatures observed by science, the passenger pigeon in order to survive had to maintain its population up to an especially high figure; it died out when the population dropped below that minimum.

But there must have been other factors also. It is not improbable that some disease—perhaps a disease already mildly endemic among the pigeons, or one brought from another continent and caught by the pigeons from barnyard fowl—may have fastened itself upon the race after loss of numbers had made it too weak to resist. Certainly a plague of any degree of virulence would have aggravated an already dangerous imbalance in the pigeon's group life.

But after all the chief disturber of this life was man. Much of

1. For a summary and discussion of views see *ibid.*, pp. 128–47.
2. *Ibid.*, p. 138.

the harm he did to the pigeon he did in innocence: even his laudable efforts to civilize the wilderness, such as logging, clearing the land, and setting up hamlets and towns, little by little forced the pigeon to retreat from its natural haunts. But none of man's acts was so violently subversive of the pigeon's normal manner of mass life as was his intemperate butchery. He had easy access to the passenger pigeon's nesting places, and he became its fatal enemy.

Chapter 10

THE GREAT DRAUGHTS OF FISHES

O N his map of 1815 Captain Owen clearly shows lying off The Bruce a line of small islands one of which is larger than any one of the others. He leaves them nameless. But in 1822 Captain Bayfield fills in the gap by writing across it the name "Ghegheto" and, close by, the words "Fishing Islands." In another document the Indian name is spelt "Gaheto." There is reason to believe that this form is none other than the Huron or Petun word for *island* or *islands*. Until 1885 the tiny archipelago belonged to the Saugeen Indians who in that year ceded them to the Crown.

A story still told among the Indians of the Reserve, but which one cannot now verify, has it that the transaction was a very shady one: the Indians were simply sold down the river by one of their own race. A resident of the Reserve (though perhaps not a member), a certain Jack Martin, a Mohawk at that, undertook without authority to act for the Reserve. According to the story, he sold the islands to the Crown at seventy-five cents apiece. But this might not have been the scandalous sell-out it seemed to be. If in a period of low water, the summit of every reef and every rock showing above water was counted as an island, the sum paid by the Crown may have been no trifling one. At any rate, it is said that to escape the wrath of the Reserve Jack Martin cleared out—with the money.

Soon after the Crown formally took over the archipelago the whole chain was properly surveyed. However, over the years the gradual lowering of the level of Lake Huron so changed the outlines and areas of individual islands that in many cases one could not tell just where the boundary lines between islands lay. Under such uncertain conditions nobody was willing to acquire an island. So in 1899 a new survey was begun and upon its completion a year later the islands were put up for sale. Fishing

Islands, in very truth! Though now long past their prime, no archipelago anywhere ever bore a more fitting name.

Even the names of the islands from the south of the chain to the north throw off little flashes of meaning. Some hint at casual episodes of local import, some at aspects of natural history, some at freakish contours and outlines. Even a passing glance at them brings out what manner of things, trivial or serious, influence the pioneer in choosing labels for the diverse places of his new-found world. Here are some of the seventy islands, which vary in size from the flat top of a dry shoal to Cranberry, the largest, with its 124 acres. Though the names seem as matter-of-fact as a laundry list, they are actually as quick with life as were the men who allotted them: Whitefish, Cigar, Whisky, Smokehouse, Squaw, the Jacks, Main Station, Cranberry, Rabbit, Frog, Rowan, Burke, Basswood, Snake, Beament, Round, and Green. On paper you may sail close to them with safety, but if you approach them by water, beware! Scout Reef, Drake and Harrison Shoals, Hattie Rock, and the long underwater arm of the Chimney Reefs are an ever present threat to those who venture rashly.

In 1831 (or perhaps a year or two earlier), just a few years after John Galt made his historic voyage on the gunboat *Bee* from Penetanguishene to Flowerpot Island and thence round Cape Hurd to the new Goderich on the Menesetung (now the Maitland) River, Captain Alexander McGregor of this lively hamlet was busy exploring the eastern shore of Lake Huron northward to the very tip of the Saugeen Peninsula. Not a bay, river mouth, channel, or inlet escaped his scrutiny. Everywhere, in off-shore shallows as well as in deep water, he found an abundance of the kinds of fish that are in commercial demand—herring, whitefish, and lake trout. But one spot was favoured above all others by herring and whitefish. Here in their seasons these two species came together in schools so dense that the fish, like Pacific salmon crowding up stream to their spawning beds, fairly lifted each other out of the water. This area was the varied waters of the Fishing Islands, their shoals, rocky banks, and the network of pools and winding channels among the islets.

But what lure was it that drew the fish hither in such huge bodies? That was a mystery. It was probably a supply of some favourite food which Nature had stored here on a scale little short of fabulous. Whatever it was, Captain McGregor saw at once that this was no time for theorizing but for action. Never before had a wayfarer on the Great Lakes in search of fish run into such luck. Here they were actually tumbling out of the water as if inviting capture. Without delay he bought a stock of seines, twine and kit for repairing them, and drying racks, added to his fleet of two-masted schooners and rowboats, and put in many barrels and a quantity of coarse salt. In a few weeks he had a camp ready for business.

Of course Captain McGregor caught fish, sometimes too many. That realization turned exultation to dismay. Like so many other pioneers who reap the rich harvest of a new territory, he found that in the zest of rapid calculation he had overlooked a vital factor: he had forgotten to obtain an outlet big enough to absorb his product. Many a frontier farmer has failed to provide in advance a market for his surplus wheat. Though this kind of situation has a tinge of humour about it, it is still too grim to be funny. Not till 1834 did McGregor find the market he needed. In that year he made a contract with a Detroit company to deliver not less than 3,000 barrels a year of salted whitefish and herring. The price was set at $1 a barrel, the company to assume the cost of cleaning, curing, and packing of all fish delivered even in excess of the quantity specified in the contract. While shipment by schooner from The Bruce to Detroit was long and, in the heat of summer, precarious, nevertheless in the main the arrangement was satisfactory for McGregor. From the start the business thrived and continued to thrive in a way that drew the eyes of envy upon it.

That the fishing was all that the fisherman himself said it was we are assured by a visitor who saw it. In July of 1838 the famous missionary to the Indians, the Reverend James Evans, when on his way by canoe to Sault Ste Marie, spent a day at the "Saugeen Fishing Island" to preach to the fishermen of "the Huron Fishing Company." "This is a fine fishery," he notes; "sometimes four hundred barrels of herring are caught at one single haul of the seine." Think of it: more than one-tenth of the minimum delivery for a year![1]

In more senses than one McGregor's course was not all easy sailing. Many a mishap befell the two-masters in which he took his packs of fish downlake to Goderich and Sarnia and thence on

1. Tradition has it that McGregor's last lift was 7,000 measures of 100 pounds each (350 tons); for lack of salt half the catch was let go.

to Detroit. In the autumn of 1835 one of his ships ran ashore thirty-six miles north of Goderich and was frozen in for the whole winter. But nothing so petty as that could daunt its owner: if he could not deliver the cargo by water he would by land. This he did by sleigh over the snow. In his diary Liard of Goderich states that on January 29, 1836, and again on March 18, he saw McGregor pass through Goderich on his way to the imprisoned schooner for a load of salted fish, each time driving a train of four sledges. How many times he made the trip unknown to the people of the village one can only guess.

Faithful accounts of the manner in which the fish were caught off the Fishing Islands are still to be had. By far the best is the one which the late Norman Robertson of Walkerton includes in his *History of the County of Bruce* of 1906. His information had come straight from the lips of McGregor's son, Murray, who was active in the fishery with his father. Murray's version calls to mind stories of the South Seas where natives, perched on high cliffs, scan the waters for signs of great schools of fish of many kinds. It was Captain McGregor's practice to post a man in a tall tree to enable him to get a clear view of the expanse frequented by the schooling fish. There the watcher stayed patiently, sometimes for many tedious hours, looking much like a kingfisher on a branch overhanging a pool. What he sought was the first glint of a sheet of sparkling silver moving swiftly over the water. The instant he spied it he shouted his discovery to the men on the ground. Without delay they launched the large heavy rowboat which, its stern piled high with the folds of a long seine, was held ready to respond to a sudden call. Guided by the lookout's signals they steered straight to the oncoming horde of fish. They dropped the net at a point from which they could begin drawing it in a great curve that would surround the moving mass. The circle completed, the animated "kettle of fish" was laboriously dragged shorewards.

Though of a race commonly accounted as stupid the fish did not submit without a struggle. "When [they] commenced to feel the pressure from the narrowing of the net," writes Robertson, "the scene was one long to be remembered. There in a small area were entrapped thousands and thousands of fish, sufficient possibly to fill five hundred to a thousand barrels. The water in that circumscribed space seemed to be fairly alive as the fish in their efforts to escape rushed madly about, causing its agitated surface to glitter with their silvery sides." Sometimes it happened that a huge sturgeon, weighing a hundred pounds or more, would be caught in the great loop along with the myriads of lesser fry. Like a salmon scaling the face of a waterfall it would hurl itself into the air in a vain effort to clear the slowly closing barrier. Perhaps several garpike, the swordfish of our fresh waters, would add to the commotion by shooting like arrows across the seething mass into the meshes of the net. But as a rule the twine was tough enough to hold them, too. Yet the fishermen did not like them, for they were always a threat to nets made with meshes gauged for smaller and weaker fish; with the philosophical manner of their guild they accepted them as among the minor hazards of their trade.

At length the net was hauled up close to the shore. Into the very middle of the seething pond which it formed strode a bare-legged fisherman armed with a long-handled scoop-net. With this he threw the fish on the beach in a slithering heap. When this seemed to contain all that the men could pack in a single day, the net was eased off shore into deeper water and the catch kept alive for packing on the morrow. Not seldom, through sheer ill luck or through lack of foresight, were the fishermen's labours brought to a rude halt by a shortage of barrels or of salt. At such times they would ruefully open the net and release the fish they were unable to handle. When a pack became large enough to make a full cargo, off it would go by schooner to Detroit.

So successful was McGregor's business among the Fishing Islands that he soon saw he needed more room for living quarters and storage than a mere camp afforded. Salt and packed fish could not be kept safely in the open air. With the quick returns from his lucrative trade the Captain built on Main Station Island, one of the largest of the group, a solid stone building fifty-seven feet long and eighteen feet wide. This satisfied all immediate needs. Today though in partial ruin it testifies to the skill and thoroughness of the pioneer mason. But its chief distinction is that it is the first building to be erected in the whole County of Bruce. As we have seen, local legends have gathered around it, all of them tinged with hints of adventure or of romance.[1] One of them has it that the building is an old trading post of the French régime. But this claim must yield to the story Captain McGregor's son, Murray, told to Norman Robertson. The latter

1. See chap. VII, "Folklore of the Fishing Islands," pp. 72–3.

"The Fort," McGregor's Headquarters, Main Station Island

inferred that the building was put up about 1834, though the year may have been as early as 1828. By 1848 the structure had acquired a notable status. In a report issued in that year Alexander Murray, a government geologist, states that "with the exception of a building which was raised by a fishing company at Gaheto, or Fishing Islands, there is not a single dwelling on any part of the coast all the way from the Saugeen [River] to Cape Hurd."

It is the tallest pine that draws the lightning, says Horace, that shrewd old Roman. So in the world of affairs striking success attracts the shafts of jealousy. Captain McGregor's good fortune was at once spectacular and unique. Here in waters very easy to command was a natural store of a staple food in quantities that seemed to be unlimited. Yes, unlimited as the armies of wild pigeons that crowded the airways and the forests of the continent; unlimited as the bison whose herds packed the broad spaces of the western prairies. Who in the eighteen-thirties dared suspect that before the end of the century the bird would have passed into utter extinction and that the beast would be on the verge of a similar fate? Whether McGregor himself believed that the schools of Lake Huron fish were inexhaustible or not, nobody can now say, but we do know that certain of his fellow-citizens did believe it. They saw other reasons also for the exceptionally profitable nature of his business: it required very little capital to

maintain; its market was rapidly expanding; returns were quick
and in cash. The lucky McGregor was indeed a ready mark for
cupidity.

The next stage was not far off. A clique of his own fellow-
townsmen cast covetous eyes upon his business. At a date now
known only approximately Colonel "Tiger" Dunlop, Dr. Hamilton, and Trader Gooding, claiming for their action the high
motive of protecting their country's interests, pointed out to the
Government that the country was suffering terrible losses of rich
natural resources. Their Exhibit A was the dumping of fish from
the prolific Fishing Islands into a foreign market. Moreover, they
charged, fishing on those grounds was under no control of any
kind. So they urged the Government to require each fisherman
operating there to take out a licence. This kind of talk, only some
fifteen years after the War of 1812, fell upon ears only too quick
to listen to representations against a former enemy. Unfriendly
words were spoken in public about that nation, but their effect
upon the relations between the two countries was as slight as
they were insincere. The real aim of the little syndicate of loyalists
was not, it seems, to steer the fishing schooners from the channels
of an alien market into the channels of domestic commerce, but
rather to gain exclusive control of the Fishing Islands industry
for themselves. It was as slick a political manœuvre as the famous
"double shuffle" of the fifties.

The outcome was foreordained: the noble band of patriots
became the Niagara Fishing Company and was given a licence
according it the sole right to fish the favoured waters off the
Saugeen Peninsula.[1] The threats against truck and trade with a
foreign power turned out to be just what they were intended to
be—threats only. The salted herrings and whitefish of the Canadian Fishing Islands were still borne into the market of Detroit.
There was one difference: henceforth the sails that bore them
were those of the Niagara Fishing Company rather than those
of Captain Alexander McGregor's Huron Fishing Company.

Before following the later career of the despoiled McGregor
we yield to the prompting of human curiosity. How did the de-
spoilers fare? "For some reason," the County's historian records
dispassionately, ". . . [the new company] did not meet with the
same success that rewarded the labors of Captain McGregor."

1. The licence was granted by an act of the British Parliament and the formal
consent of Chief Mitegual of the Saugeen Indians, owners of the Peninsula and
its islands.

There is ample reason to believe that this is a studied understatement. When Robertson wrote his history of Bruce nearly fifty years ago he knew much more of the truth than he could discreetly put in print: he had learned the whole story from Murray McGregor. Apparently, the usurpers met with failure from the outset. No mention even of the name of the company is found in the Misses Lizars' book, *In the Days of the Canada Company,* much less mention of its frustration. If it had achieved success one cannot imagine Dunlop and his partners keeping silent about it. Man is not prone to boast about his blunders. In 1848 the Niagara Fishing Company was glad to sell out for the paltry sum of eight or nine hundred pounds to Captain John Spence and Captain William Kennedy. These two, the founders of Southampton, carried on the business jointly until 1851 when Kennedy withdrew to take part in a polar expedition that set out in search of Franklin.

Dispossessed of his fishing grounds like a crofter of his lands, McGregor at once set himself bravely to the task of adapting himself to a cruel situation. He felt sure that in this vast freshwater sea there were waters never yet seined—channels, bays, deep basins, and broad inlets swarming with fish. The Indians assured him there were. First he tried the straits between the Peninsula and Manitoulin Island; then the deep waters and bays off the headland of Cape Croker on the Georgian Bay; finally, the long chain of channels and great bays along the North Shore. True enough, he found fish here in abundance, but the reward of his efforts fell so far short of that yielded by his former fishing grounds that it seemed little better than failure. There were other baffling problems too. The greater distance to good markets and the lagging pace of sail as compared with that of steam bit too deeply into an already narrow margin of profit to leave a wage worth the pains expended. McGregor did not starve, nor did he ever gain or leave a fortune. But he did leave behind him a good name, a name firmly attached to prominent places on the coasts off which he had cast his nets. Hence there is McGregor Harbour on the north side of Cape Croker, and on the North Shore, McGregor Bay, now the most famous haunt of anglers in all Lake Huron. On the banks of the Whitefish River near where it flows into this bay, which is really a deep indentation in the North Channel, repose the remains of this indomitable pioneer of the fishing industry of the Bruce Peninsula.

The story of the catches made off the Fishing Islands after the

scandalous seizure of rights is in general one of progressive decline broken now and then by spurts of recovery. One of the
spurts took place under the energetic régime of Spence and
Kennedy, but after both of them had withdrawn from the industry the curve of decline resumed its steady drop toward zero.
Today the lifts have become so lean that every fisherman makes
a joke about each lift being his last. And this is not a flippant
pleasantry but rather his indomitable sense of humour which has
kept him alive. The reason for the woeful drop from plenty to
scarcity will long remain an enigma, an enigma as baffling as is
the real cause of the extermination of the wild pigeon. We can
still only guess.

Yet guessing is not without profit; taken seriously it can train
modern eyes to look beyond any natural resource itself, and, in
advance of using it, to try to perceive a way of doing so with
intelligence and thrift. It may be that the immensity of the first
draughts of fishes, repeated as they were for several seasons,
began to cut deeply into the numbers of fish wont to spawn in
the fertile beds around the Fishing Islands. Perhaps if Captain
McGregor had been able to retain the exclusive rights, he might
have fared as badly as did his successors. But one cannot suppress
other suspicions. The spirit that fired the usurpers to an act of
grave injustice, together with the history of the usurpers themselves, leaves one with the feeling that the startling drop in the
success of the seized fishery was caused by greed and incompe-
tence. The desire to get rich quickly lifted all restraint; the in-
experience of landlubbers made a bad bungle of a business that
requires expert skill, experience, and the patient fortitude bred
by living on great waters. All these qualities Alexander McGregor
had. The story is an ancient one of human society: those who by
craft wedged themselves into his place predetermined their own
reward.

In any case, soon after this shady transaction the Fishing
Islands became "just another" fishery of Lake Huron, good but,
compared with its first yields, ordinary. Though the volume of
the catch varied from year to year, the trend, viewed decade by
decade, was steadily downward. At times the lifts were very
heavy, so heavy indeed as to raise high hopes that Nature had
recaptured her kindly mood of other days and was steering the
fish into the nets in vast schools. So too there were times when,
actually overnight, she became so miserly as to seem trying to

drag fishermen's hearts down to levels as deep and dark as the bed of Lake Huron itself. And yet, with the tenacity of fishermen everywhere, they clung to their calling and found that, in spite of the inevitable ups and downs, in the long run there was, on balance, a small margin of gain. From the larger settlements with good harbours, such as Southampton and Kincardine, deep-water fishing was carried on with schooners of considerable size. In the fifties and sixties the names of Robert and John Rowan of Kincardine stand out; Larry Bellmore had his headquarters on one of the Fishing Islands, one which long carried his name but is now known as Wildman's. In the seventies most if not all of the fishermen working off the Islands had names that revealed at a glance their bearers' Scottish origin or ancestry—McAuley, McLeod, Mc Kenzie, Morrison, and many others. And during all this period an evolution was going on, a steady, progressive change in the type of vessel employed in the trade.

The following years were marked by another change also: a new race of fishermen, who were only half professional, began working out of such Lake Huron inlets as Stokes Bay, Johnston's Harbour, and Tobermory, a race who were part of the time farmers or trappers or lumbermen and the rest of the time—at least during spells of really good fishing—fishermen. They came on the scene at sundry times during the eighties and early nineties. Hawke, Golden, McLay, Smith, Davis, Belrose, Hopkins, Simpson —these are some of the names of those who gave the breed its distinctive stamp. And a virile stock they were, adept in handling small sailing craft in the most varied and moodiest of waters. Having to adjust themselves quickly to the manifold conditions of the seasons, of forest and soil, of wind and wave, of reef and shoal, they became extraordinarily versatile and adaptable. Their bearing and their manner of speech were those of fishermen the world over, on salt seas and on fresh alike, always suggestive of calm judgment and inner poise. There is something in the daily sight of vast expanses of water that nurtures fine qualities like these. Long since has the original stock of the breed passed on; in some of their progeny one can see today a measure of their finer traits. The passing of that first generation happened to take place at the time when the gas-boat was seen to be a practical form of craft and not merely a toy. Its ability to thread its way among the devious channels of the Huron coastal waters was to spell the doom of sail and steam for commercial fishing.

In the career of one man we can see the life of the fishermen
of The Bruce at a certain stage of their industry and trace the
transitions through which it passed. In 1880 at the age of nineteen
William Simpson, a native of the Eastern Townships of Quebec,
settled in the bush near Tobermory. Since at that time there was
no road leading to this peninsular John o' Groats he travelled by
steamboat, his transport being none other than the new but luck-
less *Jane Miller*, whose tragic story has been told elsewhere in
these pages.[1]

The first winter Simpson spent with his father in the forest.
The native trees of commercial value that grew in the area were
hard maple, yellow birch, beech, red and white pine, white cedar,
hemlock, spruce, and balsam. There was also a good deal of red
oak, but as its wood is of inferior quality it was at first left untouched. The Simpsons, strange as it may seem now, during that
winter cut nothing but maple, converting huge trees into cordwood to feed the hungry furnaces of the steamers that touched at
Tobermory on their way from or into the Georgian Bay. Less than
ten years ago Captain Simpson told a friend that his memory of
the massive maples was the most vivid of all the pictures of his
early life that he carried into old age: even still, he said, the
mere thought of having to reduce to the dimensions of cordwood
a trunk three feet through and a hundred feet tall, made him
tremble. The other kind of wood in great demand was cedar. In
the course of many years the Simpsons took out of the bush
thousands upon thousands of posts and railway ties. These were
shipped by water, first from Big Tub, and later from Little Tub on
which Tobermory at last made up its mind to grow. For twenty-
two years William Simpson lumbered in this region.

However, during the larger part of this period he spent the
months of summer and autumn in fishing. In the season of 1881
Big Tub was made the headquarters of fishing activities at the
head of the Peninsula, when a number of fishermen moved their
camps here from Flowerpot and Half Moon islands. It was in that
same year that Simpson joined the guild. The general practice
was to bring catches to Big Tub, salt them, pack the fish into
100-pound bags, and deliver to a professional shipper, Gilbert
McIntosh, to be conveyed to Meaford. Two years later McIntosh
shifted the seat of his business to Little Tub.

Not long afterward another change took place, one of international import and of a kind common to those of the Great Lakes

1. See pp. 52–6.

that are shared by Canada and the United States: McIntosh, the Canadian middleman, gave over his business to a great Chicago house which deals in fish on a continental scale. This is one more illustration of the powerful influence exerted upon Canada's economic life by her rich and powerful next-door neighbour. To-day the influence continues though the effects are different in detail. The fish now go out of The Tub fresh and not in salt. Well chilled, they are sped southward by swift motor truck over a long chain of firm, smooth highways. While still fresh and in prime flavour they are delivered to their markets—most of which are still on the other side of the international frontier.

One must not hastily conclude from piecemeal records of the fishing industry in this corner of the Great Lakes that the life of the fishermen was all drudgery and disappointment and always under the cloud of uncertainty. Their existence was time and again brightened by relieving dashes—outbursts of humour and exhibitions of common human foibles. One sparkling touch was of a sort that flashes out in any new community anywhere, on the prairie or amid the woods, any community made up of people who have come from many different places. While still in the days of sail Tobermory split into two rival groups. And the matter that caused the cleavage was not a trivial one; on the contrary, it had a direct bearing upon the hamlet's chief interest. The men from Southampton claimed that their type of sailboat, one with a square stern and a large wooden centreboard, was without question the only one suited to those waters. With equal heat and earnestness the men from Meaford championed the sharp stern and a centreboard of iron. While the rival factions spun out their debate unduly, something of moment was hatching, something which at this late hour recalls to mind a fable of Aesop. As the two men of that tale wrangled over the oyster which each claimed as his own, a third party slipped in, gave each of the others a shell, and took the meat for himself. While the rivals in The Tub were haranguing, a new type of vessel, the steam tug, quietly entered their waters and began the long process which ended in the banishment of the last shred of sail. This too had its day and in time had to make way for the ubiquitous gas-boat, or, as some old-timers dubbed it in futile derision, the "contemptible sea skunk." Today in the region of The Bruce you can count the number of fishing steam tugs on the fingers of one hand; on merit the "sea skunk" is now supreme.

But after all what's the use of this supremacy now? Through

the unremitting draughts made for over a century and a quarter
upon the vast store of fish in Lake Huron, the total weight of each
year's catch has dwindled, and the roster of fishing crews and
craft has become pitifully short. The crews, now alarmed, frantically ask why a once profitable trade has collapsed. For many
years they have loudly bewailed the unfortunate situation, but
only recently have they seriously cast about them for real causes.
A department of government has long had to defend itself
against their charge that the reason for the industry's plight was
failure to put adequate curbs upon fishing in the region. Without
doubt there was right on both sides. The next scapegoat was the
Atlantic smelt. The fabulous powers of this introduced fish to
multiply and spread was the cause, fishermen insisted, of the
destruction of herring and whitefish spawn on every spawning
bed. No, they could not prove it, but. . . . Then attention shifted to
the sea lamprey which has slowly invaded the Upper Lakes until
it now is counted in myriads; its leechlike manner of attaching
itself to other fish is notorious. But when the fishermen began
calmly to review the havoc wrought by smelt and lamprey on
the grand scale of a whole lake with its billions of fishes, they
were not sure that they had put their finger on basic causes.

Yet all this searching was far from futile. It has at last brought
about a practical, voluntary alliance between government and the
Canadian fishing industry of the Great Lakes. After many years
of anxious parley government and industry are jointly employing
the most modern methods of ascertaining facts and are endeavour-
ing to discover a way that will lead to salvage and restoration.
They have entrusted the search to the patient spirit, skilled hands,
and penetrating vision of the scientist. But to recover and to
restore will not be enough. Until men learn from experience never
again to be guilty of such acts of prodigality as have sullied their
record on Lake Huron their faith in the future cannot but be
uneasy and insincere.

But why this lamentable lag in the powers of nations to learn?
The reason lies, I think, in man's habit of looking upon the past
as something that is gone. Absurd! As long as the effects of the
past are still a factor in our way of life, the past, for good or for
ill, is still here. As a sage character in a recent tale reminds us:
"The past hasn't gone anywhere. There's no place for it to go to."

Chapter 11

THE SERPENT IN THE GARDEN

EVEN the Garden of Eden had its serpent. Whether it was physically as well as morally venomous, the sacred narrative does not say. But Eden is not alone in this distinction. At least one other garden shares it. Not long ago a journalist declared that Ontario is not only the garden of Canada but a veritable Garden of Eden. Nor did he pause here, but added, with all the earnestness of parochial loyalty: "In this beautiful garden of Ontario there are no venomous snakes." Thus with a single patriotic breath he blew away the last of the barriers which, during World War II, had been holding back the incoming tide of tourist traffic. Little did he realize that before the summer was past, at least one traveller was to be disillusioned.

The scales of ignorance were rudely brushed from the visitor's eyes one day when, sauntering along a woodland path near the Lake Huron shore of The Bruce—the rock garden planted northward in our provincial paradise—he beheld a rattlesnake lying across his way. The shock struck him dumb. However, assured that the specimen before him belonged to the smaller of the two native species of the same family, he soon regained his full powers of speech in the utterance of eloquent phrases of gratitude to his Maker. Upon being told that the larger species had in historical times never been seen nearer The Bruce than the Niagara Escarpment at Waterdown, he recovered his normal poise. Later that evening before a safe indoor fire he listened, with the rapt attention one gives to a new-found theme, to a long recital on rattlesnakes in Ontario, a recital composed partly of the tales of early explorers and colonists and partly of personal experience told by some of his comrades of the fireside circle.

But at the outset let us be clear about this fact: The Bruce is *not* the only part of southern Ontario in which rattlesnakes are a feature of native wild life. The first Europeans to visit the region found two distinct species of these reptiles. One was quite large, a true Crotalid related to the Diamond Back, which sometimes was nearly six feet long and as thick as a man's arm. Happily for the traveller and the settler this was rare and belonged to only a few localities—the Escarpment near Hamilton, the Niagara Gorge, Point Pelee, and the islands of western Lake Erie. This species, now known as the Timber or Banded Rattler, still lives on in the beautiful Niagara Glen below the Whirlpool.

The other rattlesnake of Ontario is much smaller, seldom exceeding thirty inches; a friend who lives in The Bruce once told me of killing a monster of thirty-nine inches. For this species the colonists had many names: the best-known of these are Massasauga, and Black, Little Gray, and Little Swamp Rattler, all of them still used in one region or another. The scientific name is significant and interesting: *Sistrurus catenatus catenatus.* The *sistrum* was a musical rattle used in the worship of the Egyptian goddess Isis; οὐρά is the Greek for *tail*; hence *rattletail.* The Latin *catenatus* means *chained* and refers to the chainlike markings that extend along the reptile's back. The basic colour of the body is blackish-brown clouded with dull yellow; the belly is black.

The Massasauga, as we shall from now on term the species, is indigenous over a vast territory of northeastern America—from eastern Kansas to Manitoulin Island. The earliest travellers knew it on both sides of Lakes Ontario and Erie, along the Niagara and Detroit, around Lake St. Clair, at the head of the St. Clair River, in most parts of upper Lake Huron, especially the Bruce Peninsula and the eastern shore of Georgian Bay. While the chief haunts of the Massasauga are the shores of these larger bodies of water it is known also in various places inland. Within recent years examples have been taken near Bala and Gravenhurst in Muskoka District and in Minto Township, Wellington County. Three years ago I saw a specimen that had been killed near Newbury, thirty-five miles southwest of London, after it had bitten a child on the arm. Fortunately the child recovered; there is no known record of death resulting from the bite of a Massasauga. Naturally, the spread of settlement in Ontario has greatly reduced the numbers and range of this reptile. The thought should be enough to put our minds at ease.

I recall as if it were an event of last week my first experience with a Massasauga. Our family spent the summer of 1898 on the island of Minnecoganashene, which lies ten miles north of Penetanguishene. One evening at twilight as I was climbing the rocky path leading from the dock to the house, I was halted by a weird sound rising from somewhere a few steps before me. Peer as I might I could see nothing to cause it. Yet it continued without a pause. A pace or two to my right was a dampish depression in the granite carpeted with a shaggy patch of grass and weeds, and over this hung a branch of a Juneberry bush. My first thought was that a cicada had fallen from the branch into the tangle below and was struggling to get free. I bent forward to see what was there. From a tuft of grass a gaping mouth shot toward me. Even if I had not drawn my head back the swift thrust would have fallen short of my face by inches. When my wits came back I realized that an ancient wish had just been fulfilled: at last I had seen what I had long been looking for—a rattlesnake in Ontario. With a boathook that had been hurried to me from the dock I combed the mat of herbage and dragged the snake out to his doom.

The other day during a spell of desultory reading my eye fell upon a passage that reminded me of my first rattler, a passage in which the late W. H. Hudson describes the sound of the rattlesnake in almost exactly the terms I used in my boyhood: it resembles, he wrote, "muffled cicada music." This is more accurate than Galinée's comparison: "a sound like a quantity of melon or gourd seeds shaken in a box."

At least twice in later years I came into really intimate contact with Massasaugas, in each instance inadvertently stepping upon a large specimen. Once as I was hunting for marsh plants along the sedgy borders of a shallow bay on the Lake Huron side of the Bruce Peninsula, a Massasauga happened to be prowling for frogs in the same place. His path and mine crossed. At the very moment of our meeting, without knowing it and with an uncanny precision I planted a heavily booted foot squarely on the middle of the snake's body. Not a single note of warning had he sounded, so quickly had I come upon him. But as soon as my boot pinned him down his tail began to vibrate furiously. Yet, strangely enough, the sound I heard seemed to come from a distance. Bewildered I looked about me and asked my companion: "Where's that rattler?" Putting his hand to his ear he swung slowly around in a circle to detect the source of the sound. After a few moments of intent listening he stood still, looked directly at me and in a tone of mingled perplexity and anxiety declared: "That buzz is coming straight from you." One glance downward was enough. There beneath the thick sole of my larigan writhed a Massasauga well

over two feet long. One end of it was rattling madly while the
other struck viciously but vainly against the tough boot-top. But
even as I watched, the illusion continued, for the sound still
seemed to come from the dense alder thickets behind us. The
experience taught me, as a rover of the wild lands in that region,
always to stop short the instant I heard a rattler's signal. Not until
eye and ear working together have precisely determined its
source should one budge even an inch. After that one may suit
action to sight.

Although Massasaugas are usually found in swampy depressions
within areas of limestone or of granite, sometimes they appear in
quite unexpected environments. Once I caught one swimming
in the water half way across the full expanse of Stokes Bay. I was
loath to halt so adventurous a creature. Its effort to reach a new
territory illustrates one of the ways which the Massasauga must
have used in spreading his kind over the land during the long ages
that preceded the coming of men. Time and again I have come
upon one lying at full length on the summit of a limestone ridge
in the blazing sun. This seemed to be very strange, since, according to common opinion, snakes cannot stand direct, hot sunlight
for more than a few minutes at a time. Hudson observes that
"snakes are seen coiled up when they are at home; when travelling
and far afield, they lie as a rule extended at full length, even when
resting—and they are generally resting." Doubtless the snakes I
saw were wayfarers taking snatches of rest while passing over
ridges that separate one boggy spot from another.

All I have seen and heard of the Massasauga confirms the belief
that under normal conditions it is far from being aggressive except
in its search for the small forms of animal life that it feeds upon—
mice, young frogs and toads, and grasshoppers. I know of only one
instance where it has been seen to assume the offensive in threatening a human being. The witness of this rare occasion was the
teacher of a rural school in The Bruce who often goes with me on
my hunts for plants. One June day he was gathering flowers near
the lake shore with two of his younger pupils, both of them lads
under ten. By chance, one of the boys who was walking ahead of
his companions almost trod on a pair of Massasaugas. Enraged at
the intrusion, one of the pair, presumably the male, abruptly left
his mate and darted toward the youngster who only by nimble
dodging escaped from the attacker. The teacher's *post factum*
comment—discreetly made out of the hearing of his tender wards

—was distinctly to the credit of the race of rattlesnakes: "Who can deny that chivalry still lives upon earth?"

Why has Nature evolved the rattle? The question has never been finally answered. The late Dr. Thomas Barbour, the famous zoologist of Harvard, has offered an answer that seems to be more than ordinarily plausible. It is certainly not to warn away the snake's prey, he says, for the breed knows no such altruism; nor to warn man, for he is relatively a newcomer to America and was not a wholesale threat to reptiles. Probably then, Barbour suggests, it was to warn the wide-ranging bison. Ancestors of this animal do "fulfil these conditions, and we know there were still earlier bisons, for their fossil remains have been found." The hoofs of the bison must have been a source of danger to the snake and the bite of the snake enough of a bane to the bison to cause him, if he were warned, to shy away from the snake. The rattle supplied the warning. That the sound is not a warning among the snakes themselves has been proved: the rattlesnake is deaf to its own rattle.

That snakes hypnotize their prey is a belief common to all lands where snakes exist. On one occasion in The Bruce my daughters and I had reason to wonder whether it is really true. While searching on hands and knees for Coral Root orchids under a dense stand of spruces we noticed ten or eleven feet ahead of us a full-grown chipmunk standing stock still. He was not making a single one of the quick nervous little movements the chipmunk is wont to make; he neither jerked his head nor flicked his tail. We halted. He seemed quite unaware of our presence. What held him there? Nothing that we could see in the dim light that filtered through the screen of needles above us—at least at first. But shortly, and in the very same instant, we all spied the same thing. Perfectly camouflaged against the woodland floor of spruce crumble and rotting sawdust lay a motionless eighteen-inch Massasauga facing the motionless chipmunk. His raised head was two feet from the rodent, yet too far away for him to take the chance of striking. However, it was only too obvious that the snake was awaiting the opportunity of doing so, and it was equally obvious that his ambition was futile, for if he killed the chipmunk with an injection of venom he could not possibly stretch his marvellously elastic jaws wide enough to swallow him. But perhaps—just like many a human gunner or angler—he was hunting merely for the fun of the thing. At any rate, whatever process was going on in the mind of the snake, then and there we three human observers came to the conclusion that, if a snake's power to fascinate prey is only a myth, the original author was not wholly without warrant for believing that he was putting forth a truth. . . . But all things come to an end. Suddenly the chipmunk came to himself, whisked his tail, and darted away into the woods. The snake's disappointment was unfeigned: the angry way in which he flung his head and body about was nothing else than profanity without words.

Although over the years I have learned that one need have little fear of the Massasauga, yet I have never cast all caution aside. But such is the perversity of my nature that on one occasion I almost welcomed an encounter with a robust representative of its tribe.

In June, 1934, I had the honour of conducting a large party of North American botanists on a visit to the Bruce Peninsula. On arriving there we put up at the Tamarac Club for the night. After the evening meal the guests expressed the wish to tramp to a nearby glacial bog-lake where there was a gorgeous display of the Queen Lady Slipper. I offered to guide them, but on one condition: that each person must either wear high boots or protect his ankles and shanks in some other way. My zeal to ensure safety, while openly approved—doubtless, for politeness' sake—was, I felt, privately found to be amusing as just a spinsterish whim on my part.

In an extended file we trudged along an old lumber-trail to a break in the jungle of spruce and fir where the narrow path to the lake began. One enterprising visitor, in his ardour to be first, rushed ahead to the opening. But just as he reached it he threw up his hands, shouted loudly, and stopped short. Before him, extended at full length across the path, was an exceptionally large Massasauga. Its link-like chain of markings of brown and black showed up with startling distinctness against the light gray of the limestone slab on which it lay. At the intrusion the snake drew itself into an S-loop, began rattling loudly and waving its head threateningly. As if turned to stone the whole party stood in their tracks. In that tense moment only five of those zealous botanists found that they loved orchids more than they feared Massasaugas.

In a minute or two we managed to guide the snake into the gaping mouth of a large paper bag which he soon discovered to be a fatal blind alley. We took him to the Club and killed him, gingerly throwing the body out on a conspicuous flat rock in front of the club house. On measuring it we found it to be much longer than the average—thirty-two inches. In the middle of the carcass was a huge bulge whose contours, clearly sketched on the tautly drawn skin, were obviously those of a frog twice as broad as the creature that had gulped it down. The company lingered about the prey until darkness hid it from sight. It was easy to see that the feelings of the observers were of a mixed order. Everybody was manifestly conscious of a sense of relief. As for myself I was alone in suppressing an unholy impulse to shout exultingly: I told you so! And—believe it who will—I can truthfully state that the chaste silence of the night was humbly respected.

Still Waters

On two counts it is hard for anyone who has once seen Spring Creek—the Spring Creek we crossed north of Stokes Bay on our way to Tobermory—to forget its clear waters and its wild woodland setting. In the first place, its apparent promise of full creels of speckled trout makes one hanker for the excuse to come back to it soon and try one's luck. In the second place, its local name, Rattlesnake Creek, rouses in strangers an odd curiosity to explore the course of the stream and see if the name really fits. That it does fit I proved beyond cavil a quarter of a century ago: on my very first tramp up the swampy flats, where the creek empties into Middle Boat Cove, I came upon no less than four Little Swamp Rattlesnakes, or Massasaugas, in the space of ten minutes. The people of the region have named the stream most aptly.

Steve Bradley of Stokes Bay called himself a farmer; like many of his neighbours on the land he also fished at sundry times, frequently working out of Boat Coves. But his farm, I fear, was chiefly a blind: he found this sheltered little haven a better place in which to carry on his private avocation, a sideline which for success required a scene quite "exempt from public haunt." For Bradley, Boat Coves was perfect. The focus of his labours here was a spring of pure, cold water bubbling out of the rocky bank of the valley a short distance up the Creek. It was like an ancient stronghold in that it was defended, and that doubly: by a dense belt of cedars, and, from spring to early fall, by an unseen body of living guardians. The latter defence was none other than the host of Massasaugas that infested—and still infests—the approaches to the concealed woodland fastness. Though a rabble this force was as good as an ordered army.

In the midst of the cedars Steve built him a still. A crude affair it was, a curious complex of tubes and coils and ancient tin con-

tainers rescued from sundry junk-heaps, but nevertheless a contraption which, thanks to the steady flow of cold spring waters and
the direction of its ingenious maker, did well the work it was
intended to do. Later, Bradley built a log shanty near the mouth
of the creek; the remains of its foundation are still to be seen. This
contained several small rooms to serve as living quarters and—
we venture to guess—temporary storage space. Bradley's husky
daughter, Mag, was installed as chatelaine of the establishment.

That Mag was thus made an accomplice in crime never entered
Steve's one-track mind; a companion in trouble, perhaps, but
nothing worse. The truth is that Steve fancied himself a rather
brave fellow, one of the few who have spunk enough to resist a
most objectionable regimentation of society. He was really a bold
exponent of free enterprise, one with the fine qualification of
having enough sporting instinct to accept high risks for higher
profits.

For several months all went well, indeed, very well, according
to one point of view. Bradley welcomed with glee the swelling
volume of his income, while his ultimate customers were far from
disdaining even so raw a poteen as his clandestine still poured
forth. Trade was as brisk as it was risky. In order to keep the site
of his amateur distillery hidden from everybody, the artful
operator made a point of conducting all sales of his product as far
away from his headquarters as possible. Every ounce he delivered
in person to his pedlars. He was supremely confident that the battle-
ments of precautions and rattlesnakes that begirt him roundabout
were quite impregnable. Apparently he knew nothing of the old
adage: "It takes a thief to catch a thief." If he did know it he was
not astute enough to see that by the same token the most likely
person to trail a bootlegger is another bootlegger.

In his blissful cocksureness Bradley did not notice that a few
chinks were being forced in his defences from without. First one
and then another of his pals picked up short stretches of his trail
toward the bush. Piecing these together at leisure they finally, by
means of a rough and ready reckoning known to bushmen, divined
the secluded tract to which the trail led.

In the meantime the police had noticed enough irregular behaviour in the populace of the region to become suspicious. It
soon became apparent to them that a stream of something which,
though clear as water, was nevertheless not water was flowing
southward from the forest of Rattlesnake Creek. But try as they
would for several weeks to narrow the source down to one spot

they made no progress whatsoever. They worked on without taking a single soul into their confidence. At times they were sure they had come upon the right trail, but every time they lost it a few rods inside the forest boundary. At last they decided to play the role of Brer Rabbit and "lay low." Their shrewd patience paid well. The powerful spirits of illicit stills have their own way of disclosing the fountainheads from which they spring. The potency of the Spring Creek Moonshine loosed the tongues of pedlar and imbiber alike. Both, freed of the gag of restraint, told the world all they knew as well as much that they didn't know. But there was just enough in their babbling to put the foot of the law on the right track. Two special constables were detailed to raid Bradley's stronghold.

One bright morning in a mid August of about seventy years ago the officers sailed out of Stokes Bay for Boat Coves. They had first made sure that Bradley had returned to his retreat. Landing just inside the mouth of Spring Creek they moored their boat to a small rough dock of cedar poles. Being utter strangers to the terrain of this lower reach of the valley both men were shod in ordinary shoes that left their ankles and shanks unprotected. Innocent of danger they set out across the soggy beaver meadow and headed for the dense copse of cedars where they believed the still to be hidden.

The tall grasses and sedges were fairly alive with leaping leopard frogs. But the two men were not the only creatures to note that fact: the Massasaugas of the valley were noting it too. Indeed, they were having a field day of it. On their left a few feet ahead the officers heard a weird buzz. Stepping quickly aside to the right they heard a buzz of the same kind in that direction too. They were afraid to put one foot before the other. They stood as if rooted in the very middle of the beaver meadow. Any advantage they had hoped to gain by an unannounced approach to Bradley's hide-out was now utterly lost. It was they who were trapped, not Bradley. Only some desperate action could free them. As if spurred by a single will they made a dash straight to the nearest point on the edge of the woods two hundred yards away and took chances on where they placed their feet. Like wild men under pursuit they raced across the open space. When they reached the heavy cedar jungle that screened the still they were breathless and too unnerved to be in the mood to face resistance. But what did that matter now? Their bird had already flown.

They turned to Bradley's house. Somebody was at home, or had been lately, as a curl of live smoke from the chimney made clear. The officers knocked. With little delay the door was opened—just wide enough to reveal part of a woman's face.

"Is Mr. Bradley home?" the men asked.

"No." There was finality in the tone.

"Will he be back soon?"

"No." The slit between the door and its frame was narrowed slightly.

"May we come in and wait for him?"

"No."

"Well, if you won't let us in we may have to force our way in. We have a warrant to search the house."

"If you try that you'll be sorry." The uncanny confidence in the voice was ominous.

Without further ado the men stepped forward as if to prevent the door from being slammed in their faces. But far from being closed the door was thrown open as if by an explosion. Before the visitors towered the figure of a great angry Gorgon. They saw her plunge her right hand deep into a tall barrel that stood close to the door frame. In an instant up came the hand brandishing two large wriggling Massasaugas and thrusting them straight at the officers' faces. The men were petrified as though beholding the head of Medusa with its tresses of writhing serpents. But it was for a moment only that they stood fixed like figures of stone. The darting heads never touched, never even grazed their target: no human faces ever before drew backward with such celerity. The owners of the faces were in no mood to parley. They had had enough of Massasaugas for one day—nay, for a lifetime. And to reach their boat they had yet to run the gauntlet of Massasaugas through the grass. Massasaugas behind them, Massasaugas before them! Were men ever before ensnared in so desperate a dilemma? They ran as if demented, ran in the full, undiminished sense of the word, ran as fast as foot and lungs would permit. And on their heels strode the Gorgon, now waving a serpent in each hand. So close was she that the men dare not pause an instant to loose their boat. Past it they shot as on winged sandals and leaped into the water of the off-shore shallows. Medusa waded in after them. On went the pursued until the water came up to their armpits. Ignominiously they halted, turned right about face, held up their hands, and pleaded for mercy.

"All right," screamed the brawny guardian of home and father.

The "Gorgon"

"But don't you dare come ashore. I'll shove your boat over to you. And get out o' here as fast as the wind will take you." No man ever obeyed a woman's behest more gladly and with greater alacrity than these two gallant servants of the law. As they floated out on the cove they realized with a relief beyond words that it was water, and not marsh grass and Gorgon's tresses, that was waving beneath them.

To headquarters the officers reported—without humiliating embellishments—a tale of failure. If they thus misjudged their own effort one now knows why and can condone the mistake. The truth is that they did not fail. Though the law failed to seize Bradley's person it did put an end to his business, at least in that part of the world. Now that the law knew the scene of his lawless toil he saw that the jig was up. Shrewdly and quietly, like his own spirits, he evaporated from the Peninsula, leaving no address behind.

But both father and daughter did leave behind something of note: a repute that lived long in the half-legendary, half-factual history of the region. In the annals of Lake Huron shipping Bradley will be remembered as the man[1] who in 1895, along with a brave comrade, brought safely into Boat Coves Captain Silversides and the whole crew of the wrecked *Severn*. Perhaps it was

1. For the reason why Bradley just missed being a hero see p. 65.

that valiant act that led some of the recent map-makers to change the name of Boat Coves to Bradley's Harbour.

As for the doughty Mag, she turned out to be a highly adjustable character: she converted her skill in taming rattlesnakes into a profitable vocation. Perhaps you recall a travelling circus among whose advertised attractions was the Great Ranee, the Hindoo Snake Charmer? If so, you can now identify this celebrity: she was none other than Steve Bradley's Gorgon-like daughter, Mag, who with her Massasaugas stood off the law at Spring Creek one August day half a century ago. But the Great Ranee's snakes had never known the distant Orient, I regret to say: like their mistress they were just plain "Bruce," born and bred in the famous peninsula.[1]

1. Mag Bradley died on July 10, 1954, in her 88th year, and was buried in the Lucknow cemetery. She was born February 28, 1867, and married in 1889. The event at Rattlesnake Creek took place probably in 1887 or 1888.

PART FOUR: PLANT HUNTERS AND
THEIR QUESTS

The Calypso Orchid

Chapter 12

JOHN MUIR WAS HERE

THAT John Muir, the famous American apostle of conservation, early in his career drew from a prolonged sojourn on the Georgian Bay of Lake Huron a measure of the inspiration that made him what he was, is a bit of history known only to a few. Among the parts of this region in which he fared was the Bruce Peninsula. That fact is enough to entitle him to space in our pages, though he was more familiar with the territory east of Owen Sound. It is an honour to the whole region to have a valid though small claim to a great name, a name that will live as long as the Muir Glacier of Alaska flows and the Yosemite Valley retains unimpaired its imposing nobility and beauty. Of this claim our knowledge had been scant until a friend recently opened the pages of an unpublished manuscript. This, written by one in whose home Muir lived near the Georgian Bay shoreline, tells of a formative stage in Muir's life about which he himself was strangely silent.

In the *Atlantic Monthly* of February, 1913, Muir ended his account of his boyhood and youth. Here in his own fascinating way he had told of his early childhood in Scotland, of his family's migration to Wisconsin when he was eleven, of the many inventions he had made at home in his teens, and, finally, of his life and thoughts during his student days in the University of Wisconsin. When this period came to a close in the summer of 1863 John Muir stood on a hill overlooking Madison and lovely Lake Mendota and bade farewell to his "blessed Alma Mater." In the last sentence of his story he revealed the ambition—even before it was really formulated in his mind—the ambition which, like a river in continuous flood, was to carry him through life: "But I was only leaving one university for another, the University of Wisconsin for the University of the Wilderness."

After that notable declaration there is a gap, measured in years,

in what Muir tells about himself. This extends from the farewell
to Alma Mater to the summer of 1866. That so notoriously frank a
man should suddenly seal his lips has long caused many to wonder.
In 1947 his biographer briefly and reluctantly hints at the solution
of the enigma. It is now known that Muir's long silence was not
unrelated to his absence from his own country while she was engaged in a great war.

When Muir left Madison in 1863 to return to his home in
Portage, Wisconsin, his spirit was in a turmoil. His supreme desire
was to make his life one of signal service to his fellow-men; he
felt he could best achieve that end by becoming a physician. So
he planned to enrol in the autumn in the Faculty of Medicine of
the University of Michigan. But where was he to get the money?
The question worried him. But something else worried him more:
he was not yet certain that his love of medicine was greater than
his love of the wilderness. Of great moment, too, was the possibility that he might be drafted into military service. The upshot
was that he spent much of the summer, autumn, and winter of
1863–4 in exploring the wilds of Wisconsin and in scraping together money to support him in his projected course of study.
During these months many young men of the region were going
to Canada to escape the draft. This Muir manfully refused to do.
He waited until the draft had taken place before making his decision. It came about that his number was not drawn. In the relative
calm of spirit that followed Muir took advantage of the chance to
read his own mind. By March 1, 1864, he felt he knew which had
the greater claim on his affection, medicine or the wild: for the
time being the wild had won him over. On that day he set out,
apparently with his brother Dan, who was a minor, on a long
casual trek that led them on and on into the part of the "Canadian
wilderness" that borders on the Georgian Bay.

When the Muir boys left their home town of Portage on an
eastbound train John was within a few weeks of his twenty-sixth
birthday. From several extant descriptions of him it is easy to
make up a picture of him at that age. He was a fine figure of a
man, six feet tall and straight as an arrow. His chestnut brown
hair hung down to his shoulders. He wore a long ungroomed
beard which was quite in keeping with the state and style of his
clothes. He walked with the long tireless lope of an Indian on a
forest trail. A fellow-student called him "a storage battery of
energy, encased in flexible, elastic steel." Thus, plus something
added by the wear of four months in the bush, John Muir must

have appeared to his Canadian hosts when they admitted him to their hearths and hearts.

Just where John and Dan left the easy way of the rails to step out on to the rough trails of northern Michigan is recorded nowhere. We do know, however, that after a few weeks of trudging they made their way into Canada, crossing, presumably, from the Michigan "Soo" to the Canadian "Soo" over the St. Mary's River. Thence they strode eastward on the mainland. In their search for plants they hopped over to St. Joseph's Island and afterward went on to Manitoulin. At that season of the year when nothing green was left except the evergreens the young men's observations must have been limited to trees; these could easily be identified by their needles and winter buds.

Though no positive word survives stating that the Muirs crossed the fifteen-mile strait from Manitoulin to the northern tip of the Bruce Peninsula, those who know the region well cannot but conclude that they did. It is absurd to think that at that time of the year they tramped all the way around the east side of the Georgian Bay—a formidable journey of over three hundred miles —to enter the Peninsula from the south. The label on the first plant the Muirs took on the south side of the Georgian Bay is dated April 20, 1864; the place is somewhere in Simcoe County.

It was on the southern border of this same county that one evening late in June John Muir had one of the most momentous experiences of his life. While looking for a sheltered nook in which to spend the night outdoors he suddenly came upon the first specimen of the beautiful little Calypso orchid he had ever seen. For years he had sought to find one, but, timid shrinking thing that it is, it seemed, as if purposely, to have eluded him. Now against a perfect green background of bog moss it held up its dainty white and mauve head for his eyes to feast upon. Of the entrancing vision he himself wrote: "Hunger and weariness vanished, and only after the sun was low in the west I plashed on through the swamp, strong and exhilarated as if never more to feel mortal care."[1] That these words sprang from the depths of Muir's being his biographer makes clear. Long years afterward he "recalled the two supreme moments of his life. One was when he found Calypso blooming alone in a Canadian swamp. The other was his meeting with Emerson."[2]

1. Linnie Marsh Wolfe, *Son of the Wilderness: The Life of John Muir* (New York: Alfred Knopf, 1945), p. 93.
2. *Ibid.*, pp. 146–7.

The second account of the Muirs in this territory comes from two persons who became almost brothers to the young pilgrims—William and Peter Trout. From Peter's handwritten story, now spread before me—"What I Know of John Muir"—and from William's published reminiscences[1] we learn much of John and Dan Muir's sojourn and rambles amid the hills, valleys, woods, and bogs of the Georgian Bay country.

Father Trout had built a sawmill and wood-working factory in a gorge of the Bighead River not far upstream from Meaford, Grey County, where its waters empty into the Bay. By the Muirs' time he had retired from business and had entrusted the direction of the work to his elder son William. With the latter worked Peter and a partner of the name of Jay. It is only fitting that from this point onward we allow William and Peter to take up the thread of the story every now and then and together tell it, now in the voice of one, now in that of the other. With a little editing the two narratives can be blended into one.

It was in the month of August, 1864, Peter Trout relates, that one Saturday evening about four or five o'clock, a man came along who was looking for work and seemed anxious to get it. As I was not busy at the time we sat down on a sawlog and I asked some questions; who he was, where he was from, and so forth. He told me that he came from Wisconsin and that his name was Dan Muir; and that he had just come from Owen Sound, twenty miles away.

From what I learned from Dan, says Peter, he and his brother John started out on a botanizing tour in northern Wisconsin. They were collecting botanical specimens which they pressed and put in the frames they were carrying on their backs. I also understood that they botanized through northern Michigan, but of that I am not very sure. They had specimens from St. Joseph's Island, Manitoulin Island, and the peninsula between Lake Huron and the Georgian Bay. At Owen Sound, it seems, their money gave out and Dan went ahead to look for some chance to replenish their store. He came to the mill, with the result I have described.

I was very favourably impressed with him, continues Peter, although his clothes were badly worn and shabby-looking. I told him he had better stay and see my brother William whom I expected any minute; he would know what could be done in the way of giving work. Shortly afterwards my brother appeared; he

1. William H. Trout, *History of the Trout Family* (Milwaukee: published privately, 1910).

also was favourably impressed with Dan and invited him to supper, and after supper he invited him to stay over Sunday, stating that he would know on Monday what could be done about giving him work. For Dan the situation was very much improved when we learned that he and his people belonged to the same church that we did, that is, the Disciples, or the Campbellites, as they used to be called, although they never acknowledged any such name.

We always went to meeting on Sundays, and as there were only my eldest sister and brother and myself we locked up the house and after meeting we usually went to dinner at the farm where my father and mother lived. We went to the evening meeting at six and would get home before dark. We strongly urged our guest to go to church with us, but he stoutly refused because of his shabby appearance. He said he would go out into the woods and stay until we returned. He asked us to lend him a book to read; he selected *The Testimony of the Rocks* by Hugh Miller and went out into the woods. We found him at the house when we returned in the evening. Dan told us about his brother, John, and his wonderful clock and some of the wonderful things he had done. We concluded that he might be useful and so we sent for him as he was at that time in the neighbourhood.

When I first saw John his appearance was no more presentable than his brother Dan's had been; so far as his clothes were concerned he would be called "a sight to look at." But this shabby condition did not last long, for the boys had better clothes and were not long in getting them. After that we all went together to meeting every Sunday.

The two visitors stayed at the Trout Hollow mill for a short time, it seems, and then set out southward together to hunt plants in what was left of the summer. They rambled without a plan to guide them, turning this way or that according to their changing fancies. All that is known of their trail is gleaned from the labels on the few plants of their collection that now remain. They were at Niagara Falls on September 2, 1864. Then for a time they explored the river gorge together and later at a leisurely pace trudged back to the mill and home near Meaford, to "den up" there for the winter that would soon be upon them.

The Trout family may at first have taken this decision of the Muir boys to be due solely to their inability ever to be idle. But one day the boys received a letter from Portage. In it their parents commanded Dan to remain in Canada as long as the draft was

being enforced in the United States. At the same time, as William
Trout notes, they urged John, being of manhood age, to stay on
with his young brother. While John's feelings did not coincide
with his parents' wish in that respect, yet for his mother's sake he
complied. In the light of his behaviour early in 1864 one cannot
but believe that this decision left him an uneasy conscience for the
rest of his days, a feeling of mingled regret and shame that he had
ever given anyone reason to suspect him of disloyalty. No wonder
John Muir refrained, even long years afterward, from recording
the strange interlude in his life which he spent amid the peace of
alien hills and woods while vast tracts of his own country re-
sounded with the roar of battle.

After a parley with us (to take up Peter Trout's account again),
the two Muirs were hired to work at the plant. Their first task was
to help in building an addition to the shop, or rake factory, as it
was afterwards known. John worked principally at the manufacturing of rakes but spent considerable time in improving the
machinery for making them. My brother William was a first-class
hand at that sort of work, but for original ideas he was nowhere
with John Muir, for the improvements he made in the machinery
were simply marvellous. He had much to learn in the way of
handling tools, for about all the tools he used in making his famous
clock were a jack knife, a saw that had been made out of a corset
stay, and a primitive kind of gimlet. As would be expected, he
learned with amazing rapidity and he has always spoken in the
highest terms of my brother William for showing him how to use
tools, lathes, and other machinery.

But, as one may gather from Peter's story, this spell of inventive-
ness had not come upon John Muir suddenly. When still a mere
boy he had begun making, out of the odds and ends that clutter a
farmstead, all sorts of mechanical devices. Among them he turned
out a self-setting sawmill, water-wheels, odd locks and latches for
doors, thermometers, hygrometers, and a barometer. Three of his
home-made clocks became famous. The one to which Peter Trout
alludes was the first of those designed to do extraordinary things:
though in shape reminding one of a sawmill it could strike like an
ordinary timepiece, indicate months and days as well as hours,
light fires and lamps, and start stalled animals feeding at stated
times in the morning. But the clock's supreme service was to rouse
sleepers from their slumbers and send them forth early to their
daily tasks. Through a combination of levers and cogs the clock
would cause a specially constructed bedstead to throw its occu-

pant on the floor at any desired time. And all these creations were for years turned out of Muir's workshop between the morning hours of one and six. "Five huge, solid hours," their maker would exclaim. When he called his supreme contraption "an early-rising machine" his austere father actually almost laughed at the ironic humour of it all. To think the young gaffer would rise so early to make a machine to rout him out still earlier! But to John the machine was life. By selling trick bedsteads tripped by ordinary dollar clocks he paid some of his expenses at university. In the dormitory he used one himself until his fellow-students rose in rebellion at being wakened at five o'clock with a crash like that of a collapsing scaffold.

After John had been living with us about a month, observes Peter Trout, he had the famous clock and bedstead shipped to him from Wisconsin. These he set up in a room that he had partitioned off upstairs for himself and his brother Dan. I slept in it one night with Dan, who did not know I was there, since I got in bed after he was asleep. I was a long time going to sleep, but it seemed that as soon as I got asleep I dreamed that I was climbing a hill, and that the hill tipped over on top of me, and while I was hanging on for life I fell with a crash and found myself out on the floor. This was the only experience I ever had or wanted to have with John Muir's bed.

In his autobiography Muir states that he rose every morning about one or two o'clock and worked or studied all the rest of the night. When with us, says Peter Trout, he usually worked in the factory until eleven or twelve at night making some improvement. He would then go to his room and study for two or three hours longer. Four or five hours each night was about as much time as he spent in sleep; the balance of the twenty-four were spent in either work or study apparently without the loss of a minute of time. It has seemed to me that if he had followed along this line through life he would have been another Thomas A. Edison, for his ideas were of the most original and practical kind.

Although the mill kept John Muir constantly busy he was always conscious of the tug of the wild upon him. In winter when flower and leaf were dead he would let his thoughts wander out of doors by thumbing over the sheets carrying the plants he had gathered in his rambles. His enthusiasm kindled a lively interest in herb and tree in the minds of the Trout household and of their friends. Plant after plant would remind John of the various strange experiences he had had in getting them; his tales held his hearers

entranced. With the bursting of the first buds of spring the young
people took to plant-hunting as bumble-bees to red clover. Indeed,
nature study in general became the avowed hobby of the community, invading even the Sunday School of the local Disciples
church. John had agreed to lead a class of boys if he himself would
be allowed to follow the lead of his own spirit. And whither did
he lead these juvenile charges? Why, of course, as even the gravest
elders knew he would, away from the little meeting-house out into
the woods, over the hills and far away. No class in nature study
anywhere ever was given a more inspiring vision of God's ways
with the material aspects of His world.

But it was not always in company that John went out to hob-
nob with his beloved plants; every now and then, with William's
permission, he sallied forth alone, roaming up and down the wild
glens of the rolling countryside and slogging through bogs to visit
with the sundews, pitcher-plants, and water-loving orchids. It was
at such times that he wrestled the hardest with the problems of his
future that were tormenting his soul.

In May, 1865, Dan took a job in Buffalo to earn the means of
continuing his studies at college. The parting of the brothers,
though intended to be brief, threw John into a state of gloomy perplexity. Here he was twenty-seven years old, and yet not knowing
what he was going to do with his life! To think his way out of the
maze alone, in July he took a week off from the mill and spent it
in hunting plants on both sides of the great inlet of Owen Sound.
How far up the west side of the Sound he went we do not know:
at the pace he was accustomed to travel he had time to go a
number of miles north of Wiarton. Here he would revel in the
spruce and cedar jungles where the rare Alaska orchid hides; or
amid the damp dark-shaded limestone cliffs that are host to the
still rarer Hart's Tongue fern. Anyway, wherever he roamed that
week he saw about him an untold number of evidences that, ages
before, glaciers had passed that way. Already he was as interested
in the ways of moving ice-fields as he was in plants. Somehow this
lonely jaunt helped brush away some of the clouds from John's
mind, for by September he took with firmness a step which while
not final was positively forward. Whether he was to be a physician
or a second Humboldt, this was certain; he needed money for the
training to be either.

In September the Trouts offered John a contract. They proposed
that he invent devices and make other improvements in the

machinery designed to speed up the factory's production. They aimed to turn out 30,000 broom handles. They were ready to give John half the profits. Would he accept? John signed the contract and with furious energy threw his whole self into the enterprise. Through his ingenuity and driving power the output was doubled. By February of 1866 all the broom handles had been made and were already seasoning in storage. Half the rakes were completed and work on the second half was being pressed. The hour for reaping the gains of honest, hard labour was drawing nearer and John was catching glimmerings of the rosy dawn of that day when, freed from the student's nightmare, poverty, he could give every hour to preparing himself methodically for a life of service to society.

But that day, that hour, were still a long way off. One stormy night about the first of March, 1866, as William Trout sadly tells us, their works took fire, and factory, mill, broom handles, rakes, and all were destroyed. The Trouts saved nothing but a good team of horses and a wagon. All of John's collection of plants, except the part he had already sent home, and all the profits of his dreams had gone up in smoke.

There is every reason to believe that the settlement then made was an honourable one. The Trouts offered John $300, part in cash, part in personal paper. John cut the sum to $200. With the cash he paid his fare to Indianapolis and a job. The friendship between employer and employé continued unimpaired for life. "Between John Muir and myself," writes Peter Trout in 1915, "there developed a kind of David and Jonathan friendship which was considerably interrupted on account of our fields being far apart, but, in so far as the heart's affections were concerned, this close friendship was never broken, and always awoke into new life whenever, or wherever, we met."

When at last John Muir—naturalist, inventor, great exponent of applied democracy—left bench and lathe in Indianapolis to take up his true mission, he could have said fittingly and with deep feeling what he wrote later about the first great adventure of his life, leaving college to go out into the world. "Anyhow, I wandered away on a glorious botanical and geological excursion, which has lasted nearly fifty years and is not yet completed, always happy and free, poor and rich, without thought of a diploma or of making a name, urged on and on through endless inspiring Godful beauty."

Chapter 13

THE TRAIL OF THE ALASKA ORCHID

IT was in a book that I was introduced to the Alaska Orchid, and it was the author himself who opened the book for me. Though this happy event took place in the early nineties the memory of it is as fresh as if it happened yesterday. At the time it meant much to me that the author of the little green book,[1] who was my teacher of botany, had, twenty-five years before in another Ontario school, taught my father also. "The proof of the pudding" applies to teachers as well as to the sweets of a repast. Father, having partaken zestfully of Henry B. Spotton's instruction, passed on to me his proof of its high quality and thus whetted my appetite for the subject with which it dealt.

One day when we were intent on dissecting a certain flower, Spotton casually—or was it by design?—made a remark implying that orchids grew wild in Ontario. At once every ear in the class pricked up. Eyes flashed doubts that lips were too timid to speak. What? Orchids in this northern land? Beautiful orchids, we asked, in rose and mauve and green like those we sometimes see in the florists' windows? "Yes, indeed," was the reply, "many like them though not the same kinds. For instance, there's our tall Queen Lady Slipper with its large showy blooms of rose-purple and white; the deep rose Moccasin Flower; the retiring and dainty mauve Calypso and the Grass Pink of the peat bogs." Eyes opened wider and wider as doubt gave way to belief. The teacher, noting the manifest interest, adroitly led the class on to rapt contemplation of the splendours of Ontario's native orchids, and then, sure of having captured attention, quickly switched it to the study of duller and less conspicuous details which the youthful mind is apt to ignore. That was teaching!

"Some of our orchids," Spotton went on to say, "are so much

1. H. B. Spotton, *The Commonly Occurring Wild Plants of Canada and More Especially of the Province of Ontario* (Toronto: W. J. Gage, 1st ed. 1883, rev. ed. 1889).

like grass and weeds in their greenness that one might easily walk over a patch of them without noticing them. But they are just as interesting as the brightly coloured kinds, and by far the plainest of them all is the most interesting. That particular orchid," he said in a tone that gave us a feeling of awe, "is rare, very rare, just as rare in Ontario as gold is." (Little did the good man suspect that in fifteen years the Ontario northland was to become a new Eldorado.) "The only spot in the province where it grows is near Sauble Beach at the base of the Bruce Peninsula. It has two other homes in Canada, both of them far from here— the solitary island of Anticosti in the Gulf of St. Lawrence, and, in the west, the Rocky Mountains from the Alaskan frontier southward through British Columbia to northern California. How did this little plant of the far east and the far west get its roots into this out-of-the-way corner of Ontario? It's another of Nature's mysteries!"

But the good man had not yet reached what was for me the climax of the hour. "However," he went on to say, "you will not find the name of this rare plant in my book, for the very good reason that the man who found the specimen of it near Sauble Beach didn't tell me of his find till after the book came from the press. So I want you all to do something unusual: I want each of you to write this in the margin of the proper page in his copy— ALASKAN REIN ORCHID." These words he printed on the blackboard in large capitals. A few minutes later that legend was rubbed off the board but it still stands out clear on the page of my memory.

For me, from that never-to-be-forgotten hour in September, 1892, a great quest was on, the quest of the Alaska Orchid. But fate willed that many years were to pass between the acceptance of the quest and the actual pursuit of it in the field. However, throughout this interval, which I spent partly on the Canadian prairies and partly abroad, the grip of this interest on me never weakened for a moment. Not until 1919 did I even set foot on any part of the now romantic Peninsula. When at last in that year the way opened I knew exactly where I would begin the quest: of course, in the dense, dark jungles of fir and spruce that clothe the long dunes of Sauble Beach, the very ground where, fifty years before, the Alaska orchid had first been found in central Canada. Surely, I should quickly come upon at least one specimen. Of all manner of men the plant-hunter is always the most hopeful.

For an hour or more I crept, face close to the ground, over the mossy crumble of spruce needles. In my searching I came across several lovely little Calypsos and a few clumps of the Ram's Head Lady Slipper which were then in the very prime of bloom. Besides, the Lake Huron dwarf iris had unrolled its luxuriant carpets over the long strip of damp sand marking the high-water line of the Beach. But as for the Alaska orchid my only reward was heartache and backache. "Let's be off at once to the Fishing Islands," I said impatiently to the friend who was with me; "the plant has been found there too." But not a single boatman was to be seen anywhere. So there we were stranded on our mainland for lack of a craft just as Crusoe had been on his island. Now after many years I know why I had failed at the outset of my quest: in The Bruce it is not until the third week in June that the Alaska orchid dares to thrust even the tip of its leaves and its tender spike of tiny buds noticeably above ground. I had launched my quest in the last week in May.

For three summers in a row official duty gave me enough tasks with first claims to attention to keep me from visiting the Lake Huron home of the little orchid. However, in July of 1923 I again crossed its threshold and put up at my fishing camp, the Tamarac Club on Stokes Bay. There the hunt began afresh but this time not in ignorance. Now fully aware that a written list of the orchid's chief traits would not be legible in the deep twilight beneath the evergreens I learned all the facts by heart, and as I crawled along on the ground kept reciting them to myself as though mumbling a magic formula. The upshot of several days of this muttering and grubbing in the gloom was fatigue and bitter disappointment. During the last day of this methodical search I had travelled several furlongs on all fours when I came out of the woods on the township roadway that winds through the trees between Stokes Bay village and Tamarac Island. With dragging feet I turned toward the Club. On both sides of me was ideal cover for the Alaska orchid—a serried army of black and white spruces, balsams and white cedars, posted there, it seemed, as if to protect a great treasure.

While I was trudging along as in a stupor my eye chanced to fall upon some tall slender green spikes that overtopped the wild grasses and weeds on both sides of the narrow roadway—just rank, overgrown stalks of plantain gone to seed, I thought, and passed on. But what kind of plantain in this corner of the world could

The Alaska Orchid

possibly attain such a height? At the question I turned back and
of themselves my lips began mumbling. "A thin rapier-like spike
of tiny, green flowers." Often before out of the corner of my eye
had I seen these upstanding stems of green, but I had always been
too stupid—or too lazy—to observe them closely. This time I stared
until I knew I had missed nothing.

Though tingling all over I steadied myself long enough to check
details against the words of the formula which was beginning to
show that it had some magic after all. "Flowers of unmistakable
orchid shape." Yes, there's the typical orchid lip, and spur, too.
"Crowded into a very narrow, elongated spike, twelve to twenty
inches high." No doubt about the spikes and their height. There's
not a short one in the whole patch and one is even twenty-two
inches tall and has sixty-four diminutive green orchid blooms.
"Flowers give off a sickening odour of stale pollen." Whether its
source was ancient pollen or not, this noisome detail clinched
the proof for me. How I longed to check one more point—the
soft, fleshy roots and their two small, egg-shaped bulbs. But the
fear of sacrilege paralysed my hand. Why destroy a rare life
when the case has been proved? As I withdrew, I casually noticed
that I was not alone in taking an interest in the Alaska orchid:
a number of mosquito-like flies were hovering about the green
spikes as if seeking to alight on them.

The thrill this good fortune shot through my whole being has
not yet spent itself. Man knows no greater excitement than that
of discovery. Had the plant I found been the most beautiful on
earth the effect would have been the same. For me the experience
was as exhilarating as was John Muir's first sight, in 1864, of the
lovely Calypso orchid in another county of Ontario.

In the summer of 1924 I returned to the scene of my discovery,
intent on extending the known range of the Alaska in its "half-way
house" between Anticosti and the Rockies. By this time knowing
what I was looking for and where to look, I seemed to detect
stands of it almost at will. I found them here and there under the
cedars that line the woodland trail between Stokes Bay and
Gauley's Bay and also along the old lumber road that skirts the
mile-long sphagnum bog between Gauley's Bay and Greenough
Harbour. Then ten miles north up the shore at North Boat Cove
I came upon them behind Garney Hawkes's log shanty where we
often eat our shore dinners. A few years later when with the late
W. E. Saunders, the ornithologist, I was hunting for an area to

set apart as a wildlife sanctuary, we suddenly found ourselves guilty of trampling down many fine specimens of Alaskas growing right on the woodland paths near Johnston's harbour. And only two years ago a small company of us chanced upon a very rich stand of the species behind the dunes of Dorcas Bay, six or seven miles south of Tobermory.

In the meantime other plant-hunters[1] had caught the scent and were hot on the trail of the uncomely green flower. Making their way over the straits to Manitoulin they pursued the plant northward across the great island and thence to La Cloche Peninsula on the North Shore where their zeal was amply rewarded by the discovery of several stations. Their finds impressively demonstrated the great extent of the "half-way house" between the eastern gulf and the mountain chain of the west: from south to north—that is, from Sauble Beach to the North Shore of Lake Huron—the house was well over 100 miles long, no mean dwelling for a modest herb.[2]

The summer of 1925 I spent in Great Britain, but the quest in The Bruce did not suffer. One day in Scotland I happened to come upon an idea which for me bridged the Atlantic. While angling for trout in a beautiful mountain burn near Oban—later I learned that I had innocently been poaching on a preserve of the Duke of Argyll—my eye fell upon a tall, leafy-green orchid around whose flowers swarmed some gnatlike flies. Suddenly it occurred to me that this orchid and this species of fly might have a special relationship to each other. Did the plant's power to reproduce itself depend in any way upon the fly? I recalled the Yucca's dependence for fertility upon its own species of moth. Memory then made a leap overseas to the Alaska orchids of Lake Huron and I caught a vision of mosquitoes hovering about fetid green spikes. It was at that moment that a plan took form: on my return home I would transplant amid the spruces and cedars near the Tamarac Club enough Alaska orchids to make possible, over a period of years, a large-scale study of their manner of propagation.

The scheme conceived in haste was matured in leisure. Never did a dictatorship draw up a five-year plan with greater care. The Alaska orchid garden was to be ready in the summer of

1. Professor A. S. Pease and the late Professor M. L. Fernald, Harvard University.

2. Since these words were written I have found stands of Alaska orchid on Cove and Flowerpot islands.

1937. One day during my orgy of computing a visitor favoured me with an unannounced call at my office; he was an eminent scientist from a distant place who was making a name for himself and his growing botanical gardens. Here, I thought, is a rare chance to get advice from a real professional. Ablaze with an ardour that forgot caution I laid my plan before the visitor. With a keenness that matched my own he approved every detail. He too was interested in The Bruce, he said, and had long wished to visit it with his staff of assistants. If he went there could he easily secure lodgings? The obvious genuineness of his interest quickened my hospitable inclinations. So I told him to let me know when he wanted to make the trip and I would then arrange to put him and his party up at the Club. For this simple little promise I was tendered elaborate thanks and a most cordial word of encouragement that could not but be welcome to an amateur: "I congratulate you on your proposed investigation of the Alaska orchid. The best of luck to you!"

This pleasant chat took place in the spring of 1932. Between that time and the summer of 1936, part of which season I spent in fishing and botanizing in Northern Ireland, not a word did I get from my friend. Even in Ireland a reminder of my plan pursued me, for there in County Fermanagh I came across several specimens of the same kind of orchid I had seen in Argyllshire eleven years before. The important fact about this orchid was that it was haunted by what seemed to be the same kind of fly. In late August I returned to Canada, my mind filled with pleasant thoughts of The Bruce and of the execution of my plan the following summer.

But a few weeks later thoughts of a very different order were thrust upon me. In October I received a letter whose contents affected me as would the bursting of a bomb. The text is imprinted indelibly on my memory. Here it is—abridged.

DEAR FOX:

I have never forgotten your kind offer to provide lodgings for me at the Tamarac Club at any time I wished to make a botanical survey of the Bruce Peninsula. Only last July did I make up my mind to make the trip and to make it at once. *En route*, I motored to London to see you but to my regret I found that you were overseas. However, your secretary telephoned to the Club's president in Port Elgin and arranged with him for accommodations for me and my party.

You will be glad to know that all of us were deeply impressed with the Peninsula's marvellous combination of natural wonders. We regard the ten days of our sojourn as eminently profitable. We were so fortunate as to get together a collection of 192 living plants, nearly half of which were splendid specimens of the rare Alaska Orchid which we found in a remarkably large station beside the roadway leading to Tamarac Island. All of these are now thriving in the Botanical Gardens at home. . . . All the members of my staff who accompanied me join me in thanking you for your generous hospitality.

Need I quote more? The restraint now exerted upon my pen has no effect upon my memory. The last words of this remarkable message still echo and re-echo in my mind: "generous hospitality"! Were they meant to be as ironical as they sound? Against all my life's training there arises in me an unholy desire to make a secret visit to those distant gardens; secret, I say, for the reason that I fear an announced and conducted visit would be much like a conducted visit in Russia where the powers-that-be show the visitor just what they want him to see—and no more. I should like to sneak unseen to the plot where my precious Alaska orchids now repose and with my own eyes see what legend is inscribed on the signboard that marks their present resting-place. Does it say, I wonder, that they came from Anticosti? Or from the Rockies, or, perhaps from. . . ?

At last, you say with a sympathetic sigh, we have come to the end of the trail! No, I cannot accept that word. The trail will be taken up again just where it seemed to be broken off and it will be pursued as long and as swiftly as the zest of three-score years and ten permits. I cannot bear to think of giving those Bruce mosquitoes reason to believe I could go back on them!

Chapter 14

"*THE HERB CALLED HART'S TONGUE*"

THE same teacher who in my teens kindled my zeal to follow the trail of the Alaska orchid also launched me on the quest of another unusual plant of The Bruce. This, in the quaint words of a Welsh folktale, is none other than "the herb called hart's tongue." Actually this "herb" is a true fern, though at first glance few people would know it as such. "It is very rare in North America," said our teacher, "and grows among the rocks and forests of the Bruce Peninsula." These words, coming from one who had the gift of making even the mention of cold facts inspiring, seemed almost like the command of a master. To me, at least, it was as if he had said, before Kipling, "Something hidden. Go and find it." Never for a moment did I dream how long, how varied, how fantastic that quest would be.

Not until a year or two ago did I find, in its haunts in the Peninsula, the thing I sought so ardently. Only another naturalist can understand how even decades of frustration can be enjoyable. That quest turned out to be a veritable flying carpet. In a series of zigzag courses it bore me, in mind, over a large part of the globe, into the weird fields of folklore and primitive medicine as well as into the realm of scientific fact; it carried me, in fact, into every section of the Peninsula. For all the many years of unrewarded effort I have not the slightest regret; on the contrary, never have I had more wholesome fun than in this protracted and baffling chase.

What does this interesting "herb" look like? One can find no better description of it than that given by the British botanist, John Gerard, who brought out his massive volume, *Herball,* in London in 1597. The antique flavour of the language and spelling adds a touch of charm to the clarity of the passages quoted.

The common kinde of Harts tongue, called *Phyllitis,* that is to say, a plant consisting of leaves, bearing neither stalk, floure, nor seed, resembling in shew a longue tongue whereof it hath been and is called in shops *Lingua*

The Hart's Tongue Fern

cervina, that is, Harts [deer's] tongue: these leaves are a foot long, smooth and plaine upon one side, but upon that side next the ground straked overthwart with certain long rough marks like small worms, hanging on the back side thereof. The root is blacke, hairy and twisted, or so growing as though it were wound together. . . . It is green all the yeare long, yet less green in winter: in summer it now and then brings forth new leaves. . . .

As one would expect, so odd a clump of herbage was thought to possess strange powers. Three centuries before the Christian era a great Greek botanist wrote that a dosage of its leaves would dissolve the spleen. A famous physician of Nero's reign warned women not to eat them for fear of becoming sterile. John Gerard has a great variety of things to say about the plant. "It is of a binding and drying facultie," he notes. "Common Harts Tongue is commended," he advises in a bedside tone, "against the laske and bloudy flix: Dioscorides [the Roman physician to whom reference has been made] teacheth, That being drunke in wine it is a remedie against the bitings of serpents. It opens the hardnesse and stopping of the spleen and liver, and all other griefes proceeding from opilations or stoppings whatsoever."

It is clear at once that these notions had their origin in folklore untold ages ago. It was from that source that medicine, when still only slightly removed from witchcraft, borrowed them. Indeed they lingered on in medicine long after Gerard's day, even crossing the Atlantic, until at length, like a spent candle, they sputtered out. There is actually a record of their last flicker in America. As late as 1833 the United States *Dispensatory* mentions that Hart's Tongue leaves in decoction may be used to stop bleeding and fluxes but confesses that "their properties are feeble, and they have fallen into neglect." The edition of 1839 states that "they have been superseded by more active medicines."

However, only a few years ago Robert Gibbings, on one of his rambles in the highlands of Wales, found the Hart's Tongue still rooted in an ancient folktale of the region. The gist of this is worth telling if for no other reason than to show how false ideas concerning natural objects live on through the centuries.

Of the many lovely lakes in Wales, we are told, the most famous is Llyn y Fan Fach, the Lake by the Little Hill. Like other lakes it was the home of a beautiful fairy sprite. Once, long, long ago she rose from the waters, went ashore, and was wooed by a mortal man. After a time she wedded him, bringing with her from the depths of the waters a rich dowry of horses and cattle. As man and wife, mortal and fairy settled down on a farmstead about a mile distant from Myddfai. Here three fine sons were born to them.

But all was not happy with them "ever after." Just as in a wholly human household unity does not always prevail, so this household was often divided by hasty differences over the merest trifles. The delicate spirit of the fairy could not endure the discord forever; at the third tiff over a trivial matter she fled the family hearth and plunged into the lake, taking her herds with her but leaving her sons behind. They, overcome with grief, day after day roamed along the borders of the lake hoping to find their mother.

One day, to their great joy, she reappeared at a place called The Gate of the Physician. There she told her sons that her mission was to bring healing to the bodies of men. This she asked them to take as their calling in life. She taught them the recipes for many remedies and showed them the potent herbs that grew in the region roundabout. By dint of hard study the sons became the most famous healers in the land. To preserve their precious knowledge for those who would come after them they wrote it down in a book. What they wrote has been put into print by the Welsh Manuscript Society. The list of herbals prescribed by the fairy lady of the Lake of the Little Hill is long and wonderful. One of them in particular is of great interest to those who are following hard on the trail of the rare fern in the Bruce Peninsula.

To preserve chastity. If you would always be chaste, eat daily some of the herb called hart's tongue, and you will never assent to the suggestions of impurity.[1]

If ever any plant deserved to be called ubiquitous, it is the Hart's Tongue fern. It is rooted in all three major land masses east of the Atlantic and in some of their satellite islands. Take up its trail in Ireland, follow it across to Scotland, to Wales, and then eastward across England; there "the common harts tongue," as Gerard remarks at the close of the sixteenth century, "growes by the way sides in great plenty, as you travel from London to Excester, in shadowie places and in moist stony vallies and wells."[2] Fly over the North Sea to Scandinavia, and south to the Spanish Peninsula, skirt the mountainous north coast of Africa, and then speed on to Italy and the Balkans; thence across the blue Aegean, over northern Persia and central Asia to the Pacific and Japan. In many parts of the great tract over which you have flown this modest herb the Hart's Tongue abounds. The length of the living cord thus flung across space staggers the imagination.

But there is yet more to be said. Nature cast frayed ends of this cord over the Atlantic to North America. One tiny strand she dropped in a lonely little valley of New Brunswick; a couple of strands among shaded limestone outcroppings in New York State south of Syracuse; a mere thread in an out-of-the-way limestone sinkhole in Tennessee and another in a faraway corner of Mexico near the frontier of Guatemala. Could the distribution of anything seem to be more haphazard or capricious? But that is not the end of it. With a great flourish Nature strewed other loose ends of the living cord northward along the craggy, scalloped edges of the Niagara Escarpment in the province of Ontario. There they took hold in a loose chain of crannies in the dolomite of several counties. It is in the peninsular part of Bruce County that this fern is found in its greatest plenty in America.

But the first visit I made with a friend to that land of promise fell far short of our dreams. With that infallible plant-guide in our hands—our botany teacher's own text—we invaded The Bruce in high hopes. But alas! faith was rudely shaken. All the precious

1. Robert Gibbings, *Coming down the Wye* (London: J. M. Dent and Sons, 1942), p. 25.
2. In the *Atlantic Monthly*, June, 1950, p. 35, Donald Culross Peattie states that, since the bombing of London in World War II, Hart's Tongue fern has grown up in abundance in the craters and cellars.

little volume had to say of the Hart's Tongue was: "Gladed ravines and limestone cliffs; not very common"; just a vague, tantalizing generality with not one definite direction in it. No needle was ever lost more effectively in a haystack than the Hart's Tongue in the Peninsula's 500 square miles. So ended the first search. Ten years later, even with Gray's *Manual* as guide, the second search ended in the same way.

But during this period of seeming failure progress was being made. From time to time snatches of good news came in from various niches along the Escarpment. One day the postman brought a parcel, postmarked Collingwood, Simcoe County, containing a fresh, green clump of Hart's Tongue. Was a third county now to be added to Bruce and Grey? No such luck! The specimen though mailed at Collingwood had been found on the Escarpment above Meaford in Grey. But the catalogue of sources was not to remain long static. One sunny morning a few weeks after, the ardent naturalist, Will Saunders, hailed me exultingly across a busy down-town street: "Yesterday I found Hart's Tongue north of Orangeville." So Dufferin came into the honours list of counties. In May of 1951 James Soper entered the name of Peel County.

My first view of the Hart's Tongue growing in its native soil came unheralded, in a land very far from The Bruce. In August of 1936 I spent a fortnight in Ireland fishing and plant-hunting. One afternoon as I was travelling eastward in a bus through County Leitrim on the way from Sligo to Enniskillen I glimpsed on the roadside a healthy bunch of long, straplike green leaves. I knew them at once for Hart's Tongue. I shouted loudly enough to awaken the long-dead Irish kings. The driver, thinking there had been an accident, halted the bus abruptly; the passengers were given a violent jolt. As one body they turned and glared at me. When I leaped to the ground they looked relieved. Good riddance, they seemed to say; upon my reappearance moments later they made no attempt to hide their disappointment. However, that did not last long. Such is the Irish spirit that when my fellow-travellers saw the triumph wreathing my face and the trophy of green in my hand, instantly they sensed that I had found a treasure and openly showed me that they shared the exhilaration of discovery with me. Yet they were cheerful and clever dissemblers. As we went on our journey one by one they confessed to me that though they had lived all their lives in Ireland they had never really noticed the Hart's Tongue before nor had ever heard its name until they heard it from me. What a commentary upon the average man's power to observe the commonplaces that surround him! It was a friendly company that exchanged farewells at the bus stop in Enniskillen.

When after returning home I put pressed specimens of my County Leitrim Hart's Tongue beside those from Tennessee and Collingwood it was easy to detect differences between the two groups: the fronds of the Irish plants are noticeably longer and somewhat broader proportionately than those of the American. Besides, minute differences in the fruiting bodies are brought out by the microscope. It was manifest that the professional botanist is right in counting the trans-Atlantic Hart's Tongue as the type of the species and the American as a variety.

Early the following summer clues began to come in. "You will easily find the Hart's Tongue," a wise old botanist assured me, "in the wooded southeastern corner of the Peninsula. It is sparsely scattered among the damp, shady crevices of the dolomite near Purple Valley. There's lots of it in the woods southwest of Hope Bay." That seemed to be the last word on the subject. I was buoyed up by a feeling of confidence such as crowns the end of a long hunt. But I exulted too soon. What seems clear indoors today, is tomorrow in the field often as inscrutable as a signpost in a fog at midnight. The morning after the old man sent us on our way rejoicing my companion and I found to our dismay that even the common little word "near" can be without real meaning. "Near" might be a matter of half a mile or five miles. Of a sudden, a suspicion dawned upon us: possibly our accommodating guide had been vague by design. We could not brush the idea away. Was he trying to steer us away from his treasured rarity? So we set out on a long tedious trudge from farmhouse to farmhouse. At each door we asked the same question: Does anyone here know where the Hart's Tongue fern grows in the neighbourhood of Purple Valley? Certainly the name was no "open sesame": nobody had ever heard it before. One kindly housewife cheered us with a hearty "Yes, I'll show you." The good soul limped ahead of us to a shaded corner of a lovely garden and proudly pointed to a bed of gorgeous pansies—heart's ease, of course.

Balked but not beaten we turned, still hopeful, to the heavily wooded tract southwest of Hope Bay. But "southwest" proved to be as vague a directive as "near." We saw clearly we must change our way of approaching people. So instead of trusting in the magic of the plant's unusual name to open up a lead, we had recourse to description. We aimed to make our word-pictures so vivid that even the simplest rustic who had ever seen the Hart's Tongue growing would recognize it at once in our portrayal of it. We stressed its unique features—its long, straplike fronds, its resemblance to garden herbs, its love of dim, secluded nooks in the forest. But we made no more headway than before; in every doorway we met a blank uncomprehending face. Our pride in an ability to command words was a pricked bubble. And to think that this was the last day of that year's quest! We gave up and returned to the Club.

The news awaiting us there was not such as to banish all disappointment. A passing party of American botanists had left a message for us: only the day before they had found a stand of Hart's Tongue *near* Sydney Bay on Cape Croker. And that was not all: a Toronto friend had come upon one *near* Berford Lake. Once more those baffling approximations! However, the reports were fundamentally encouraging: they brought assurance that the Hart's Tongue still had roots in the Peninsula.

In the summer of 1951 the quest was taken up afresh. Again the mode of attack was changed. Now we resolved to resort to stealth, to steal up, as it were, upon the plant itself in its fastnesses. Our cunning was businesslike. On a single card we jotted down brief notes on all the features of the Hart's Tongue's haunts in this region. Outstanding were: *dolomite cliffs of varying height; horizontal ledges, clefts, or fissures; damp and very rich leaf mould; a dense overshadowing canopy of hardwood trees.* Then we put ourselves through a quiz. Do we know of any single tract on the east side of the Peninsula, we asked, in which all these features are ideally combined? We took our time to think it over —two whole days. Our answer was a positive "Yes." But—here's the rub—the spot is two miles away from the nearest station previously reported.

To that spot we repaired next morning early. Our first view of it was gratifying; it seemed to be all we had hoped for, nearly ideal. A low limestone cliff, no higher than twenty-five feet and somewhat more than two hundred yards long, lay squarely across our line of vision. At no time of day in any season could a direct ray of sunlight strike its face, so thick was the network of branches and twigs that overhung it. The two of us parted, my companion to scale the south end of the little cliff and I the north. It was only seconds later when a voice on my right rang out: "Here they are, a whole settlement of them!" Yes, there they were, fine, healthy clumps of them hob-nobbing in the twilight with companies of Holly ferns. The sight was as beautiful as it was thrilling. In an instant the load of accumulated disappointments of many years was lifted from our minds; only the satisfaction of achievement remained. And there was sound reason for triumph: in finding our way, as it were by dead reckoning, to this solitary stand of Hart's Tongue we now had in our hands the key to other stands.

But has our story given the key to all the world also? When I say that I hope not, the motive is not a selfish one. On the contrary, it is thoroughly altruistic: I am moved by the desire to help save for the people the Hart's Tongue and the other rare plants of the Bruce Peninsula. The vagueness with which the sage old botanist veiled his reports on the rare fern's stations was the product of a ripe experience in Europe and in North America. The good man had learned that when Nature's prized rarities are placed within easy reach of the public hand, that hand is apt to feel no restraint. The hand that has to toil hard and long to discover Nature's treasures is likely to value and preserve them. That the Hart's Tongue of this region has already suffered from the lack of restraint is no fiction. Before me as I write is a depressing entry in a diary; the diary is that of the man who nearly fifty years ago found the Hart's Tongue stand near Owen Sound. "July 24, 1931. . . . I visited 'the spot' and even in semi-darkness got three small Hart's Tongues. . . . Visitors seem to have taken all the large plants. Even last year specimens were scarce. Sent some last summer to Ottawa. . . ."

Time and again my thoughts dwell upon the astoundingly various properties which for more than two thousand years witch, seer, wizard, and physician have attributed to "the herb called hart's tongue." That Science has now branded them all as vain delusions I cannot accept without some lingering regret. Only think: if they were true, the abundance of the plant in The Bruce could make the place even more remarkable than it is now. With a quick "remedie" at hand no longer need the wayfarer fear the Massasauga's fang nor sudden seizure by "the laske and bloudy flix." Besides, there remains the comforting assurance of the spirit lady of the Welsh Lake of the Little Hill. If she is right, then any inhabitant of The Bruce who suffers from the torment of unchaste impulses could blame no one but himself.

Chapter 15

ORCHID AND FLOWERPOT

W ELL, now that at last you have found the "big thing," is there anything around here worth looking for?" That question was thrown at us the morning after we had found the Hart's Tongue fern in its native lair in The Bruce. It nettled me a bit, probably without real reason; I seemed to sense in its tone a hint—no more than a hint—that for a man on the far side of seventy to take on another long chase was the height of rashness. My reply was quick though perhaps too sharp: "Yes, there is something else; and the old man can take it. The chase is on right now!"

That something had long been in our thoughts, one of the loveliest of our native North American plants—the Prairie White Fringed Orchid.[1] In its true home in the swampy flatlands of the Mississippi Valley and adjacent regions it grows lush, tall, and in abundance. In the northeast—scattered spots in Nova Scotia, New England, New York, and eastern Ontario—it is rapidly dying out if it is not already dead. In the thirties it was found in the Bruce Peninsula by the lynx-eyed Krotkov. Its mere presence here so far away from its usual haunts adds to the wonders of this great rock garden of the north. The appeal of this new wonder was too strong for me; to my friend's gentle taunt what other retort was there to give than the one I gave him? Besides, a shrewd observation of that famous rover, George Borrow, had long ago fixed in me a conviction that the quest would not be utterly unrewarded: "The dog that trots about finds a bone."

For many years this note, made up of the remarks of several observers, has been reposing in my files:

From its soggy bed among pitcher-plants and sundews the Prairie White Fringed orchid lifts aloft a straight green, leafy stem which sometimes reaches a height of four feet. This culminates in a spike of gleaming white, a pinnacle of flowers that seem to be molded out of foam. This effect is

1. *Habenaria leucophaea* (Nutt.) Gray.

Prairie White Fringed Orchid

produced by the finely-cut petals of the individual flowers. From the spike floats off a dainty perfume, half-strange, half-familiar, but always intriguing. Some say it reminds them of the fragrance of elder blossoms. But whatever it be, one who smells it carries away a pleasant wonder.

When a party of three of us set out on our new mission we put on a bold front to conceal a question that sorely puzzled us. The directions that Krotkov gave me by word of mouth in the thirties were indeed gloriously vague. He had come across the rare orchid near a lake in the northeast corner of the Peninsula. That was all he said; and now he was long dead. Only count the lakes in that corner; here are but a few of them: Shouldice, Crane, Gillies, Britain, Marley, George, Emmett, Lower and Upper Andrew, Umbrella, Moore, enough to keep a large company hunting all season. The old gentleman—God rest his soul!—had a keen sense of humour.

Two things were plain: a plan was needed to save time and effort; if any of the lakeside bogs were dry it was useless to press the search. A visit to two or three would soon determine our course. With the new large-scale government chart before us we laid out the route for the day: to Shouldice and then on to Crane, Marley, George, and, last of all, back southwards to Britain. One

look showed that the floor of the small bog at the east end of
Shouldice Lake was caked hard and cracked. No orchid could live
there. In the great broad swamp east of Crane conditions were
even worse: one could walk halfway across it dryshod. Returning
to our car we were about to turn north towards George and its
neighbouring lakes when a native kindly warned us that the rough
trail was blocked by a fallen tree.

So it was with very dim hopes that we coasted down the last
slope of the winding road into a parklike property on the east side
of Lake Britain. Its owner—who, as it turned out, was a fellow-
citizen of our own home town of London—greeted us cheerfully
by name and welcomed us to his summer demesne. We told him
our errand. "Hopeless, utterly hopeless," he said; "this year the
water in the lake and adjacent bogs is at the lowest level I have
ever seen it. See for yourselves." We did: a few glances up lake,
down lake, and at the broad bog on the far side were enough.
Nature's decree was plain to read: the quest, barely begun, was
already off—but, of course, for this year only. Hope returned when
we thought of the late Frank Morris's long search for the very
same orchid that we sought and the feeling words he wrote under
the inspiration of final success. "But there's joy in the chase as
well as in the kill; and it certainly has been no end of a chase, over
many a season and hundreds of miles."[1]

As we were about to bid our kindly host farewell he exclaimed
in a tone that revealed a desire to spread salve on the wound of
our manifest disappointment: "But you haven't seen the Monument yet." "What monument?" we asked naïvely. "Why, a remarkable rock formation—a great limestone column standing on the
face of the cliff. If you haven't seen that you haven't seen the
Peninsula." Thereupon our friend pointed out the way to the
marvel. "Drive east," he said, "across yonder newly-mown hayfield,
then walk the rest of the way. When you get to the brink of the
cliff you can easily get down to the Monument; an old iron fire-
escape leads to it."

At the far side of the field a snake fence in the last stage of
decrepitude halted the car. The sag in this barrier at which we
stopped had obviously been a gate long years before. Clambering
over the ancient rails we found ourselves in a rank, dense tangle of
staghorn sumac, wild roses, and chokecherry trees heavily laden

1. Frank Morris and Edward A. Eames, *Our Wild Orchids* (New York: Charles
Scribner's Sons, 1929), p. 153.

with fruit. Through this we pushed slowly and with great caution, for the exceptionally heavy curtain of foliage hid the ground ahead of us. We knew we must be very close to the scalloped edge of the precipice. Parting the curtain carefully we suddenly gave ourselves a glorious surprise: a broad, gorgeous scene of cliff, trees, water, and sunlight.

As a picture it was perfectly composed: from one side to the other was the blue expanse of that inland freshwater sea, the Georgian Bay, and in the distant background to the north the vision was blocked by the clear-cut silhouette of Cabot's Head and its lofty bluffs. Though the day was by no means windless, not the faintest sound of lapping waters rose to the height where we stood. But it was neither the breadth nor the depth of the scene that held us transfixed: it was the spectacular object that lorded the foreground—a huge vase-shaped pillar of stratified stone. With one voice we shouted: a Flowerpot!

So this was the Monument. And a massive stately pile it was. Indeed, together with its setting of craggy cliff it seemed like the remains of a turreted corner of a ruined medieval castle. Into my mind flashed the words in which Duncan expressed his pleasure at the sight of Macbeth's battlemented home:

> This castle has a pleasant seat, the air
> Nimbly and sweetly recommends itself
> Unto our gentle senses.

The Monument! And well named it was—the only monumental example of the "flowerpot" formation, so far as we knew, on the whole mainland of the Peninsula. Our elation could be forgiven: in trotting abroad that day the dog had really found a bone. We had set out to find an orchid and had come upon a "flowerpot." How strange that in many years of trotting we had never chanced upon it before. And yet it had been there for thousands of years. But strangest of all was it that, as we learned later, only a few local inhabitants who had long known the Monument had ever seen in it any special reason for wonder. Familiarity even with an exceptional phenomenon had made it just an "unassuming commonplace of nature."

But, unlike the Monument, the famous "flowerpots" which many years ago gave Flowerpot Island—four miles off Tobermory—its unique name, had not thus been left unhonoured. Indians of the region have said that for ages their forefathers offered to them the grim reverence of fear. They shunned them as though they were

living agents of evil. Even many a modern Indian avoids Flowerpot Island unless driven by night or storm to take refuge there.
The earliest white explorers as they paddled that way noticed
three oddly shaped columns of rock: since their day one of the
three has been toppled over and shattered. In 1827 John Galt,
sailing on the gunboat *Bee* from Penetanguishene to the Canada
Company's infant settlement at Goderich, turned aside to visit the
curious formations. In a few years they became an attraction for
tourists. In the course of time the government of Canada became

The Monument or "Devil's Pulpit"

aware of their significance and took special measures to protect
them against the ravages of the elements and of thoughtless
vandals. Flowerpot Island, with its 300 acres of cliffs, caves, dales,
and forest, is now set apart for the people forever as a national
park.

Seeing these great, queer stone shapes for the first time, each
flaunting on its summit a shrub or a small tree, you would probably agree with John Galt that the name fits. The two "flowerpots"
that now survive differ in size and form from each other. One is
tall—indeed, about fifty feet in height—and graceful in its lines.
The other is shorter by twenty feet and in form is stubby, dwarfed,
and rugged. On its several sides one can see weird, cruel human
profiles jutting out. Can we blame the unschooled red man for
his fear of the island?

On my first visit to Flowerpot Island I stumbled—literally—upon an enlightening experience. The goal I sought immediately after landing was a cave that opens high up on the southern face of the island. The job of clambering up to it was not hard. But the descent was a very different matter, a problem in mechanics for one carrying more weight than that prescribed by a discreet doctor. Thus encumbered I found I could not make the return journey downhill with a comfortable degree of control. In spite of desperate efforts to use my heels as brakes I half-slithered, half-

Larger Flowerpot   *Smaller Flowerpot*

ran down the declivity toward its abrupt terminus, which was nothing less than the brink of a "tall cliff vertiginously high." In my frantic wriggling I had managed to put myself flat on my back. But this position was a menace rather than a help, for it made me a human toboggan sliding downward over the smooth ground-cover of fallen leaves and pine needles. Conscious of gaining speed I gave up hope. At last, however, I passed the zone that favoured swift descent and shot out on the bare limestone shelf. Its roughness slowed me down enough to enable me to straighten out my legs and brace my feet.

Of a sudden I was brought to a rude but welcome stop: one heel had dropped into a fissure nearly a foot wide and held there firmly. For several minutes I lay without moving, giving my lungs a chance to gather breath and my mind to reap a few sober thoughts.

Apparently, if we are to accept the assurance of the great naturalist, William Beebe, the position in which I was is one that encourages philosophic meditation. "In the world of nature of the naturalist," he observes sagely, "to lie supine, even to have slid violently into that posture, is merely to be presented with a fresh, new view of the world."[1]

Struggling to my feet I gazed with gratitude at the breach in the rock that had saved me. Though agape like the mouth of the dumb, it seemed to say something about the making of a "flower-pot." On the surface of the shelf above the cliff the fissure had the outline of a half-circle. But the gap was far from being super-ficial; with the almost uniform width of nine inches it dropped down into the rock farther than one could see. Plainly, it cut out of the face of the island a solid block of many strata. This mass was now a separate unit in itself—the rough material out of which some day a new "flowerpot" may be sculptured. What force severed it? And with what tools? What hand and what skill would give it its final form?

Probably the initial fissure of each of the existing "flowerpots" was caused by the tort, or twisting effect, of a glacier as it forced its way along the edge of the island's southern cliff. After the retreat of the ice Nature had a chance to begin her long patient work of shaping the rude block of stone and shales that had been left behind. First she wielded her lighter tools: with the constant drip and seepage of water she slowly widened the space that now separated the block from the island; when that became wide enough to hold great volumes of water she poured into it torrents of rain and melted snows. Then with the fine chisels of wind, sleet, and frost she set herself to chipping away at all the exposed sur-faces of the huge mass until it began to take on a few of the finer features men were to behold and wonder at in a later era. But Nature was not yet done with her heavier tools. At the base of the new towering shape she hurled the waves of great storms and the battering rams of winter ice-fields. The hard Lockport dolomite on top resisted the impact with some success, but the soft strata below were worn away until all that was left of them was a slender stem holding aloft a body of rock whose lines and proportions remind the common man of today of some familiar article of domestic use.

1. William Beebe, *High Jungle* (New York: Duell, Sloan & Pearce, 1949). p. 139.

Different travellers of the early days saw in these striking formations different things. Some saw in the larger formation a Roman wine jar, but others a kind of Greek vase; still others, noting the tree or shrub that adorned each summit, saw in both masses nothing but flowerpots. To the unschooled pioneer classical comparisons meant nothing. So, with him, the modern commonplace won out over the refinements of antiquity, and to this day the shapely stone columns of Flowerpot Island are just plain flowerpots.

In form the Monument resembles both its counterparts on the island: it has the slim stem of the larger and the harsh profiles of the smaller. Like both it displays a clump of green foliage; this is dappled with little spots of red. With the naked eye one can easily identify the species: it is that now common European stowaway, kindred to the tomato and the potato, the Nightshade, sometimes called Climbing Bittersweet. Its touch of colour tones down the glare and softens the lines of the gaunt stone form.

The Monument seems to be the product of the same order of natural forces that fashioned the long-known "flowerpots." In general it consists of the same materials, but in one respect it is conspicuously different: its body, which is made up of members of the Medina-Cataract series of strata present in the Escarpment, lacks the hard protective shield of Lockport dolomite that caps each of the island forms.

But the Monument, we find, is not after all the sole formation of its general kind known on mainland parts of the Escarpment. When, a year or two ago, the press and the grapevine telegraph told the world of the Monument's presence on the Peninsula, reports of other pillar-like rocks began to come in from several quarters. Simcoe County proudly reported a "standing rock" within her borders, one that looks like a cylinder standing upright on one end in a rough deep notch in the edge of the Blue Mountains eight miles south of Collingwood. In its turn, Grey County pointed with spirit to its *authentic* "Standing Rock" that overlooks the Georgian Bay five miles west of Collingwood. Students of the history of ancient Huronia believe this to be the Standing Rock near which lay Etharita, the village of the Petuns, or Tobacco Nation, to which the Jesuits gave the name, Mission of St. Mathias. The last word came from Halton County, many miles to the south: on the sheer face of the cliff at Mount Nemo, it said, is poised a ten-foot "flowerpot" shaped like a chimney. Of these three stone columns, one must observe, not one seems to resemble in its making the "flowerpots" of The Bruce and of the island in the straits. However, the "Standing Rock" of Etharita has long been known to have a special significance: for the Petuns it marked the wild tract in which dwelt the spirits of their departed. This belief and the fact that a village was established near it illustrates a notable contradiction typical of the primitive mind. While repelled from the great pinnacle of stone by his fear of it, at the same time the Indian could not resist an influence that powerfully drew him towards it.

As we looked long and intently upon the Monument on the day of discovery thoughts crowded into our minds. This massive shape in stone is more than merely a scenic wonder and a subject of the geologist's study. Perhaps it has an historical, even an archaeological, significance as well. We know that the early Indian shunned the island "flowerpots"; we know too of the Petuns' paradoxical attitude toward "Standing Rock." If Du Creux's outline of the Bruce Peninsula is even approximately correct, then one can infer that somewhere in the region of the Monument was the Petun village which became the Mission of St. Simon and St. Jude. Is it absurd to expect that the Monument, though an object of awe, could yet attract to it settlements of the very people who dreaded the sight of its uncanny form?

There are—a flash of memory reminds us—signs near Gillies Lake, only four miles distant, of an ancient Indian occupation thereabouts. The possibilities of discovery are fascinating. We feel a strong impulse to go and see forthwith. But, happily, a mentor within us intervenes in time—a remnant of common sense. To yield to the prompting now would be nothing else than the launching of a third quest in a single day. In the morning we set out to find an orchid[1] and before we knew it we were probing into the natural history of "flowerpots." Are not two quests between sunup and sundown enough for anyone in his right mind?

1. In mid-July we found it on the shores of a lake several miles north of Lake Britain.

PART FIVE: FOREST AND WOODSMAN

"Camboose" Camp, No. 1, Shouldice Lake

Chapter 16

AND THE TREES TROOPED OUT

A ND the trees trooped out! Yes, they trooped out in companies, in battalions, in divisions, in armies. Then, mustered afresh in certain strategic places, they were reformed and sent forth over many routes to diverse destinations. The process of evacuating the forest stronghold of The Bruce did not last many years (though longer than seemed possible at the start), but when it came to an end it was alarmingly near to being complete. In but few areas was there left any reason to expect that some day they might again raise a force of the most sought-for trees—the pines white and red—to hold the place of those that had marched forth into the outer world. Some tracts were now deserts of slash, tangles of windfalls, fire barrens, and solitary trees too twisted or dwarfed to interest the axeman. Elsewhere nothing remained but bare expanses of limestone pavement, the sight of which recalls a Cromwellian description of County Clare: "Not enough timber on which to hang a man, enough water to drown him, or enough earth to bury him."

Of what trees did the original forest garrison consist? "The men of the trees" would answer that it consisted of two classes: "the conifer woods of the Canadian zone" which mark the Lake Huron side and the north half of the Peninsula, and the "deciduous" (i.e. leaf-shedding) Alleghenian woods of the Transition zone which are characteristic of the east side. But this is too general an answer; only a dry, specific list can, I fear, tell us what we wish to know. In the first class we find the three pines— red, white, and jack; the two spruces—white and black; white cedar, tamarac, and hemlock. In the second class are hard maple, beech, white elm, red oak, white and black ash, grey birch, and basswood; scattered here and there over the Peninsula are the elms, rock and red, and, on the east side, the butternut; anywhere, especially where fire has raged, one may expect the "indomitable white birch." Of course, not all of these trees were in equal demand.

Manifestly, trees do not troop out of themselves; they need human marshals. These taken together are an interesting type of citizen, a citizen who can be recognized anywhere by his garb. By the sixties and seventies when the woodsman began to storm The Bruce this garb had virtually become a uniform for his whole guild, a uniform which had slowly evolved out of two centuries of forest experience of the Canadian *habitant,* the New Englander, and the English-speaking colonist of Upper Canada, as they hewed their way westward. For many years numbers of husky men, as it were labelled by this uniform, could be seen every autumn before freeze-up in all the ports of the Georgian Bay, including Owen Sound and Wiarton. Here they made their last preparations before setting out by water for their winter camps up the Peninsula or beyond.

But not all the men who marshalled the trees of The Bruce came in each season from outside. A goodly company of them were already there, families who had lived on the land since it had been opened for settlement. It was their chief occupation, especially in winter, to cut down the trees on their own holdings. The piecemeal subdivision of the surface of the Peninsula imposed upon it, in general, a small-scale type of lumbering. But far more restricting was a practice that did the settler a grave injustice, a practice that robbed him of the natural right to be master of his own property. This deplorable wrong has been almost wholly forgotten; any mention of it in print is brief. Only now are the main facts coming into the open, and that just because a few old-timers[1] (members of families once engaged in the making and shipping of timber and lumber, and men old enough to have seen with their own eyes something of the things they tell about), have exceptionally keen memories. And how they revel in telling of these things! But it is with no little heat that they recall the great wrong that caused the settler grievous hardships and was at long last righted in a highly dramatic manner. The small part of this long tale for which there is room on these pages is enough to show us how the big pines of The Bruce trooped out over its borders.

1. In order of seniority these are: William Gilchrist, 93, and Robert Lymburner, 88, of Owen Sound; Charles Williams, 80, of Lion's Head. Charles Williams died on January 15, 1952, and William Gilchrist on February 28, 1952.

The big pines? you ask in a tone of doubt; were there many? Though not as numerous or as large as the pines of the Ottawa or the Trent, many more of them grew in the Peninsula than tradition suspects; certainly, there were enough of them to excite the cupidity of big timber operators. Today's ignorance of the facts is easily explained. When in the middle fifties the Crown took over the Peninsula from the Indians, the sale of lands to settlers and the issuance of timber licences were put into the hands of a local agent of the Department of Indian affairs. At one time the agent had his office in Owen Sound and later in Wiarton. His duties were prescribed by Ottawa. Not unless the Department requested reports upon special cases did the agent have to send to Ottawa records concerning timber leases. So the renewal of these leases each spring became in practice a routine matter. The germ of trouble in this quite legal course was that the pines on the settler's land that were big enough and good enough to make square timber for export to Britain belonged not to the settler but to the big company that had been given the licence to cut the pine on the area involved. One licence noted in the records covered fifty-one square miles; the amount asked for was seventy-five. Of the pine on his holding the settler was allowed only barely enough for the erection of permanent buildings, such as a house, barn, and a small sawmill. The settler's grievance was a real one, but all his protests were in vain. The evil lasted, as we shall see, until early in the eighties.

The pines marked for export began their exodus from the Peninsula in the first years of the sixties. They were cut and squared in Keppel and Amabel townships by a large operator who held the licence for that territory. They were landed at Oliphant and then sent in rafts to Collins Inlet, now Tobermory. There they were loaded through stern-ports on to three-masted schooners and conveyed to Toronto and, ultimately, probably in rafts, to Quebec.

Later in the same decade and through the seventies the same company secured a succession of leases to work in the north part of the Peninsula where grew the largest stands of prime pine. Here operations were conducted on so extensive a scale that the operators found it necessary to build a full-fledged "camboose" camp of the type common in the eastern forests. The spot where this camp stood is now a half-grown-over clearing at the east end of Shouldice Lake. Camp Number 1 it was called by its

owners; whether there were others of its kind in the region no
one seems to know. It sheltered a staff of eighty-two hands, all
skilled in the making of square sticks. No wonder the pines
marched out of The Bruce in veritable armies! No wonder, either,
that the settlers' complaints had become a chorus!

At first the men working out of Camp No. 1 drew the squared
timbers over iced snow trails through the forest and across
frozen Gillies Lake to Wingfield Basin at Cabot's Head. Where
the sticks went from there we can only conjecture. Probably they
were taken to Collingwood by schooner or raft and there loaded
on flat cars of the Northern Railway. As yet the rails had not
reached Owen Sound. This we do know: square timbers were in
that period unloaded from the cars at the Northern Railway's
dock by the Queen's Wharf in Toronto and there made into large
rafts to be towed to Quebec. During two latter phases of the
industry in this region—1882 and 1888—the sticks were landed on
the shore of Dyer's Bay where the village of that name stands
today. From there, as my informants often saw with their own
eyes, they went in rafts to Owen Sound to be forwarded by railway to Toronto.

Over the years novelists who have pictured the life of the
North American woodsman have cast an aura of romance around
the name of the "camboose" camp. This has drawn attention
away from evils that almost always followed in the wake of its
operations. The truth is that the making of square timber, whether
by large gangs or by small gangs, was appallingly wasteful. For
this purpose only the largest and finest pines were chosen. The
operators well knew that the ultimate purchaser would reject any
stick that failed to meet his most exacting requirements; the
presence of more than two black knots in any stick was enough
to condemn it. By sounding a tree with the back of his axe a
skilled axeman could nearly always tell its quality. Sometimes,
however, he found after felling a tree that its wood was below
standard; its fate was to be left prostrate on the ground to rot.
Even the felling of sound trees was wasteful, especially in the
early days when all felling was done with the axe. The chips
produced by the chopping and by the squaring were left just
where they fell; masses of these, together with the slash of
branches and tops and the rotting remains of whole trees, became enormous tinder-boxes. In this inflammable stuff was kindled
years later many a fire that brought ruin to the settlers over
whose lands and homesteads it swept.

By 1880 the settlers found themselves driven to resort to almost desperate measures. In a council of war they decided to demand the abolition of a practice that stripped their land of its natural wealth. Enlisting the aid of members of Parliament who were in favour with the Government they took their grievance to Ottawa. To give point to their plea they named one firm in particular as affording a convincing illustration of the kind of harm that was being done by the "big fellows." This operator, it seems, was the successor to the company that had built Camp No. 1 on Shouldice Lake. But the successor was no longer an individual or a family; it was a recently incorporated company of British investors. Had the original operator, one wonders, seeing that the big pines were almost all gone, unloaded upon others who lived far away the burden of ownership? In any case, the new owner resisted the efforts of the settlers, but with so little tact as to get under the Government's skin. At long last, the petitioners secured the ear of the Prime Minister, Sir John A. Macdonald. Very quickly he perceived the justice of their case. So—by this time it was 1882— he summarily cancelled the lease complained of and put an end to the issuance of that kind of lease in The Bruce. Thus what might fitly be called the Peasants' War of the Peninsula ended in complete victory for those who launched it to right a great wrong.[1]

But not all the blame for ravaging the forests of The Bruce can justly be laid at the doors of big business. Many small operators and the settlers themselves seemed in their own modest way to be no less obsessed with the same passion: to keep the trees marching out into the world at the double quick. The joint advance of camp and sawmill over the face of the Peninsula was as ragged and random as the front of a guerilla army. A few dates together with a little geography will make that clear. Before 1860 a sawmill was at work on Colpoy's Bay in Albemarle, which is north of Amabel, whereas William Street's mill on the Sauble River in the latter township did not begin sawing until September 1862. In 1872 a saw-and-shingle mill was set up inland on the Crane River ten miles south of The Tub; The Tub itself got along without such an installation until 1881, the year in which Horace Lymburner and his sons started their mill at "Ghost Lake,"[2] that is, Gillies Lake, between Dyer's Bay and Cabot's Head on the Georgian Bay side of the Peninsula. In 1874 a water-run mill was turning out lumber at Barrow Bay farther south on the same shore. About 1892 two important plants began operating

1. See Appendix.   2. See chapter XVII, "The Mill at Ghost Lake."

on the Lake Huron side, the one àt Big Pine Tree Harbour which handled soft woods, the other at Stokes Bay[1] which was chiefly concerned with the hardwoods commonly used in the manufacture of furniture, notably maple, beech, grey birch, and ash. Both these mills had checkered careers, passing in succession from one owner to another, bringing sometimes the heartache of loss, sometimes the comfort of profit. In the main, their story is the story of most of the other mills of the Peninsula.

These are only a few of all the mills that busied themselves over the years with turning the trees of the whole Peninsula into timbers and lumber. Of the total the historian[2] of the industry in this region makes the astounding statement that the logs from the Peninsula "fed the *eight* mills that in the early days encircled the lower end of Colpoy's Bay, besides some *thirty* smaller mills which dotted the shores of the Georgian Bay, Lake Huron and numerous inland lakes of the Peninsula."

To see the trooping of the trees to the best advantage, we should keep our eyes on Wiarton. First, let us watch them troop in. Most of the logs that went into the town's mills came as great rafts towed in by tugs during the season of calm, open waters. In those months the lower part of Colpoy's Bay was for long periods a vast expanse of logs marshalled into large booms; they extended from the town dock far down the Bay. The sight of these acres upon acres of logs brought forth the same anxious question year after year: How long can the supply up country stand the drain? Some said ten years; others, fifteen at the most. One operator reckoned that his corner of the forest would last for twenty-five years; this shrewd prophet actually worked it for twenty-four and then cannily sold his holdings and his risks.[3] The proved volume of the supply amazed all observers: it lasted until 1914, well over thirty years. In that year the decline was so obvious as to herald the end: there were no more trees to troop out.

But the moving-picture of trees on the march is not complete until we see the great army actually in motion out of Wiarton. It was composed not only of what was once red and white pine but of products of other kinds of trees as well. Of these hemlock was one, a common species of the virgin forest. It marched out in two forms, square timbers and tanbark. At one time 4000 cords

1. See chapter XVIII, "The Mill at Stokes Bay."
2. Mr. Walter M. Newman, J.P., of Wiarton.
3. See chapter XVII, "The Mill at Ghost Lake."

of bark were shipped out in a year by a single company. The white cedar, too, joined the great exodus in the guise of posts and ties. In this, the heyday of railway building, the demand for ties was greater than the supply. In one season alone the Grand Trunk Railway mustered out of Wiarton 300,000 ties cut in The Bruce, in addition to tens of thousands of others that had been borne by boat to Wiarton from Manitoulin Island and the North Shore. Wiarton was then indeed a haven of job-seekers; there were more jobs than men to fill them.

The memory of this stirring scene remains vivid in the minds of some men and women still living. In the printed record set forth by Walter Newman, who himself played an active part in the industry, we can gain a clear vision of it. "During the six or eight months of the summer session," he writes, "twenty-five carloads of ties and timber were taken out of Wiarton daily, besides large quantities of posts, bark, wood and other products of the mills, and the children of that day watched with interest when the locomotives (sometimes three to a train) snorted and groaned in their efforts to haul the long trains of lumber and ties up the heavy grade leading out of the business section of the town."

However, not all the output of Wiarton mills and the labour of Wiarton hands went out over the rails: one contingent sallied forth by water on a long and hazardous voyage, its destination being the Canadian "Soo." Newman himself helped in forming it and preparing it for its journey; today he delights in telling the story of it.

In 1891 the young Wiarton lumber company of Seaman and Newman was honoured with the award of a contract of notable importance: to supply half a million feet of squared hemlock timbers, in lengths of twenty-five and thirty feet, for use in the construction of the Canadian canal at Sault Ste Marie. Delivery was to be made by raft, an undertaking which, because of the exceptional risks involved, called for skill and courage. These, as the outcome proved, were not lacking.

A raft consisted of a crib made of the timbers to be transported; it was 125 feet long and 25 to 30 feet wide according to the length of the timber in the consignment. The basic framework of the crib was a rectangular boom floating on the water. Into the logs of each long side was bored a row of perpendicular holes, the space between each pair of holes being equal to the thick-

ness of a single timber. Through each hole was thrust upward
from the underside of the boom-log a heavy iron rod about
thirteen feet long. This was really a bolt with its head under
water and its thread aloft. On each pair of opposite bolts was
laid a timber whose ends had been bored to receive them. In
this manner layer after layer of timbers was piled up to a height
of thirteen feet. Nuts were then screwed tight on the projecting
threads of the bolts. This bound all the timbers together into a
firm single unit—into a solid rectangular raft of hemlock drawing
nine feet of water! It was virtually a tow-barge in itself. But like
a horse it could not be allowed out on the highway without its
"bridle." This was a very simple but ingenious device made of
heavy chains to which was fastened the hook of the towline. The
bridle was attached to the forward end of the raft in such a way
that the raft instead of slewing from side to side at the slightest
turn of the tug followed the turn at once.

The success of Seaman and Newman's experiment was indeed
brilliant; it gratified both the partners and the Department of
Public Works in Ottawa. During the next six years the company
rafted 6,000,000 feet of hemlock timber to the "Soo." Only once,
despite many a violent storm, did the firm suffer any serious loss.

This was not the only type of rafting known to the people of
the Peninsula. In the eighties and nineties they often saw passing
westward through the strait off Tobermory rafts of a different
order. These were not made up of logs taken from the hills and
dales of The Bruce; rather, they were "logs for Saginaw," brought
from the French, the Wahnapitae, the Spanish, rivers that empty
into the northeast corner of the Georgian Bay. The magnitude of
the undertaking staggers the imagination. The distance from the
mouth of the French to Saginaw is more than 230 miles. The size
of raft used was enormous. "A raft containing three million board
feet of logs," writes an authority, "covered an area of about ten
acres, while an eight-million-foot-raft would be as much as twenty-
five acres in area. Probably the largest raft seen on Lake Huron
during the 1890's was one towed from Georgian Bay to Tawas
(Michigan) in 1892. It contained 91,700 logs, scaling about ten
million board feet and needed three tugs to handle it."

The volume of this traffic varied with the legislative changes
in Canada and the United States in regard to tariffs on the movement of pine between the two countries. The peak was reached
between 1890 and 1898. In the former year Ottawa removed the

export duty on pine logs, and in the latter the Dingley Tariff, which imposed an import duty on Canadian pine, began to make itself felt. The greatest volume of this wood to go in one year from Ontario to sawmills in eastern Michigan was rafted out in 1894: a grand total of 301,000,000 feet. What interests us now is the fact that the greater part of these vast quantities went out under the eyes of the inhabitants of Tobermory. Often have I heard some of the older folk of that place speak in sad tones of the impressive spectacle of whole Canadian forests being borne away from the land that grew them.

But the picture of the great exodus of the trees from The Bruce is even yet not fully drawn: a few minor touches are lacking. Among these are several typical figures. "I can well remember," writes Walter Newman, "when it was not unusual for one of the mills to ship in one season from Wiarton several cargoes of the best no. 1 com. and better maple at $9.75 per M. and the choicest hemlock at $5.50 and $6.00 per M. feet. The greater part of this found its way to Detroit, Windsor and Chatham. Soft elm, which at that time was much in favor for the manufacture of furniture, was produced in large quantities in Wiarton and on the Bruce Peninsula, and brought as low as $9.00 per M. feet good grades."

These figures, for major products of the mills, help to illustrate the changes that have taken place since the turn of the century; perhaps one of the lowliest products will serve the purpose still better. Sixty years ago for a cord of four-foot soft slabs loaded on the car one could not get more than fifty cents. So little above cost was this that in the long run it was much more profitable to use the slabs in the making of docks. To this grim fact Wiarton owed the convenience of three long slab docks on its water front. Today in any Ontario city a small bundle of thin slab kindling eighteen inches long sells for twenty-five cents; there was a time when in Wiarton for that paltry "two bits" you could have purchased half a cord of whole slabs.

While we have been discoursing about the protracted mass flight of many generations of trees from The Bruce, our thoughts have really been chiefly concerned with generations of men and women, and with two in particular. One of them is the generation who have inherited the patchwork of wilderness, arid barrens, small farm clearings, and a struggling second growth of forest. The other is the generation who left the legacy. The latter it is very easy to judge harshly; they are really better than they seem. From the point of view of today they were wasteful of Nature's bounty, being anxious only for the morrow and without thought for the day after tomorrow. But we must remember this: they were trail-breakers in a new land and were like all others of their kind anywhere: immediate ends for them were food and life itself. It is unjust to appraise them by the standards of long-settled communities, rural as well as urban. An endeavour to see them in the light of the austerities of life that confronted them on the frontier will bring reward. We shall then come to know a generation of men and women of great industry, courage, resourcefulness, and warm-heartedness. So young is the frontier of The Bruce that some of that generation are still spared to us. Moreover, in a goodly number of their children we see reborn into new lives the quality of the parents.

Chapter 17

THE MILL AT GHOST LAKE

COULD a zealous angler ever bless the day when his luck utterly failed him? The very idea seems preposterous. Well, I did once; indeed, I still do. If the fish had been biting on the day when I first cast a line in Ghost Lake I could never have known the halo of lore and authentic history that surrounds the name of a remarkable lake.

The Indians of the Bruce Peninsula called this unusual body of water Ghost Lake. Today the prosaic white man knows it as Gillies Lake, a name which though it fits the history of the region fails to arouse any feelings of wonder. The Indian name suggests the marvellous, if not the unique. The truth is that this lake *is* unique among the lakes of this remote recess of Ontario. It is only natural that the unschooled Indian felt its wonders to be the creation of unseen cosmic powers.

But he had a graver reason for disquiet. Long, long, ago, the lake, as with one gulp, swallowed a whole company of his folk. One day in late winter, the legend has it, nearly half the people of a nearby village were fishing through the ice. Their rough bark shelters dotted the lake's glistening expanse. Suddenly, there was a loud report; it sounded as if the whole forest round about had crashed in a single instant. Rushing out, the fishermen beheld a fearsome sight—the great solid sheet of ice was shattered into hundreds of small floes. No more than half a dozen of those who were fishing escaped; being nearer shore than the others they managed, by jumping from floe to floe, to scramble to land. Now the white bones of all their unfortunate fellows add to the eerie whiteness of the marly bed of Ghost Lake's deepest abysses. Yes, the Indians had reasons for looking with dread upon these waters and their surroundings.

The very situation of the lake arrests attention. A body of water two miles long with a maximum breadth of half a mile, it reposes close to the scalloped edge of the high, precipitous cliff that over-

181

looks the Georgian Bay. What keeps the lake's waters from cas-
cading over the precipice? How can the lake, being where it is,
remain a lake? The name "Hanging Lake" would be just as apt as
the Hanging Gardens of Babylon.

Besides, Ghost Lake is a place of the most startling contrasts
by reason of its extensive shallows and stupendous depths. From
its western end its glistening floor of chalk-white marl drops
imperceptibly from zero at the rate of little more than an inch
in every hundred feet. In the broad basin at its eastern end and
not far from the coastal escarpment, I have failed in many efforts
to touch bottom with a heavy weight attached to a fishing line
150 feet in length. Who can blame the Indian for attributing to
invisible spirit forces the scooping of this phenomenal hollow out
of the limestone? Only recently has geology offered a simple and
convincing explanation of the lake's origin. At one time before the
ages of ice came to an end the deepest part of what is now the
lake was an immense cavern in the heart of the many strata of
limestone, a cavern so lofty that only a relatively thin ceiling
separated it from the surface of the ground above it. One—but
which one we cannot say—of the several ice-fields that ruthlessly
ground their way southwestward across the Peninsula either
sheared the ceiling off or crushed it in. The retreat of the ice
left a vast gaping basin. This, filling with water from springs and
surface drainage, in time became a lake. Quite rightly did the
Indian see a mystery here. And a mystery it still is even to the
white man with all his knowledge.

The abundance—indeed, the superabundance—of marl in the
upper half of the lake must have intensified the Indians' notions
of the part played by weird, unseen potencies in its making. The
bottom, or floor, of this area and a wide margin of its shores are
as ghastly white as wraiths are supposed to be. Viewed from an
aeroplane the lake looks like a long, narrow splash of shiny white
enamel dropped on the mottled, green-grey pavement of forest
and limestone. The aquatic plants that project above the surface
of the water are coated as with the dried spray of whitewash. The
many kinds of tiny molluscs that are seen throughout the shallows
are glaring white. Even the fish living in the deep waters of the
eastern end of the lake are, except for the jet-black back, of a
ghostly pallor; belly, sides, fins, flesh are snow-white. It was
reports concerning this strange denizen of its waters that first

drew me many years ago to Ghost Lake. Natives and tourists called it "mountain trout," a species unknown, except as a local name, to science and anglers alike. The very inappropriateness of the designation was a lure I could not resist. By a route which in those early days was both devious and rough I forged my way in to the lake with several companions and found its mysterious fish to be only a local type of the lake trout of the Great Lakes and of many inland lakes, just the ordinary *Cristivomer namaycush*.

No one who has seen a fish of this species drawn up from the depths of Ghost Lake fails to wonder how it and its kind got there in the first place. In no other lake of the Peninsula does the lake trout exist; yet here in a basin delicately poised on a narrow ledge at least two hundred feet above the Georgian Bay it is abundant. The most absurd questions flit into the mind and, just as quickly, flit out again. Did fish ages ago have the power of flight? Or of climbing, as a certain tropical species has today? The answer most people give themselves is that Ghost Lake is a left-over corner of a vast preglacial lake in which the lake trout was native. If that be true, it was a body older than Lake Algonquin, whose beach lines to be seen in The Bruce today are lower than the level of Ghost Lake.

Another answer persists in certain quarters, the kind of answer that catches popular imagination, glibly offered in many other places on this continent to explain the unexpected appearance of a fish in a region far from its known habitat. Robert Lymburner, who helped his father build the mill at Ghost Lake, submits an observation of his own which seems, to the uncritical, to support it.

In the autumn of 1881, according to Lymburner's interesting account, their millwright, Richard Townsend, was compelled by a prolonged spell of wet weather to postpone the work of setting the foundation for the turbine. So he and Lymburner decided to use the idle time for a visit at their homes in Big Bay. To get the steamer *Jane Miller* that would take them there they had to go on foot four miles to Cabot's Head. While still near the shore before climbing the escarpment to the overland footpath they suddenly saw a large bald eagle take wing ahead of them. As it flew up the face of the cliff and thence northward right over Gillies Lake they noticed something like shreds of flesh dangling

from its talons. Reaching the spot on the waterline from which
the bird had risen they found the carcass of a lake trout three and
a half feet long; little remained but the nearly stripped backbone, head and tail. Now this happened to be the very season
when on favourable days the lake trout come close to the shore
of the Georgian Bay to spawn. Plainly, the fish whose sorry remains lay before the two men had come too close. As they mused
upon what they saw the thought came to them that possibly
among the fragments they had seen hanging from the eagle's
claws were lumps or strings of spawn. Perhaps the sight they had
just seen showed just how in a long-past era Gillies Lake had
become stocked with lake trout. The suggestion, though alluring,
forces still another question upon us: Is there an authentic record
anywhere of the hatching of unfertilized spawn?

Probably nobody will ever be able to explain conclusively
how the lake trout of the big waters became established in
Gillies Lake. All one can say with certainty is that it has been
landlocked in that lofty basin since long before man, Indian or
white, first knew its glistening expanse. At all events, it has lived
here long enough in an environment thoroughly impregnated
with lime to become, inside and outside, preternaturally white.

But we have not yet done with the wonders of Ghost Lake that
roused the awe of the Indian: the most awesome wonder of all
remains—the outlet. This is startlingly abnormal: unlike most lake
outlets it is more audible than visible. At its eastern end Ghost
Lake tapers into a charming little stream which seems bent on
speeding through the dense forest to the brink of the precipice
that overhangs Georgian Bay. It leads the visitor along for about
fifty yards and then rudely abandons him as it abruptly disappears
in a cleft at his feet. If he stands there motionless and silent, he
hears, to his surprise, weird reverberations deep down in the rock
below. Thirty rods further on, at the very edge of the perpendicular escarpment, he will hear, if the rush of the wind through
the forest is not too loud, the sound of water breaking out into
the open two hundred feet below and dashing noisily down the
remaining slope of broken rocks to the Bay. Such phenomena
have always stricken men with awe. The mere thought of the
legend of Kubla Khan which told of the sudden plunge of "Alph,
the sacred river" of Xanadu, into "caverns measureless to man"
gave Coleridge the inspiration for the creation of one of his most
fanciful poems.

> But oh! that deep romantic chasm which slanted
> Down the green hill athwart a cedarn cover!
> A savage place!

Can we wonder that the soul of the Indian was stirred to its depths by what he saw and heard on lake and cliff? Can we wonder that he believed the eerie sounds to be the voices of especially powerful spirits who had performed the miracle of creating, against extraordinary odds, an outlet for a lake which had been denied such an essential by the normal processes of nature? To the Indian the name, Ghost Lake, was laden with ominous meaning.

If the waters that fell from Ghost Lake spoke to the Indian, they spoke also to the white man, but they bore a different message. A certain Captain Port, who with his little steamer, the *Jane Miller,* during the eighties plied the route between Owen Sound and Manitoulin Island, caught the message. A white man with a white man's bias, he gave it, of course, an economic rather than a mystic interpretation. He relayed it to a friend who could understand it and profit by it. The friend was Horace Lymburner, father of Robert, the operator of a sawmill at Big Bay in Grey County, eighteen miles north of Owen Sound. The Captain told the miller of the abundant discharge of water bursting forth from the base of the escarpment on Dyer's Bay. This, he pointed out, was the novel outlet of the large, deep lake perched on a lofty shelf above the cliffs. The water emerged from the steep face of the rock at a point quite close to the Bay and high enough above it to give it a sufficient head to run a small sawmill. As for the timber for the mill, it was, like the lake itself, spread out over a great expanse of the plateau behind the escarpment, and in considerable abundance, chiefly pine, basswood, cedar, and hemlock. The Captain's account was really an invitation to explore; the miller accepted it gratefully.

About June 1, 1881, Horace Lymburner landed one evening at sundown from the *Jane Miller* on the rough shore of Dyer's Bay. With him were his son Robert[1] and three mill-hands. At a glance all saw that a steady supply of water-power for a modest mill was assured. What about the supply of food for the mill? Next day

1. It is to him, now eighty-eight years of age, that the writer is indebted for most of the details concerning the lumbering and milling operations at Gillies Lake and Dyer's Bay. His narrative and other papers are now in the library of the University of Western Ontario.

Horace and one of the hands clambered up the face of the rock
and began a survey of the timber standing on the lands surrounding the lake. In due time, like Caleb and Joshua, they reported
on their land of promise. The stand of timber, they computed, was
great enough to keep a small mill in operation for twenty-five
seasons. Their accuracy of observation and keenness of judgment
were amply verified by results, for the mill ran on this supply
for twenty-four successive years.

There was nothing romantic about the beginning of this new
venture—just the hard slogging labour that marks the pioneer
phase of life in any new rough country. Yet even the dullest of
its details show at least how intelligently the pioneer economizes
his time and adjusts himself to the limitations of his resources as
well as to the unusual and unforeseen obstacles that confront
him. In the cycle peculiar to his way of life there is a season for
every task; if that task is not done in its proper time then that
whole season is irretrievably lost.

The Lymburners realized the truth of this. Once their explora-
tion was over they saw before them a multitude of tasks all of
which had to be completed well before their first season came to
an end. They set to with a will. First, a site had to be cleared for
the mill, accessory buildings, and lumber yards. This they hewed
out of the dense jungle of underbrush and trees on a slanting
ledge lying not far from the shore of the Georgian Bay and some
few feet above it. Here too they hollowed out of the broken surface limestone and scant gravelly soil a shallow basin in which to
catch the lake water that gushed out at the foot of the cliff. The
remainder of the summer was spent in erecting a mill beside the
basin, and a dwelling to serve as winter quarters for the lumbermen. The beams, studding, boards and planks for the building
were brought from the old mill at Big Bay.

That was an easy task; more troublesome was the attempt to
convey the heavy sections of the machinery to the new millsite.
The *Jane Miller* was chosen to be the transport. It so happened
that this trip was the last she was destined to complete before
her mysterious disappearance. Because of the good landing facili-
ties at her home port, the water-wheel and the ponderous saw-
frames were quickly put on board. But it was a very different
matter to get them ashore at their destination for as yet there
was no dock there. After many fruitless efforts all hands gave up
and the load was taken to Lion's Head and left there till the first
heavy snowfall. All the machinery was then drawn on sleighs to

the millsite. In the spring it was set up, a dock was built, and sawing began. The first two shipments of the new mill's output were sent out on the schooner *Nellie Sherwood;* of her unhappy fate a word will be said later.

On the whole the first and second winters were normal cutting seasons for the woodsmen: the trees were felled and the logs so placed that they could be readily delivered to the saw when required. But there was a novel feature in the placing of the logs: they were tumbled indiscriminately over the precipice on to the huge jagged chunks of limestone that lay in a vast disorderly mass some two hundred feet below. Here they were gradually piled up until they formed a towering, tangled heap which sometimes contained as much as 200,000 feet of board lumber. The logs lay close to the mill to which, it seemed, they could be readily rolled by hand and canthook whenever needed. What a saving of time and labour, one is prompted to say. But the saving was illusory. The terrific crash of the logs falling on the huge rocks and on other logs so mutilated many of them that their wood was rendered useless except for fuel. Besides, the progressive deepening of the snow and ice of winter cemented the logs so tightly together that the heap did not thaw out till midsummer, thus causing a great loss in time. Worse than that, a great danger was involved as well. Could a lumberman fear anything more than to have to stand at the foot of a mountain of logs precariously balanced on a steep slope and from that perilous position pry out individual pieces? It was even more hazardous than loosening the key-log of a jam in a rapid river. This risky game of jackstraws on a mammoth scale was repeated for two seasons, until the Lymburners plainly saw that they must quit it at once. But how? Here was a tough problem. To understand their solution we must first note how they controlled the mill's water-supply.

It had been clear at the very outset of their operations that the place at which to effect control was the fissure down which the water in the lake's short outlet disappears underground. The first step was to trench the outlet from the lake to the fissure, straightening and deepening the channel, and thus increasing the volume of flow. By planned experiment they found that in about an hour and a half any change in the quantity of water admitted into the rock at the fissure showed itself at the vent at the foot of the cliff. This meant that the descending subterranean passage was many times longer than a straight line joining the fissure and the vent, was probably, indeed, a long winding chain of caverns "measureless to man." It also permitted the inference that through countless milennia fragments of bark, lumps of mud and rotted wood, matted bundles of twigs and leaves sucked down by the descending water had in many places obstructed the underground channel and slowed down the stream flowing through it. The next step toward control was the erection of a sluicegate between the lake and the fissure. The gate was closed every night to conserve water and was opened every morning early enough to allow the water to make its roundabout and mysterious passage through the earth and to begin moving the mill-wheel at the hour when the hands were summoned to work.

This arrangement sufficed for the first season of sawing. During the second season the Lymburners extended the trench past the fissure in the rock to serve as a temporary flume in which to float logs toward the cliff. Later, this was deepened stage by stage and floored with heavy planking. Where the surface of the ground dropped below the horizontal the flume was carried on simple though strong trestles of heavy timbers. It terminated at the brink of the precipice in a slide or chute of normal construction. Yet, although the flume was a credit to the skill of its makers in overcoming formidable natural obstacles, the uncontrolled fall over the high cliff still caused an alarming loss of great quantities of valuable timber.

After a thorough study of the problem the operators decided that the line of descent for the logs must be changed from the vertical to a slope. But how move hundreds of tons of hard dolomite without powder or dynamite? The determined pioneers drew upon the power of their wits rather than upon the power of explosives, which would have to be fetched from a distance at the cost of time and money. To the power of wits they added the power of water. The plan of operation was simple and direct.

The flume, being four feet in width and three and a half in depth, carried a large volume of water of great potential power. But the chute, as we have noted, ended at the edge of the cliff; hence the water that passed through it was shot out into mid air and dropped down in foam and spray upon the jungle and boulders below. The result was a sheer waste of water-power—just an idle sprinkling of an almost sterile wilderness. The idea that broke of a sudden upon the Lymburners was to apply the lost power to the solution of their problem. They lopped off the terminal section of the chute so that the end was now twelve or fifteen feet from the edge of the precipice. Water spouting from the flume would fall, not into vacant space as before, but upon a single spot of ground. Applied there long enough and in volume as well as at a high speed, the Lymburners argued, it would rend even rock asunder with almost explosive power. The reasoning was sound: in ten minutes the thrust of the water rushing from the full flume with the swiftness of a cascade tore away seven hundred tons of hard dolomite strata, gravel and soil, and hurled them down the abyss. Another section of the timber framework was knocked off and the flood was turned on again: the result was equally gratifying. Yet a third time this was done. In the end, after not more than two hours, more than two thousand tons of material had been removed. Triumphantly, the hardy men of the frontier saw before them, not a fearsome perpendicular drop, but an even gradient of fifty-five degrees down which logs of all sizes could slide to the mill-pond undamaged. Even now, sixty-eight years after the event, Robert Lymburner still feels a thrill when he recalls the sight and the roar of the colossal mass of limestone and earth hurtling into the depths below.

The water of the lake was so well controlled that, without the use of much more than the volume needed for generating the power, it served two other essential purposes also. At stated times it floated the logs through the flume and sent them slithering down the slope; it also kept the mill-pond filled to a depth that cushioned the fall of the logs and saved them from damage. The penstock in which the water fell upon the wheel was perpendicular and offered alternative heads of power, a normal one of twenty-eight feet, and a special one of thirty-three feet. Under the normal head the Lymburners cut as much as twelve thousand board-lumber feet in a day, and under the other, to meet unusual situations, twenty-five thousand feet in a day of eleven hours. The output of the mill was loaded on steamers and schooners and shipped to the more important ports on the Georgian Bay. In the latter days of the enterprise a strong flume was run across the pond and through it logs were floated to a slide that shot them into the water of the Bay. From there they were towed in booms to Lion's Head and Owen Sound.

The mill, as mills of the Ontario northland go, was a very modest one, but its size was in proportion to the volume of the forest resources upon which it drew, and, above all, it was efficient

The Mill, Georgian Bay Shore, below Ghost Lake

and was thriftily operated. In all this it reflected the skill and resourcefulness of the men who built and ran it.[1]

The story told by Robert Lymburner is, in general, one of which he may be justly proud. But it is not wholly free of the shadow of tragedy. The little steamer *Jane Miller* that landed father and sons on the site of the future sawmill in the spring of 1881 went to the bottom in November of that year. The memorable storm of September, 1882, that destroyed the *Asia* and many another craft of the Great Lakes also sank the schooner *Nellie Sherwood*, which had carried from the mill its first two cargoes of lumber and shingles. Ironically, these were the last cargoes she delivered, and, besides, she went down virtually in sight of the mill. Finally, in the years after the mill had changed ownership, a sawyer was drowned from the small steam-tug, the *Gertie*, that plied the waters of Ghost Lake, the second steam-powered vessel ever to sail on any inland lake of the county. So "Ghost Lake" it became in fact to the white as well as to the Indian.

Of the speed and thoroughness with which The Bruce was

1. Robert Lymburner has recorded all details of the devices used to make as simple as possible the whole process of conveying the timber from Gillies Lake to the mill. These details include the dimensions of the many forms of wood and iron employed. Although of too technical a nature to be given here, they deserve a place in the archives of Ontario's lumber industry.

stripped of its trees there exists a record little short of appalling; it was written in 1879 by county valuators concerning the well-timbered townships whose lands had been put up for sale only in 1870. "It would be very difficult," they reported, "to place any value on these townships, as we have not seen any land fit for cultivation. . . . The greater part of the land . . . was bought for the timber, and when that was taken off the land was abandoned. We set it down at $1.50 per acre." About ten years ago Robert Lymburner wrote me his own judgment in the same vein: "The millsite [the mill at Ghost Lake] is now a forlorn vision of waste—house, mill, cottages and mill all burned. There is no timber of value other than firewood that I know of on the whole peninsula. In the spring of 1920 I spent a month after the snow was gone estimating the assets of the man who bought me out in 1905. . . . I could find only $30,000 worth . . . between Hope Bay and a point within five miles of Tobermory."

Today, despite the softening rains and thawing snows of nearly seventy years, the gradient constructed by the Lymburners, now covered with a binding mat of interwoven vegetation and shrubbery, still maintains the angle of slope its makers gave it. It may be scaled or descended with ease by those who have not left youth too far behind. In summer not a few tourists make a pastime of climbing it from Bay to summit. Significantly enough, the point at which they start is to this hour commonly known as Lymburner's Dock—just a few straggling, charred, and rotting planks and timbers of what was once a firm landing place for ships of deep draft. Thus historical names often outlast the material objects on which they have been based.

The tale of the Mill at Ghost Lake covers the period between 1881 and 1905. By reason of its closeness to our own times it may not seem to illustrate the pioneering of Ontario. Unfortunately, the common habit of thinking of the pioneer stage of this province as belonging exclusively to the early decades of the last century has warped the historical perspective of most people. We must remember this: the pioneer stage can be repeated at any time in any unoccupied region, even though this should lie geographically close to long-inhabited areas, whenever brave and farseeing souls become the first to explore and develop its resources. The Lymburners were pioneers because they brought to new lands the spirit, intelligence, and industry our forefathers brought to their uncleared tracts farther south a century before.

Chapter 18

THE MILL AT STOKES BAY

AS we know, the mill at Ghost Lake was not the only sawmill of the early days of The Bruce. Of the others not a few have left behind fragments of stories telling of mingled success and failure. Some of these are written in the form of ashes, rotten logs, and crumbling stone walls and foundations spread over the barren surface of unsightly clearings. Indeed, several of these stories of unlucky venture can be found, in certain files, recorded in the red ink of still unpaid bank borrowings. One of the brighter tales, though not wholly untarnished by spells of discouragement, concerns the sawmill whose buildings still stand on the west side of Stokes Bay. Though lacking the glamour that gives a unique glow to the name of Ghost Lake, its story is well worth telling if only to underline something that is already obvious: that different people adjust themselves in different ways to the stern challenges of the frontier wilderness.

Stokes Bay, as has been said, is by far the largest of the deep indentations in the Lake Huron shore of the Peninsula. It lies, most conveniently, almost midway between the base of the long arm of limestone and its tip; it is dotted with islands divided from one another by channels of fair depth. Its main channel is deep enough to float safely modern lake vessels of moderate draft. This fact and the presence on its shores of heavy stands of mixed softwood and hardwood made the bay a natural scene of a lumber industry.

How soon after 1870, the year when the lands of Lindsay Township were first put up for sale, the first mill was built on Tamarac Island, no one now remembers. It is enough to know that at some time, apparently in the eighties, a St. Catharines man was operating a mill there on the spot where the present buildings stand. It is an ideal situation. The island is separated from the mainland by a channel easily spanned by a bridge of long pine trunks. In those days before man began tinkering with Great

Lakes levels the depth of water in the channel did not vary as much as it does now.

Tamarac Island is a long narrow limestone ridge, to which the last glacier neatly gave an outline reminding one of the sole of a shoe, rising to a height of between thirty and forty feet above the normal level of the lake. Of its sixty-odd acres fifteen at the north end were cleared, these affording ample space for all requirements: mill, boiler-house, office, houses, barn, narrow-gauge tram lines running on wooden rails, a limited area for piled lumber, and, finally, a slab dock. The mill proper was erected close to the end of the bridge, while most of the other buildings were set upon the summit of the island overlooking Stokes Bay. On summer evenings the workers could from the front windows of their dwellings see the flashing of the Southampton light thirty-five miles to the south, a reminder that, after all, the wild is nearer to the collective life of organized society than it may seem to be.

Despite its advantages, however, the first mill at Stokes Bay did not prosper. Evidently its owner limited his interest, as the demands of the time dictated, to pine. His failure was probably due to lack of care in estimating the amount of that kind of timber in the region; the fact is that hereabouts nature had been rather niggardly in her distribution of it. Besides, the best of the pines she had planted there had been cut before the mill was built. The upshot was that the builder-owner sold out to a well-known company. The experience of the purchaser was as unhappy as that of the vendor had been. The mill, its accessory buildings, and its adjoining forest were soon abandoned and allowed to lie idle for many years. Anyone who has ever seen a long-abandoned property of this kind and its carelessly cut-over lands with their tangle of slash will need no description of its condition when in 1899 a prospective buyer looked it over.

As usual, it was a pressing economic need that prompted the bold thought of acquiring so unpromising a property. By 1899 the furniture manufacturers of Ontario using great quantities of hardwoods were confronted with a dearth of supplies. Central Ontario had been stripped and importation from the United States was so costly as to kill all chances of profit. New native sources must be found. An enterprising firm of Western Ontario[1] sent into The

1. For some of the details of this story the author is indebted to a souvenir pamphlet, *Our Rise from the Ashes*, published in 1901 by this company, the forerunner of the Knechtel companies now operating in Hanover.

Bruce its chief officers and several experienced hands to make a careful survey of hardwood resources. In the language of the lumberman, hardwood is, strictly speaking, any wood that is not red pine or white pine. Actually, many woods that are as soft as pine (basswood, for example) are classified as hardwoods. But the firm really sought in this instance genuine hardwoods, the kind to which the veriest amateur would apply that term. After many weeks of exploring the investigators purchased the now prematurely old and decrepit mill at Stokes Bay and a large tract of timbered lands. They could not help coming across many a rattlesnake—the small Massasauga of the Lower Lake region; indeed, so numerous were they on Tamarac Island that it seemed to be the capital city of that species of reptile for the whole Peninsula. But that did not retard in the slightest the decision to buy; in fact, it appeared to be just another challenge of the wild to add to the romance of a struggle against heavy odds.

The decision, taken in the light of two lamentable failures on the site, was in large part an act of faith. But the buyers were also influenced by the magnet of speculation; there was reason to believe that something might happen which would sooner or later enhance the value of their purchase and enlarge their prospective field of operations. In new lands the usual bait is the promise of a railway dangled before colonists' noses, and this was the very bait used here. It worked, too, not as the chief factor, but rather as that additional element men welcome as a bolster to an already reasonable hope.

At the turn of the century there was a growing demand for railways to open up new lands and to shrink distances. This was true of the nearer west and farther west alike. The prairies were rebelling against the alleged tyranny of their only transcontinental railway, a private company; they clamoured for a second line and for answer got the promise of the Grand Trunk Pacific and the extension of the Mackenzie and Mann rails. Sault Ste Marie, in the new territory of the nearer west, had but one rail connection with eastern Canada—the Canadian Pacific—which afforded only a long, roundabout service to Toronto and the populous southwestern peninsula of Ontario. It was natural that Mr. F. H. Clergue, the energetic and far-seeing head of the Algoma Steel Corporation, should desire a short route from "The Soo" to this latter region.

The Grand Trunk railhead in Bruce county was at Wiarton,

where half a century later it still is, at the very base of the Peninsula. To extend the rails for fifty miles to Tobermory and its deep, safe, and spacious harbour, at the tip of the Peninsula, involved no great difficulties of construction. Equally easy was the laying of a line across Manitoulin Island and the bridging of the narrow North Channel at Little Current to carry the rails to the North Shore and to connect them there with the already existing service. The only serious problem was that presented by the fifteen odd miles of straits separating "The Tub" from the Manitoulin. But the precedent of the train-ferry service on the United States side over the Strait of Mackinac erased this difficulty from the promoters' blueprints.

Encouraged by his careful calculations, Mr. Clergue was by 1901 holding out to the people of the Peninsula the bright hope that in two years he would have his railway actually operating between lower Ontario and the North Shore. That his intentions were serious seemed to be confirmed by the fact that he took the time and incurred considerable expense to have two separate surveys of alternative routes made in the space of two or three years. The new owners of the mill on Stokes Bay seized on the promise and with pardonable jubilation announced to their public that the survey of the new line "runs almost through the centre of our timber lands. The construction of this railway will enable us to ship logs and lumber from our own reserves and from other peninsula and North Shore points to the doors of our Hanover Mill and factories without transhipment." Altogether the expectations of things to come were as rosy as a Lake Huron sunset.

The reference to sunset is a prophecy after the event. The Bruce and North Shore Railway experienced an early sunset— a sunset without a sunrise that ever got past the stage of sanguine hope. Like many another project of its kind, it began to run impressively on paper from Somewhere to Somewhither, but ended by running from Nowhere to Nowhither. The worst that can be said of the effort is that it failed; it appears to have been free of high-pressure stock salesmanship and of the scandals that so often go with it. What happened? One can only wonder: probably a few factors of insignificant appearance but really vital for the profitable and continuous operation of a railway had been left out of the initial calculations. Happily, they were detected before it was too late.

But, railway or no railway, the owners of the mill sawed wood.

The Mill, Tamarac Island, Stokes Bay

They rebuilt the run-down mill and the other buildings. They laid the four-by-four square cedar rails on which to run the tramway carrying lumber or slabs from the mill to the bayside. Of the slabs—all waste then—they built a wharf to which tugs or rafts could be moored for loading with sawn lumber. Some of the rails are still in place, a tribute to the workmen who laid them and to the lasting qualities of our native white cedar. Under the direction of a young and vigorous superintendent who was "thoroughly up in milling, timbering and rafting in all their branches," they turned out their products in abundance and prospered, as the record quaintly puts it, "in the home of the deer, the bear and the rattlesnake." The chief woods taken out of the forest and passed through the mill were yellow birch, beech, ash, elm, and maple. Of the last there was not a great quantity, since it is much less common on the Lake Huron side than on the Georgian Bay side of the Peninsula. There was a good deal of hemlock and a little jack pine, but a paucity of white pine.

Of the hardwoods both logs and lumber were shipped to Southampton by raft or steamer as required. Some of the wood was used in the company's factory at Southampton and the remainder was transported by rail to its factories in Hanover and Walkerton. The soft woods, for which the company had no direct use, were disposed of in various ways.

You cannot eat your cake and have it too. The old adage is especially applicable to industries that rely upon the forest. It has taken the people of Canada a long time to learn even the rudiments of this lesson, and even yet they have not learned them well. Only now are they in the first stage of making restitution, through systematic planting, for their wanton plundering of the forest. The millers at Stokes Bay, denied the fulfilment of the railway's promise of supplies from the north, soon realized that their timber "limits" were really limits, that their boundaries contained just so much wood and no more. In a few years there was no longer any hardwood left in commercial quantities. The mill simply closed itself. One of two courses was open to the owners: to follow the bad example of their predecessors by abandoning the mill to the ravages of the wild, or to preserve the plant by adapting it to some novel use. Prompted by a sound business sense, which, after all, is only another form of honest thrift, they summarily rejected the first course. There remained a real problem to solve. But the persistence and imagination of an honest pioneer spirit solved it.

A systematic accounting of the whole situation was set up. The liabilities bulked large and foreboding: long distances, poor roads that were no more than rough trails winding through forests and swamps and around dolomite ridges, inadequate sources of food supplies, and the slow pace of horse-drawn vehicles. No "horse and buggy doctor" was ever confronted by worse roads. The remaining approach to the mill by water from Southampton lay over thirty or more miles of open lake and was therefore not encouraging, either for sailing-craft or for the still experimental and untrustworthy motor-boat. On the other hand, there were the assets: an excellent plant consisting of a mill of two storeys, an engine-house, a barn, several houses, a slab dock, all compactly grouped together in a single unit situated on an island approached by a bridge which guaranteed complete privacy; in adjoining waters black bass in numbers beyond the southern sportsman's wildest dream, and, each in its season, wild duck and other waterfowl, partridge, deer, and bear; above all, there was the sure promise of complete change and rest for the man jaded by the labours and

strains of town life. On balance, the assets won; that is to say,
sanity, a true sense of conservation, and a sound knowledge of
human instinct prevailed. The mill was to become a sportsmen's
club.

To the planning of this the management gave the same careful
thought that it gave to its prime concern—manufacturing. And
why not? The transaction was but another phase of the company's
affairs. A penny saved here was a penny earned for the business.
The policy was dictated by a shrewd moderation which gave it
the double aim of guaranteeing a sale and of putting the club on
a sound foundation. The price was made temptingly reasonable
and the scale of payments easy. The immediate result was to band
together a group of business men infused with the enthusiasm
common to anglers the world over. That at first all these were
leading representatives of the furniture industry was only natural;
the law of propinquity and community of interest is more des-
potic than we generally think. The fact that in later years the
membership degenerated through the admission of a few aca-
demicians and professional men is not to be counted a blot on
the founders' escutcheon.

But the founders effected a still greater result, one which they
probably never dreamed of, but the credit for which we must not
grudge them. The spirit of conservation which impelled them to
salvage a very doubtful asset, such as any old sawmill in the
bush really is, infected the whole membership of the club. It
spread to the inhabitants of the region and touched even the
casual tourist who came that way. So a new community grew up,
a community that is still growing. From it has emanated an influence which has helped inspire the entire county to make a
survey of the Peninsula's unique variety of resources and at length
to adopt policies definitely aimed at conserving the resources that
remain, and also at restoring, so far as possible, those that have
been impaired by the thoughtless rapacity of the first generation
of bush-raiders. The promise of a new-old Bruce is alluringly
bright. The people of the county have caught the vision of it
and in its light have seen their duty to their children and their
children's children. Already they have bought in the region of
Miller Lake—about midway between Stokes Bay and Tobermory
—7,200 acres of burnt and cut-over wilderness. On this "Miller
Lake Reserve" the skill of the trained forester and Nature's own
woodcraft will work together to restore, as by instalments, its

plundered wealth of trees. Within the limits of the reserve a suitable area will some day be set aside as a sanctuary in which a unique wild life—plant and animal alike—will be allowed to strike its own balance and to serve as a lodestone to draw to it all citizens who find in its wonders a tonic for spirits jaded by the affairs and works of men.

A year or two ago an old member of the club, a professional man who lives in one of the great American cities, said to the writer: "In August of 1911 I was present at the mill when the whistle blew to stop work for the last time. Everybody there knew what it meant and we were all solemn. Although I was a kid I was solemn too. Somehow we felt that in that little world of rock, water, and exhausted forest a new local era was beginning; in short, we felt that somebody had 'started something.' But little did we realize that that something was much more than a mere band of anglers and hunters bent apparently only on health and pleasure, but rather a progressive and contagious influence working towards a sound restoration of the wealth of the wilderness."

PART SIX: SKY PILOT AND SETTLER

Old Log House with Guardian Lilacs

Chapter 19

PILOTING ON THE NEW FRONTIER

A FTER the Jesuit Mission to the Hurons came to its tragic end in 1650[1] nearly two centuries passed before the white man renewed his efforts to bring his religion to the Indians of the Peninsula. In 1834 the Reverend Thomas Hurlburt, a Methodist, started a mission among the Saugeen people on their lands near the present Southampton. He must have been a man of great energy and tact and of self-effacing devotion, for when after three years he moved to another field he left behind him a congregation of about one hundred persons. To this day most of the Indians of the Saugeen Reserve belong to the United Church of Canada, the successor of the Methodist body.

Early in the 1850's the Methodists established a mission to the Ojibways living on the tract on the south side of Colpoy's Bay on which the village of Oxenden now stands. The headship of this outpost of the church was entrusted to James Atkey, a newcomer from the Isle of Wight and a man of apostolic zeal and initiative. He divided his time between caring for the needs of his flock and earning a living by doing the odd and sundry public chores common to frontier settlements. Irked by the sluggish pace of sail he saw in steam alone the means of broadening the range of his pastoral travels. With a steamboat, he reckoned, he could easily visit Christian Island and help open a mission station there. So with a local "jack-knife carpenter" and a few Indians he set himself to the task of building a steamer.

In the last weeks of a winter—the year now unknown—the hull of a twenty-five foot craft was completed at Oxenden and the engine and boiler, brought from Toronto, were installed. The little steamer's maiden trip to Owen Sound was most satisfactory. Tying her up to the dock the builders spent a restful night in town. But what they saw on the waterfront next morning was anything but restful: their proud queen of the waves lay many feet out of sight

1. See chap. III, "An Unknown Land."

on the bed of the Sydenham River. Her missionary service was ended before it had begun. Her engine was taken out and put to work in the town tannery. A fiasco? Not at all: Mr. Atkey's enterprise established the Indians' confidence in him as one who spared himself no effort to promote their welfare. Besides, the good missionary made history: his nameless steamboat was one of the first to have been *built* on Lake Huron.

When the white man took over the former Indian lands of The Bruce, the record of the Sky Pilot at every stage of settlement was as notable as it was noble. Indeed, he made himself as much a pioneer as any member of his flock, in the field of soil and stump as well as in the field of the spirit. His people's life was his life: when they exulted over the good fruits of their toil and anxious thought, he exulted with them; in their griefs he sorrowed too. In only a few settlements did his person fail to become the living symbol of the frontier.

In the diary[1] of William Simpson, the first settler of Amabel Township in the Peninsula, the role of the Sky Pilot in the frontier community stands out as sharply as do the struggles and hardships of the settlers themselves. In 1855, as soon as the former Indian lands were offered to the public, Simpson chose his tract (near what is now the village of Parkhead) and signed for it. In the very next spring he began the work of removing the brush and trees and built himself a log cabin. His first harvest yielded 105 stooks of good wheat; his great delight in this success banished all his fears for the long years ahead. The second and third harvests were equally good and hopes rode high like the sun at noon in a clear sky. Of a sudden came the chill and darkness of clouds and the crash of storm. The item in Simpson's diary for July 16, 1860, makes sad reading. "A thunder shower about daybreak was followed by a tremendous hailstorm, the hailstones being about the size of small hens' eggs. The storm almost destroyed the whole crop . . . wheat, peas, corn and potatoes, and caused a great deal of destruction in the whole settlement." For the comforting words of a Sky Pilot the settlers had to wait a whole year.

Their first parson (who was also reeve of Amabel Township) was the Reverend Ludwig Kribbs of Colpoy's Bay; he conducted occasional services, now in the settlers' homes, now in the school-

1. Parts of this diary are quoted by Simpson's daughter, the late Mrs. B. C. Ashcroft, of Howdenvale, in certain papers she read before local historical societies.

house. After Kribbs, the settlement was served by a series of other devoted men. The variety of the ways in which they ministered to their people was amazing. Most of these were of the kind one would normally expect of the cloth, but many were spontaneous, generous responses to the urgent call of unforeseen emergencies. There was never any lack of will or effort.

The experience of the Reverend Mr. Colling one Sunday in September of 1863 was just part of the day's work. He had come on horseback to conduct an afternoon service in the Simpson settlement. As he was approaching the place of meeting somebody spied a bear in a nearby oatfield. For a time the animal, without marked alarm, kept eyeing the assembling people and then started to shuffle off toward the woods that bounded the far side of the field. Flouting the ancient commandment forbidding physical labour on the Sabbath, the young parson and William Simpson made up their minds that the creature would never reach the shelter of the trees. Stealthily they made a broad encircling movement and placed themselves squarely between the bear and the woods. Each of the men picked up a field stone small enough to be grasped firmly in the hand but large enough to deal a heavy blow. Thus armed they attacked the bear. Three or four well-directed clouts stunned the animal and a few more killed him. As if nothing unusual had happened the two men went to the place of worship, the one to preach, the other to hear the message. The service over, parson and layman skinned the bear with their pocket knives. For many winters thereafter the Reverend Mr. Colling drove abroad in his cutter under the comfortable cover of a bearskin robe.

One of the virtues the frontiersman anywhere has to acquire is the habit of waiting patiently. The Amabel community had to wait for a regular house of worship all their own, as they had had to wait for a Sky Pilot. In 1867, with the advent of a new minister, their waiting came to an end. From the adjoining frontier township of Brant the Reverend David Williams brought with him a gift just as essential to the discharge of his duties as were his native vigour, clear vision, and vibrant leadership: this was actual experience in raising the lowly logs of the forest to the high dignity of homes, schools, and houses of Christian worship. Just as the people of Jerusalem under Nehemiah rebuilt their city with sword and trowel, so did the people of this pioneer township of The Bruce build, on the Simpson homestead, their first meeting

house with axe, saw, and hammer. In every stage of the work the
Sky Pilot was a pilot indeed: it was he who showed the way. With
equal skill and energy he aided many of his parishioners in erecting domiciles on their new acres. Need we wonder that he held
his whole flock, youth and adult alike, in the hollow of his hand?

When at last the time came to dedicate the church the spirits
of the people of the whole region were low: a series of storms and
late frosts had made the prospects for the crops very dark. Some
of the weaker souls were beginning to murmur aloud against
Providence, to charge their Land of Promise with breaking its
word. The prevailing mood plainly called for a balanced mixture
of rebuke and encouragement. To be effective the message had to
come from one who was known to be acquainted with the facts
and fears of the settler's life. Manifestly, this was David Williams'
supreme opportunity. The crisis itself, not his studied choice, put
into his mouth the text of his dedication sermon, these words in
the eleventh chapter of the Book of Deuteronomy.

> For the land, whither thou goest to possess it, is not as the land of Egypt,
> from whence ye came out, where thou sowedst thy seed and wateredst
> it with thy foot, as a garden of herbs;
> But the land, whither ye go to possess it, is a land of hills and valleys,
> and drinketh water of the rain of heaven;
> A land which the Lord thy God careth for; the eyes of the Lord thy
> God are always upon it, from the beginning of the year even unto the
> end of the year.

Often in later years did Simpson, as his daughter, Mrs. Ashcroft,
used to tell, recall, with amusement and approval, the new spirit
instilled overnight into the whole countryside by the first sermon
delivered in its first house of worship. The text was itself a sermon;
the preacher's part lay in his skilful play with emphasis, his control of a good voice, the manifest sincerity of his sympathy, and
his unshaken faith in the bright promise of the land which God
had given his parishioners.

But, you protest, this story is no new one; during the whole
nineteenth century the role of the parson on the frontiers of
settlement was the same everywhere on this continent; conditions
are different now. But are they different? Assuredly not, even
today, in the upper townships of the Bruce Peninsula. I am speaking of what I have seen and know. The Sky Pilot whom I saw in
the midst of his labours on this frontier only a few short years ago
followed the pattern set by his forerunners on the older frontiers;

and the influence of his example has passed far beyond the borders of his ample parish. Of such moment was it to his diocese that he was accorded the title and function of Canon. After twenty-two years of self-effacing service he was moved, in succession, to two large rural parishes in old southern Ontario. Not long since, still running strong on the last lap of the seventies, he was permitted to begin enjoying (but, true to himself, far from idly) amid a scene of hills, woods, and waters dear to his heart, a well-earned withdrawal from the ceaseless round of pastoral cares.

It was as recently as 1911 that Parson James went to the Parish of Lion's Head with its Home Station of Christchurch and its widespread cluster of mission stations. Lion's Head is a village that lies at the head of Isthmus Bay. Though small in size, it has always been important in its region as a port with a two-way traffic, at once a depot and a point of distribution for the fishing industry, and more recently as a growing rendezvous for tourists and campers. In the full circle of the year it is concerned with a much greater variety of interests than its size would lead one to expect. In short, it is a place where human relationships are numerous and complex, the very kind of place where the hand, heart, and head of the Sky Pilot are sorely needed.

When posted to Lion's Head by his bishop Parson James exulted in the opportunity opened to him, for he is one of the few who know without being taught that of all places on earth it is on the frontier that one can best see the tremendous power that one man can become. Keenly was he aware of the great length and breadth of his parish—almost the southern half of the Peninsula. Apart from his sundry visits of duty to many widely scattered homes he had a preaching schedule which, be it summer, be it winter, sent him forth in the short span of a fortnight over many scores of miles of atrocious roads. But thought of the repeated ordeal did not cool his ardour.

Here, in the barest detail, was his itinerary as he sketched it for me only a short while ago: to get its true measure read it with the map before you. "In my time we usually ran the Lion's Head service in the morning, Hope Bay in the afternoon, and Purple Valley at night. The following Sunday we held the Lion's Head service in the evening, Hopeness in the morning and St. Margaret's, which was called McCallum's schoolhouse in the old days, in the afternoon. At first we used to go to Stokes Bay on the

The Sky Pilot on His Rounds

other side of the Peninsula on a weekday, usually Wednesday, and
conduct a service at eight o'clock in the evening. But later when
the timber had been about all cut and fishing was poor, we had
to give up regular services. But I did continue to visit their sick
and needy besides, as you know, catching the odd fish. . . ."
Of course, Parson James was not the first man of his calling to
have an experience of this kind; it was the experience common to
the "circuit riders" of all faiths on the outer fringes of settlement
in America. But that does not lessen our wonder and gratitude
that despite the strain of ceaseless travel he was spared for almost
a generation to carry on his paternal ministry with unimpaired
zeal and health.

A man's true self is many a time shown up by matters that seem
of little account. This is most apt to occur in cases in which an
ethical principle is suddenly involved, especially in cases where
the difference between right and wrong is so slight that some
minds are highly amused to think that anybody can see it there
at all. It was a trivial affair of this sort which, so long ago that
Parson James has forgotten it, revealed to me his real fibre. He
himself was blissfully unaware at the time that he was revealing
anything but two or three speckled trout under legal size.

All his life an ardent addict of the angle, he took me one day
to a unique watercourse famous for its trout. Most of its water
comes from a single spring, a phenomenal pool in the limestone

that is fully a hundred feet across and thirty feet deep. The stream that empties it runs north for several miles into Judge's Creek. What makes it unique is that for the last mile before its confluence with the creek its waters have at some time been diverted by road-makers into a deep straight ditch that parallels the road. One cannot help suspecting that in planning this great rearrangement the workmen had an eye chiefly to the convenience of anglers!

And how that artificial watercourse teemed with trout! In that long-past day when the road was new, clumps of lush grasses hung over the edges of the ditch like seaweed over tidal rocks. There were great mats of watercress there too. No brook trout anywhere ever had more lairs from which to choose their watchful stations. For the angler who does not spurn the lowly worm the setting was perfect. You stood dryshod on the firm edge of the road, dropped your hook straight into the ribbon of running water below you and at your ease drew up your fish. In a jiffy, it seemed, you had filled your creel. Only one obstacle hovered between you and perfection: there were too many under-sized trout.

A silly objection? Far from it. The excess put the angler in a most embarrassing dilemma. He could not prevent the greedy tiddlers from biting; on the other hand the Law said: put back into the water unharmed any trout under seven inches. The angler's mind became an arena in which conscience fought against herself. With one voice she said, "Obey the Law," and with another, "It is wicked to waste good food." It was really a lesson in human nature to observe how summarily most of the anglers that lined the ditch resolved the dilemma: "The small trout won't live anyway," they said, "so let's take a chance with the Law."

And one day the Law came, came riding in a chariot so marked that even the most careless eye could not miss it. Cunningly it parked by the column of anglers' cars in such a way that none could slip out unchallenged. A visible shiver of anxiety passed down the extended file of sportsmen ranged along the ditch; the Parson was the only one of them that showed no concern. The Law took pains to display a game warden's badge and ostentatiously drew from a pocket a notebook in which in a workaday fashion it proceeded to write copiously as it examined one creel after another. Harsh sounds of angry protest and argument reached our ears. For us at the south end of the file there was no escape, for the Law was operating between us and our car. As for myself I fished on as though deaf, dumb, and blind.

At last the Law strode up to us; fortunately, it looked at the Parson first. The guileless smiles that wreathed his face were completely disarming. Without waiting to be questioned he reached down into a deep pocket of his Norfolk jacket and drew out his morning's catch—three tiny six-inch trout. So badly wounded were they that to throw them back into the stream would have been nothing else than an absurd, pedantic act of conformity to the text of a statute. Plainly, the Law had a sense of real justice; as it stood by this unique trout brook it looked the Church squarely in the face and found it honest. With a cordial wave of the hand that carried acquittal at once to the Church and the Church's companion, the Law pocketed its notebook with an air of finality, turned right about face, and walked away. Throughout this informal trial under the open sky not a word was spoken, except perhaps a "good morning." Never in all my days have I felt more ashamed of myself: during all this pantomime my creel containing half a dozen illegal fish lay hidden beneath a clump of grass almost at the Law's very feet. I had been shielded by a frankness ,and an honesty that neither I nor any others of that long column of anglers possessed. Here, I said to myself, is a man untainted by hypocrisy, a minister worthy of his cloth. No wonder he is loved and trusted. But was his action just a "trivial" thing? For the answer, ask any angler. Then consider this a moment: a fortnight after the Law's visitation we heard its result: three costly angling outfits—rods, reels, and creels—became the property of the Crown.

On the margin of the wilderness there is only one accepted measure of a Sky Pilot's qualification for his mission—the way in which he responds to the calls of need and of anxious hearts. When in deep distress the common man anywhere finds no real solace in nice pulpit homilies and· the recital of pious texts; prompt, heartfelt sympathy in the form of action is the only pastoral offering that means anything. If given even at the cost of slight sacrifice, its genuineness is established forever in the mind that sorrows; if given without thought of risk to body or health, it wins lifelong devotion.

It is an ancient way of human society to desire to honour its dead in burial even at the cost of great inconvenience. Many years ago during the period of autumn storms a worthy matron of Lion's Head passed away; her husband expressed to Parson James the wish that she be buried in the family plot at Clarksburg sixty miles away on the south side of the Georgian Bay. Distance and the state of the roads forbade the journey by land. The storm then raging over the Bay made the bravest spirit think many times before boarding a vessel. Yet the water route was the only route feasible. "I'll go with you," said the parson to the husband, "if you can find a crew." Inspired by this lead a crew formed at once and out into the storm they went on a steam fishing-tug.

The greatest danger that confronted the skipper was not the seas but the dense fog. In passing out of the harbour he was unable to see even the faintest outline of the towering bluff with the lion's head. Invisible too would be similar landmarks along the route, Cape Croker and Cape Rich, for instance. He could make his course only by dead reckoning. At best he could advance only at a crawl and could not hope to reach his port before the blackness of night would be added to the deep grey of the fog. With skill and intelligent boldness he steered the tug straight to the little dock at Clarksburg as if he had had the full light of day all around him. But it was beyond his power to provide a calm landing; the waves surging shoreward lifted the tug high by the stern and thrust her bow up on a flat rock. However no serious damage was done to man or property, and all on board went ashore safely. Then in affectionate tribute to a worthy Christian soul and her loved ones the parson gladly did his duty.

But for Parson James that test of wave, wind, and fog lasted only a day. Later there came a test that was drawn out for many days and many nights: it was truly "the terror by night . . . the arrow that flieth by day . . . the pestilence that walketh in darkness . . . the destruction that wasteth at noonday." It was the influenza epidemic of the winter of 1918-19, the first winter after World War I. In the summer of 1919 I was fishing for bass out of Stokes Bay; everybody in the region was talking of the beloved Sky Pilot, of how, as many persons in one, he had brought the population through the plague in the winter just past. As yet I had never set eyes on the man but when I met him not long afterwards I felt I knew him already. Even the first words I heard him speak threw light upon his real self. Embarrassed by a stranger's comment upon the great part he had played in ministering to the needs of the whole community during the recent ordeal, he dismissed the implied praise with a wave of the hand. "I was nothing

more than a hybrid between a parson and a taxi driver. Now,
let's go fishing!"

When at last the "flu" broke into the fastnesses of The Bruce
it took everybody by surprise. The great headland was so remote
from crowded centres, where the plague was raging, and its air
and waters were so pure, that it seemed assured of complete im-
munity. At any rate for a number of weeks its people were spared
the horror that scourged the rest of the country. But one day the
dread infection broke through the wall of isolation. It was brought
in from the outer world by some one who was quite unaware of
the viper that lurked in his person. Suddenly stricken with a
strange debility he called the doctor. The doctor was baffled and
while he was making a vain study of the case two other cases
were reported. Then without warning he himself became a fourth
case and the members of his family followed him in rapid succession. Now he knew what his patient's trouble was. How foolish
to think that a plague that leaped over the Atlantic could be
stopped by a strip of forest and highlands!

The distress in Lion's Head and its hinterland was appalling.
No qualified doctor, no nurse could be brought in from outside
because all outside was in the same plight. Scarcely a home in the
spacious tract of field and bushland between Georgian Bay and
Lake Huron entirely escaped the pest and in many not a soul
had sufficient strength even to crawl from bed. In some households food lay spoiling in kitchen and larder, while in others
foodstuffs of all sorts had been consumed and no one was in a
state to sally forth and replenish the store. Stoves went out, some
because no fuel remained indoors, others, because there was no
one able to feed them. Farm animals were starving in stall and pen
and men and women and children were dying. This was the news
that flooded the village telephone exchange over the long many-
party rural line. The horror of the reports was frightful enough
but it was magnified by common knowledge that all the roads
were buried deep in snow.

Somehow every crisis in human affairs discovers its own leader.
In its dire trouble Lion's Head was no exception. Its leader was
already there—Parson James. With quiet though firm power he
took over; as if it were a daily routine the community accepted
him, not as one man, however, but as a host in himself—doctor,
nurse, deliveryman, handyman, stoker, regional relief officer, and,
all the time, as comforter of grieving souls. At night he was nurse

to the doctor himself, alert to stave off the critical stage of haemor-
rhage. By day, sometimes alone, sometimes with companions, he
made as many calls with team and sleigh as any doctor would
have made within the limits of physical strength and so far as
snow and roads permitted. Outwardly the good man seemed to
have no fear for himself. Years ago I asked him this question,
rather bluntly, I fear: "Is it true that you were not conscious of
fear of catching the 'flu' yourself?" The reply was clear-cut: "It's
not true at all; of course I was afraid. At first I was ashamed, but
when it dawned on me that fear of that kind is perfectly natural
for anybody I saw it would be crazy to fight it. So I took it for
granted—like an ugly wart or a birthmark—and forgot all about
it. I soon found that at every crisis there was within me a strength
I never knew I had."

Parson James's efforts were rewarded by the recovery of most
of his patients. But one phase of the situation in particular dis-
quieted him: he saw that the period of slow convalescence from
the extreme weakness left by the infection was going to be long;
there was a shortage of hands to carry on the ordinary tasks of the
community. So he took on himself a new duty—to spur his fellow-
citizens to appeal to the provincial Department of Health for
an experienced physician. Still not a single qualified man could be
found, not even a nurse. But the Department did post to the
emergency a young graduate in medicine who as yet had not
obtained his licence to practice. He, poor fellow, though still
youthful and vigorous, soon wilted under the strain of making
his visits in the company of the parson. Sometimes the two made
as many as thirty calls in twenty-four hours, driving through deep
drifts and over the Forty Hills and back. Into the young man's
place soon came a successor, then another and still another; in
the course of the next six months a veritable procession of medical
recruits filed into Lion's Head and out again in rapid succession.
Measured by the gravity of the need most of these fleeting
guardians of local health fell sadly short of the ideals of the pro-
fession they were planning to enter. Some of them refused to
make night calls. Some charged fees that would have strained
city purses. One had to be dragged to attend a patient whose life
was ebbing fast. Yet even with such uncertain associates at his
side Parson James gave leadership in a work of mercy and healing
that was worthy of one who had been trained in the art.

Many of the scenes he witnessed were harrowing; many were

bewildering enough to break the mind of a man devoid of poise
and a quick sense of humour. In not a few of these Parson James
perceived amusing incongruities that for the moment made sights
of pain and sorrow less hard to bear. Often the irony was grim
indeed. One instance is a classic of its kind in illustrating the
curious genius of the rural party-telephone. One pitch-black night
in mid winter at the peak of the epidemic a telephone call for
help came from a home several miles up country. "Yes, we'll go,"
replied the Parson, "if the horses can pull us through. But mark the
way into your place by hanging out a lantern." When the two
messengers of mercy had floundered a mile or two along the road
they realized, to their consternation, that the way into every home
was marked by a lantern!

At long last the epidemic, like a forest fire, burned itself out.
One could almost hear the sigh of relief that passed like a sooth-
ing breeze over the Peninsula in the wake of the certain knowledge that the great fear had gone by. But its end was not the end
of the appeals for the Parson's help in meeting emergencies. Indeed, they seemed to increase in number and variety. An example
of the unexpected throws light upon the kind of response to them
given by the rectory. One day a few years after the epidemic the
Parson heard his telephone ring long and frantically. It was a
call from the doctor. "Get ready to go with me up the Peninsula
at once," he said; "Greene's boy has broken a leg—a pretty bad
one, the old man says." "I'm ready any time," was the reply,
though James was sorely puzzled to know how he could be of
use in the case of a fracture of any kind. Once at the farm the
two men learned the particulars of the accident.

Greene's boy, a grown man, was leading out a colt for exercise
when the spirited creature suddenly reared up. The young man's
first impulse was to try to pull him down. He succeeded better
than he thought: he put so much power into the effort that he
dragged the colt over sideways. The beast fell across young
Greene's legs. Something was heard to snap; the victim was left
to lie helpless on the ground until the doctor could see him. The
latter saw at once what had happened: the man's kneecap had
been split clean across. It was clearly a case for a hospital. That
meant Owen Sound, of course, fifty or more miles away. For the
journey—none too smooth in those days of unimproved roads—
the injured leg must be held firm in a splint. With manifest

chagrin the young medico frankly confessed he did not know what to do; in his haste he had forgotten to bring any splints with him and did not know how to improvise one. Meanwhile the patient lay on the bare ground suffering agonies. "But surely," interposed Parson James, "you can at least tell us what a knee splint is like." Following the doctor's brief description the Parson called for a couple of light boards, a saw, a hammer and some nails. In a few minutes the splint was made and set on the leg. Later, the doctor reported the hospital surgeon's comment: "It was the best knee splint I have ever seen."

The day came when, naturally enough, the parishioners of the Cape Chin region keenly felt the need of a church building in which to worship. Though free to go on using McCallum's school-house as long as they wished, they craved for their services an atmosphere that a plain, secular building of that order could not offer. For many months the subject was a common topic of con-versation in all the households concerned; but, as usual in the first stages of such matters, no orderly attempts were being made to bring the talk to a focus. To effect such a result, a definite plan, however crude at first, was needed. Once again the pastor's duty stood out clear as a signpost on a highway.

Even a shepherd of souls has to have near him some kindred spirit with whom he can talk freely and fully about his problems and his visions of the future. Straight to such an assured source of strength and counsel went Parson James—to a gifted architect who was at the same time a devoted churchman and a truly philanthropic spirit. "Cape Chin wants a church, and of course one built of stone, the stone of its own hills and valleys. Its plan and lines must be in keeping with the best Anglican tradition. There's no excuse for making a house of God in the wilderness as uncouth as the wilderness itself. Now won't you sketch me a plan of just such a church to crown the crest of a hill near Cape Chin? And don't forget lancet windows!"

So Architect James—there may be something more in names than we suspect—drafted a plan for Parson James. Together the two pored over it, modified it in a thousand and one ways, and at last put down boldly in cold figures what they thought the cost would be. "Even in those days,' the good pastor wrote me years afterwards, "the figures were terrifying to a country parson. The two of us decided we would try to close our eyes to them. So I

went to the people and said: 'Here's a plan for a new church and
here's what it will cost to carry it out in money and in labour.
What will you do?'

"The responses were prompt and as various in form as they were
noble. The owner of the chosen site said at once he would give
that. Others who had but little money promised to give of that
little gladly and sacrificially. All these and still others pledged
themselves to gifts of labour of hand and horsepower. The outcome of the appeal surpassed our most sanguine hopes."

The order of the steps to be taken in the progress from bare
site to roof was plain. The first was to get together a supply of
stone. In a certain sense that was an easy job, for the whole region
is in itself a vast quarry of dolomite limestone. Through untold
centuries the glaciers and the winters that came after them had
torn out from their strata great rectangular chunks of this stone
and strewed them all about. Some of these weighed as much as
two tons each; those not exceeding this weight served the builders'
purpose well. The task, no hard one for a couple of teams with
logging chains, was to drag a suitable block *upside down* to a
spot where it could be easily worked—*upside down,* since the
underside, having never been exposed to the hardening effect of
the air, is the soft side. (To think of stone having a soft side!)
About once a month the Parson would "line up" four men and
two teams to draw blocks to suitable places. One month it would
be, say, the Hayes and the Morrows, the next month the McLays
and the McDonalds, and so on down the roll of willing hands,
the McArthurs, Wests, Rouses, and still others. Small groups of
men with hammers broke the blocks into pieces of the size
required for the walls. Not the least energetic among the stone-
breakers was Parson James himself who with good effect regularly
swung a nine-pound hammer, or, if a soft side proved to be less
soft than it should be, a twelve-pounder borrowed from a fellow-
workman. And when the building stones were ready it was the
Parson who in a little trailer towed behind his old Ford coupé
conveyed them to the place where they were to become church
walls. Two professional masons, assisted by a mortar-mixer, then
laid them in their courses. In the main, the building of this church
in the wildwood was an achievement of amateurs.

"In the first year (1925) we got a good start; in the second year
we laid the corner stone, and in the third year we put the roof on.
As for the timber for joists and rafters," we read in the parson's

record of progress, "some of it was taken out of the forest near the church. Yes, it was just as simple as that."

But was it "just as simple as that"? And are we ungracious in questioning a Sky Pilot's word? The good man's modesty has glozed over the vital fact that in his own person Parson James was a whole construction staff. He was a feller of trees, a hewer, and a sawyer—a full-fledged lumberman—as well as quarryman, stone-mason, and superintendent of works. He was also owner and operator of the sawmill that converted into beams and boards the trees of the adjacent forest. The mill was nothing else than his own Model T Ford coupé which he had commandeered to serve him in a novel form of pastoral duty.

A level, low-lying tract near the site of the church was chosen as the source of the wood to go into the edifice; in it stood sound trees of the kinds needed. Into a little clearing of solid ground beside this tract the Model T was backed. Its front wheels were firmly blocked before and behind. The rear wheels were jacked up well clear of the ground. The power plant was now ready. The sawing unit was deftly improvised by the "boss" and one of his laymen. From sundry junk piles was salvaged the gear for transmitting the power of the Model T to the saw: an inch and a half steel shaft and three pulley-wheels. Two of these were fitted to the shaft so that each made contact with a jacked-up wheel of the car; on the third, fastened to the projecting end of the shaft, ran the bolt that rotated the saw. The bearings on which all moving parts turned were as makeshift as any other part of the whole ingenious contraption.

And what a "plant" it was! It turned out material as fine as the product of a trade factory. With its rear end lifted jauntily aloft it reminded one of an untethered colt joyfully disporting itself in a woodland clearing. In the sound of its saw, whether ripping or cutting across the grain of the wood, there was not the faintest hint of a whine; rather, the buzz seemed to be the voice of a creature conscious of making a joyful noise unto the Lord. Once again was the Parson guilty of understatement when he wrote: "We 'butchered up' quite a lot of timber of various sizes to fit different parts of the building"; with my own eyes I have again and again seen in the charming little church the fine product turned out by the improvised mill and the master sawyer who ran it.

During this period the enthusiasm of the pastor and his

St. Margaret's Church at Cape Chin

parishioners rose at the same rate as the walls. In time it reached
a pitch that infected beneficently the whole community, even the
members of other faiths. Passing strangers who saw the charming
stone edifice taking form in the rough hilly woodland up the
Peninsula were touched by the courage of the effort and gladly
gave their bits. But the highlight of aid from without came from
an unexpected quarter and had results that even the most romantic
mind could not have conceived beforehand. A small company of
anglers from a distant city who were fishing for lake trout off
the Head heard Parson James tell the story of the parish's enterprise at Cape Chin. Caught by his zeal they volunteered small
contributions to the cause. Out of this simple, matter-of-fact cir-
cumstance sprang up a legend, a legend of the kind which endless
repititions of the real truth can never suppress; it seems now to
have become a part of the slowly growing folklore of the
Peninsula.

Gossip had it that these contributions toward the erection of a
house of God were really the proceeds of a poker game. Absurd,
of course, for the proceeds of a poker game played to its limit
represent the acquired gains of one person only—the winner.
But the donation that gave rise to the legend was a group affair:
to that I can take my oath. However, whether the tale was true
or not, there was in it an incongruity that tickled everybody's
sense of humour. In time the tale reached the anglers' home town.

The laughter it created was extraordinarily fruitful. The head of a large glass company offered to glaze all the windows of the new church free of cost. A wealthy widow promised to provide the seating. And thus it was that, when in 1928 St. Margaret's Church at Cape Chin was dedicated by the Bishop of the Diocese of Huron, the congregation of parishioners and friends who came together for the service sat in comfortable pews of solid oak and saw the sunlight softly filtered through the cathedral glass of the lovely lancet windows.

Such is the humility of the man whom many in The Bruce, in deep affection and admiration, still speak of as "Daddy" James, that he would attribute the success of his ministry in the Peninsula to inspiration and strength vouchsafed him from above. And who would have it otherwise? Yet to those of us who have had the privilege of observing many phases of that ministry, the part of the human agent in this fruitful mission of the new frontier is manifest. If we seek a reason for its fruitfulness we can quickly find it. Indeed, it has already been put into print for us. One of the world's greatest missionary leaders of modern times, Dr. Albert Schweitzer, whose mission lies on "the edge of the primeval wilderness," not long ago wrote these words: "But it is just by means of the Christian sympathy and gentleness that he [the missionary of the frontier] shows in all this everyday business that he exercises his greatest influence; whatever level of spirituality the community reaches is due to nothing so much as to the success of its Head in this matter of—*Preaching without Words*."[1]

1. *On the Edge of the Primeval Forest* (London: Adam and Charles Black Limited; Toronto: The Macmillan Company of Canada Limited, 1948), p. 109.
Canon James died on September 28, 1961.

Chapter 20

LILACS AND LOG CABINS

A weed-grown wound between time-blighted trees,
A crumbling chimney that now stands alone,
Show where a home that faced the summer breeze
Has turned a cenotaph of scattered stone.

Where once a proud house stood is emptiness,
The roofless cellar now a cave of gloom,
Yet round its rim brave hollyhocks still press
And on the rubble valiant lilacs bloom.
ARTHUR STRINGER, *"The Abandoned Farm."*[1]

THE Bruce has many notable traits, but one stands out above all others: her spectacular ways of proving the indestructibility of life, its refusal to be smothered out by any conditions, however adverse. On every hand she parades her proofs of its tenacity. Let every tree be laid low on any given tract of the Peninsula until nothing but bare ground and naked rock is to be seen: yet, after no more than two summers, the unpromising surface is green with the tender foliage of seedling aspens, pin cherries, and birches, under whose shade will be nursed the young of a forest of pines and firs yet to be. Or let fire sweep away all signs of plant life, even consuming the last grain of humus on the underlying limestone pavement: yet, in the very next season of growth, you will see dense bunches of grass forcing their way upward through countless crevices and waving their plumes aloft. Or, again, let the face of the cliff that towers off Lion's Head crash to the Georgian Bay shore in a million fragments: yet, in but a short span of years, those bits of sterile dolomite will become the verdant home of myriads of ferns.

But despite its manifest proofs of the will to go on living The Bruce has not been able to ward off a succession of blows

1. A few months before his death Mr. Stringer, on his own initiative, sent me a typewritten copy of this poem and accorded permission to quote from it in this chapter.

that have seared her face with the lines of an old age that has come before its time, for among the frontier settlements of Ontario The Bruce is a mere child. Some disfigurements, of course, will come to the face even of a wholly unpeopled land through what the law terms "acts of God"—the ravages of lightning, fire, flood, and wind. But the most unsightly scars that mar the features of The Bruce are not such as these: rather, they are the evidences of man's effort to wrest a living from her wealth of wood and her deceptive soils.

Of these the most appalling are the remains of human habitations that one comes across here and there in the Peninsula. The visitor's eye can hardly avoid them since they hug close to the highways of today, the old trails of a pioneer yesterday made broader and smoother even if not always straighter. These remains are in all stages of decay—from erect, staring skeletons of abodes to the scattered stones of crumbled chimneys and foundations that lie round about like disjointed bones.

But here is matter for wonder! Nearly all of these relics are marked as though they were once scenes of historic events or of rare natural beauty. And in each case the marker is not an inert thing like a monument of wood or of stone, but something patently infused with life, something which stands for the triumph of life over powers that would insidiously destroy—a stately, vigorous clump of lilacs. If you go about The Bruce seeking the spots where men and women and children once had homes, look first of all for tall, flourishing thickets of lilacs, and not far off you will find the sorry vestiges of what you seek.

These decayed homesteads must have a story to tell. Sad to say, only a few of them can tell of early and continuous success. By that we mean a success which, thanks to sheer good luck as much as to skill and grit, lasted long enough to be counted as a spell of comfortable prosperity. As a rule, old Bruce homesteads of this class may be known at a glance, for they are labelled. And the labels are, most fittingly, trim modern abodes that flaunt their fancy gables above the squat shelters of the days of pioneer toil and hardship. But why have these ugly relics been left to harrow the spirit of every passer-by? Through indolence, perhaps; or because of utter indifference to the looks of things? Or can it be by design, so that the glaring contrast may proclaim to all and sundry how far along in the world the occupants of the proud new houses have forged their way?

But the mere presence of the new hard by the old is not necessarily a mark of solid achievement; I can myself point to one dismal instance in which it is an obvious monument to failure. In this case both old and new have been abandoned to crumble at leisure into shameful ruin, and the clearing in which they stand has been recaptured, foot by foot, by the relentless encroachments of the forest. For me this distressing sight has an historical significance. Not more than three decades ago I saw the "new" home of this pair, stylish with its two storeys and its then up-to-date coat of golden shingles, ostentatiously reared in front of the flat-roofed log shanty that preceded it. It was the owner's pride and the township's envy. But today mansion and shanty are homes no longer except to the small rodents of field and wood and to the great horned owl.

The first to invade the fastnesses of The Bruce were men who sought to cut its trees into lumber. Many of these came as "hands" in logging-gangs who accepted as a matter of course the rough though hearty, barrack-like existence provided by their "boss." But there were some who could not be content with anything short of family life, though lived under the crudest of roofs. Besides those who came in organized groups as hired men on a pay-roll there were a number of "lone wolves": unable to team up with others they must have a field of labour all their own where each in his own person could be both "boss" and workman. At great pains they acquired for themselves small family-sized limits, so to speak, situated in odd corners among the large limits worked by gangs.

Without delay all who were domestically inclined proceeded to set up their cabins on the ragged edge of the forest. At first these were placed near the scenes of the men's daily labours. But little by little this advantage waned. The harder men worked with axe and saw and team the more swiftly did the wall of the forest retreat. After a few seasons of cutting it was so far from the workers' bed and board that the daily trudge outward to work and homeward at dusk was too hard to endure. Any one of these loggers could truthfully have said with Goldsmith's traveller: "By every remove I only drag a greater length of chain."

At length the day came when the last tree of the limit had been felled and the last log drawn to the water. There was no longer need for axeman, sawyer, or teamster. No tenants were left for the crude homes straggling along the fringe of the wilderness. These lonely, simple structures stand out against a dreary background of stumps, deformed trees, slash, and sky, reminding one of the battered hulks of ships that lie stranded along the coastal shoals and craggy ledges of near-by Lake Huron. Come close to any one of them and listen. What you hear is the wind working its will upon the ghost of a house, hooting down the chimney as in derision and with weird fingers clawing at the windows and trying the latches of the doors.

But timber was not the only lodestone that drew men into these rugged northern parts. For many it was the prospect of possessing land. To them the forest was a foe since it kept from them the thing they coveted—an expanse of tillable acres to be had for little more than nothing, acres that a man could call his own and not a landlord's. The fierceness of the hunger to become independent proprietors warped the judgment. Not many of these seekers of cheap land brought with them any experience with soils and all seemed to nurse the naïve belief that any patch of earth, if merely scratched, somehow yields a living. All one need do, it appeared, was to barn-storm the wilderness boldly enough. Impetuously these men staked out their farmsteads on the first unclaimed tracts they chanced upon. In the building of their cabins even greater leeway was left to luck. Few signs survive that these domestic sites were really selected. In many cases even the assurance of an available water supply was neglected.

Scarcely any of these callow adventurers could do more than guess what manner of soil would be brought to light when the trees came down—whether sterile rock and gravel or workable loam. They plunged doggedly ahead, raising shelters for themselves, and, if they were not too lazy, unfeeling, or pressed for time, for their animals also. Whatever they put together to serve as barn or stable was rough and rude beyond words. Since no effort was made to pack the spaces between the rough logs the oxen and cows were exposed to almost the full blasts of winter's winds. A roof of bark kept the snow from falling directly upon them, but what benefit was that when driving through the gaping walls it would pile up all about them? But few indeed were the cattle that in the first stages of a mid-forest farmstead had even a vestige of shelter. Until their owners had time to mow and stack marsh grasses they lived their winters in the bush browsing like deer on succulent shrubs or on the tender twigs and leaf-buds of trees cut down to feed them.

After a few feverish weeks of strenuous toil there would rise in each little clearing some form of shelter for its human occupants. Thankfully and fondly they dignified their new quarters with the name of home, and, as if to signalize their faith in the happy family life that lay ahead, they planted a lilac bush at their front door. Unwittingly they were treading the path of ancient European custom, a custom sprung from a primitive folk-legend which held the lilac to be the guardian of the household. Many a flower-loving emigrant housewife carefully tucked away lilac cuttings among the household effects put aboard ship and lovingly bore them westward to the new home overseas. Today follow the lilac thickets of the countryside and you will find yourself treading the trail of our pioneers.

The mind of man is a ragbag of contradictions. All too often the assurance of a roof over his head created in the tenderfoot proprietor a spirit of cocksureness not warranted by the facts of daily experience. As the forest was pressed back rod by rod the discoveries made should have been disturbing. Here where earth of some kind was to be expected the spade struck solid limestone. Yonder where soil of no mean depth was actually found it turned out to be boggy and sour. A feeling of disquiet stole slowly over once bold hearts. This at length gave way to alarm and their early confidence began to slip away. The last stage of this sorry course of life could not be far off. Soon a melancholy inertia numbed the spirit of the whole household and thenceforth every action, in the field and indoors alike, became merely the listless ritual of daily life.

And then the end! The heartbreak of proven failure and the prospect of unrelieved poverty left but one path open for the man who had once exulted in the promise of becoming the free master of his own domain. Denied food for the table of his household and fodder for the mangers of his beasts, he cursed his acres and all upon them, nailed up his lowly manor as though it were a coffin, and slunk away overnight into the vast blank of "elsewhere." But there was one living thing he left—the undying lilac by the door.

Such are the abandoned homes of The Bruce. Their desolate remains haunt the mind of the visitor because of the shocking contrast between them and the tidy domiciles of pioneers who did win and hold a genuine success. Deserted by woodsmen and by husbandmen these forlorn relics of defeat still tell their tale. Of any one of them that remain erect Adjutor Rivard could have

written as he wrote in his charming *Chez Nous* of an ancient
haunted house—a *maison condamnée*—of his own Quebec:

So there it was at the edge of the road, like a tomb. A few hastily nailed
boards barred the door and the windows of the sad abode. Never even a
wisp of smoke from its chimney of stone; never a ray of sunshine crossing
its threshold; never a glimmer of light in its closed eyes. Blind and deaf
the deserted habitation stood there indifferent to the spacious motley pattern
of the tilled fields as to the ceaseless rustling of the meadows. Cold and
mute, nothing can rouse it from its torpor and no human voice awaken its
echoes. No human voice, . . . but, of nights, has not one heard borne on
the wind from the dead house long cries like the wailing of one who
laments?[1]

With like finality spoke Edwin Arlington Robinson of the house
on the New England hill:

> There is ruin and decay
>   In the House on the Hill:
> They are all gone away,
>   There is nothing more to say.[2]

But there is something more to say—so many things that we
cannot say them all. And one of them must be said at once. The
picture we have drawn is sombre, indeed it seems almost too
sombre to be true. Yet it is true so far as a single sketch may
suggest the collective ill fortune of a whole class of individuals.
And this ill luck was that of men who pioneered, not in some
far-off ancient time nor in some distant land, but within the lifetime of many of us, near our doors and under our very eyes. We
have often smugly said: "Never will the blunders and wasteful-
ness of the early colonists occur again." But they have occurred
again and we have seen them. And yet again will they occur
until we learn to translate into constructive social action the facts
of a history of which we have ourselves been witnesses.

Still another thing must be said: the sketch we have presented
is only a part of a picture; there remains the other part —the
happier aspects of the peopling of The Bruce. It is a smaller part,
so small indeed that one can easily overlook it. Yet it is a most
welcome high light in a scene which, so far as human comfort and
the satisfaction of human aspirations are concerned, is for the
most part an expanse of unrelieved shadow. It is welcome because
it is true, just as true as the tale of mistakes and misfortune told

1. By permission of the publishers, McClelland and Stewart, Limited, Toronto.
2. From "The House on the Hill," by permission of Charles Scribner's Sons.

by the dumb faces of the abandoned houses, for a goodly number of those who trekked into the Peninsula to win livings from its trees, soils, and great surrounding waters reaped at least a measure of the reward they sought.

Here is a bright, cheerful spot in the picture. Henry Whicher took up land at Colpoy's Bay in Albemarle in 1867. On December 3, 1870 he jotted down in his diary: "One of the best farms in Upper Canada, and that is saying a great deal, may be made of this lot [of 153 acres], either for the raising of grain or for stock and dairying. I value the lot now at $10. per acre, paid $3. for it 2½ years ago." Eighty years have proved the soundness of his hopes and judgment: he and his tribe flourished here and of his children's children some still reside in the region. Nor let this be overlooked: the land in this area is yet good. Truly here is a family who lived long enough to behold in the recurrent leafing and flowering of the lilacs by the door no longer a symbol of faith in things to be but a banner of pride in things achieved.

WHEN SIR JOHN A. PUT HIS FOOT DOWN*

A T Manitowaning, Manitoulin Island, on August 9, 1836,
the title to the Peninsula (plus an additional tract immediately south of it) was surrendered to the Crown by
the Ojibway Indians. The consideration involved was the Government's pledge to pay the tribes "twelve hundred pounds per
annum, as long as grass grows and water runs." Provision to set
aside areas for the Indians of the Peninsula was made in a "Royal
Deed of Declaration" on June 29, 1847, which solemnly reaffirmed
the right of the Ojibways to continue to possess and enjoy the
Peninsula, "or the proceeds of the sale thereof for the benefit of
the said Ojibway Indians and their posterity."

Herein lurked a germ of future trouble: the subtle suggestion
that the Indians' ownership might not be as enduring as the
Royal Deed declared. No less ominous was a certain major
aspect of administration: the government bureau that acted in
such transactions was the Department of Indian Affairs instead
of the Department of Crown Lands. Thus for some time there
existed side by side two separate bureaus for the administration
of public lands. Added to this unsatisfactory arrangement was
an even worse one: the Department of Indian Affairs was a
branch of the British War Office and the Governor-General's
secretary was ex-officio Superintendent-General. Thus this department was not responsible to the Government of Canada or
to the Indians. This situation lasted until 1868.

Fulfilment of the Royal Deed's hidden omen did not lag long.
The increasing demands for new lands for settlement turned

---

*The material in this appendix was first presented in summary form to
Section II of the Royal Society of Canada in Quebec in 1952. It was printed as an
article in the Owen Sound *Sun-Times*, June 14, 1952, in *Inland Seas*, Spring 1955,
pp. 3–9, and Summer 1955, pp. 103–110, and as no. 29 of *Western Ontario
History Nuggets*, 1961. I had hoped to include the information it gives in the
chapter, "And the Trees Trooped Out," in *The Bruce Beckons*, but the material
on which it is based, and for which I am indebted to the Public Archives of
Canada, was not available in time.

covetous eyes toward the Peninsula. In 1854 the Indian chiefs were invited to a parley to discuss the possibility of the surrender of the tract to the Crown. On October 13 of that year a treaty was signed to effect the transfer. The Indians consented to yield the entire peninsula except certain reserved areas, on the understanding "that the interest of the principal sum arising out of the sale of the lands be regularly paid to the Indians or to their children in posterity, so long as there were Indians left to represent the tribe, without diminution, at half-yearly intervals."

In April, 1855, Lord Bury, Superintendent-General at the time, authorized the survey of the townships of Keppel and Amabel and soon afterward advertised that the tract would be put up for public auction on October 17 of the same year; unforeseen delays put off the event until September 2 of 1856. On paper the result was satisfactory; of the 144,000 acres offered only about one-quarter failed to fetch bids. The average upset price for farm lots was 10*s*. 3*d*. an acre whereas the average rate paid at the sale was 18*s*. 6*d*. The total sum realized, including cash down and pledges on future instalments, was £119,332. In the light of present knowledge of the nature of the land purchased, the figures reported are monstrously absurd. In a brief word on the times O. D. Skelton (*Railway Builders*, pp. 84–5) tells us what had happened. "A speculative fever ran through the whole community . . . and land prices soared to heights undreamed of. The pace quickened till exhaustion, contagious American panics, poor harvests, and the Crimean War . . . brought collapse in 1857." The war ended on March 30, 1856, only five months before the auction at Owen Sound. The country was nearing the end of its mad descent to financial disaster.

But stern facts soon brought speculator and settler alike back to their senses. Many of both groups, shocked by the grim prospect into sobriety, summarily forfeited their cash payments and threw up their contracts. The courageous few who stayed by their bargains forthwith began to flood the Department with appeals for relief. They were, they pleaded, only the innocent victims of a universal hysteria. Their plea was not unheeded; some easement in the conditions of purchase was granted. But this did little more than add to the grievances of the settlers, who held that the adjustment favoured the speculators unjustly. This bitter difference continued unabated for many years.

The painful revelation that followed hard upon the fantastic sale of the peninsular lands and the grave depression of 1857 disclosed also a number of fundamentally unsound conditions. The most illogical of these was that the ultimate authority over the Indian's interests lay in the distant British War Office. This great drawback was only diminished, not removed, when in 1868 an act of the Parliament of Canada created the Department of Secretary of State and appointed the holder of that portfolio Superintendent-General of Indian Affairs; the office to administer the Indian lands was set up in Toronto rather than in or near the territories concerned. Not until 1878 was an office established in Wiarton and an agent posted to it. But the effectiveness of this arrangement was gravely impaired by a weakness which research brought to light only recently: copies of the licences issued by the agents on the spot were not sent to Ottawa, it seems, except when requested by the Indian Department. The result is that few copies of the licences are on record today. Strangely enough, the Indian Department has none dated before 1900; the Archives has only about fifteen for the Bruce Peninsula, and all are within the period from 1873 to 1876. These relate to the townships of Amabel, Albemarle, Eastnor, and St. Edmunds, and also to Wiarton and Cape Croker. There is only one conclusion to be drawn: the controlling authority, the Department, made very few requests for copies of licences issued locally. The agents, all honourable men, did faithfully what they were expected to do. It was the system that was wrong; its weaknesses are too obvious to need singling out. Our story as it unfolds affords ample illustrations.

There is no more fruitful source of information, though far from complete, than the files of the licences themselves. This is a group of books kept by the Indian Department which contain references to timber licences and to revenue from timber. These volumes the Department has entrusted to the custody of the Public Archives. They are: (*a*) Timber Ledger, 1863–1864; (*b*) Timber License Ledger, 1871–1874; (*c*) Timber License Book, 1853–1894.

Big timber operators invaded the Peninsula much earlier than all but the oldest of the old-timers now suspect. The paucity of extant records forbids one ever to expect to see the full tally of the names and numbers of these aggressive outsiders. In the minds of the earliest settlers two names (which, as we shall show, were really one name) stand out above all others. These are Cook and Brothers, and the corporation to which they assigned

their licences. When at long last the harassed land-owners got
the ear of Sir John Macdonald it was these two companies that
were charged as the chief cause of the pitiable condition for
which relief was sought.

According to an item in an Indian Department timber ledger
of 1864 now in the Public Archives at Ottawa (the only record
still existing of timber licences issued for the Peninsula during
the sixties), Messrs. Cook Brothers of Barrie began cutting in
Keppel Township in 1863. At the start the firm carried on its
operations simultaneously in widely separated parts of the township, on the east side not far inland from the shore of Owen
Sound, and in the southwestern corner near the Sauble River.
They took a small amount of ash, large quantities of oak (presumably red), many elm (presumably of the species called rock
or cork which is still abundant in the region bordering on
Amabel), and an enormous proportion of pine. The dues the
Cooks paid for the oak and the pine seem to indicate that the
greater part of these two species cut in Keppel was made into
square timber for export. That at least some of this reached
Quebec one may infer from a ledger item of this same time that
records a draft drawn on Cook Brothers, Quebec.

Not long before his death in 1952, an Owen Sound citizen,
William Gilchrist, gave me his recollections of these operations.
In 1865, when he was a boy of five, his parents took him with
them to reside in Keppel. The new home was near Lake Charles
in the northern part of the township. During the second half
of the sixties young Gilchrist saw many of the Cook gangs at
work on several tracts of the forest. They took out many prime
examples of rock elm to be made into ship masts, and vast
quantities of red and white pine. The elm and the pine, the
latter in great squared sticks which were felled in the southwestern corner of the township, were conveyed over the snow
to the Sauble River and then in the high water of spring floated
down to Lake Huron. The squared pines were assembled at
Oliphant and from there towed in bag-booms to Tobermory
where they were loaded on schooners and taken by way of the
Welland Canal to Toronto or to Garden Island near Kingston.
At either place square timbers were made into great rafts which
were taken down the St. Lawrence to Quebec. The hazard of
taking immense rafts of very valuable timber down the rapids
of the St. Lawrence was always great; but greater still by far
was the hazard involved in traversing nearly two hundred miles

of open Lake Ontario between Toronto and the head of the River. Enlightened by long experience the Calvin Company of Garden Island adopted the policy of avoiding the long and dangerous haul on the lake. But others, including the Cooks, closed their eyes to the risks, and, sometimes, to their sorrow, made up their rafts at Toronto.

Once again an eye-witness gives precision to our story. Charles Williams, a resident of Lion's Head since 1877, lived as a boy in Toronto, at the corner of Front and Portland streets. Opposite his father's home and tavern were the docks of the old Northern Railway where the Cooks and other operators constructed their huge rafts of square timbers. Not far away was the residence of Hiram Henry Cook, the eldest of the Cook brothers. The removal of the Williams family to Lion's Head gave the lad Charles an opportunity to witness what was to him a new phase of the Cooks' business—their activities in the primitive forest and the removal of its trees from the Peninsula. From what he overheard of the heated conversation of his elders and from what he himself saw from time to time he soon became aware of the grievous plight of the settlers, of their dogged but vain fight and of their bitter hatred of the Cooks who were denuding potential settlers' lots of their most desirable wealth, their pines. Now it so happened that 1877 was the beginning of a crucial era in the affairs of the Cooks and of the settlers in the Peninsula. In reviewing the period one should bear in mind a certain fact which may have been a relevant factor in the situation—Hiram Cook was a member of Parliament from 1872 to 1878. During these years he represented the North Riding of Simcoe; later, from 1882 to 1891, he sat for the East Riding of the same county.

How long after 1863 Cook and Brothers carried on in Keppel no record is left to tell. In 1870 Lindsay and St. Edmunds, the two northern townships of the Peninsula, were opened for settlement and lumbering. Here was a great opportunity for a company used to working on a large scale. Contrary to the tradition persisting in the Peninsula to this day, the primeval forest of the upper townships abounded in pines of a size and quality suitable for making into the square timber keenly sought by the British lumber trade. If the present tradition were true the Cooks would never have given a moment's thought to the region. As for prospective settlers in this area, they in their eargerness to become their own landlords did not always pause to calculate what a paralysing handicap the possible loss of their pine would prove to be when they actually began clearing and occupying their farm lots. The system was essentially unjust though it was the fruit of good intentions: by sale of the former Indian lands the Government aimed to augment as rapidly as possibly the capital fund held in trust for the Indians.

Through an analysis of the Cook licences made in May of 1882 for Sir John A. Macdonald by the then Deputy Superintendent-General of Indian Affairs, A. Vankoughnet, we now know the history of the Cooks' association with Lindsay and St. Edmunds. On February 4, 1870, Cook and Brothers applied to the Superintendent of Indian Lands in Toronto for a licence to cut timber on 71 square miles of these townships. The application was relayed to Ottawa; the Honourable Joseph Howe, the Superintendent-General at the time, ruled that the area requested was excessive and that the applicant must be content with 50 square miles. This, one cannot refrain from observing, was one-tenth of the area of the whole Peninsula. The Cooks accepted the decision and the licence was issued in 1871. The licensees, shrewd though they were, failed to read the wording of the licence carefully; later, this oversight turned out to be fatal. As Vankoughnet pointed out to the Prime Minister, the licence permitted its holder to cut on the limits specified *square timber and sawlogs of all descriptions of timber*—that is, of all species of trees—*and not specifically pine.* Actually, however, for years the Cooks sought and cut nothing but pine.

In May, 1871, a separate licence was granted to Simon S. Cook to separate limits of 47 square miles in the same two townships but it restricted him to *pine sawlogs alone*; not long afterward the permit was enlarged to include *squared pine timbers.* In September, 1875, and October, 1874, respectively, the Cook Brothers and the Simon S. Cook licences were renewed.

When they took over their new ample limits the Cook Brothers began operating on the grand scale long known on the Ottawa and the Trent. At the southeast corner of Shouldice Lake, in Lindsay, they built a huge "camboose" camp; its main building housed a full gang of 82 men. Charles Williams says that it was a typical "camboose" shanty; this means that it was rectangular in plan, about 46 feet long and 38 wide. In the centre of its roof, which was made of log "scoops," was a square opening between 8 and 10 feet broad. Directly below this was an earth-floored fireplace on which fires of great logs served for heating the spacious single room and for cooking the loggers' meals. Tiers of double bunks lined three walls of the room. This building, with its accessory cabins and sheds, was designated Cook Bros. Camp No. 1. For all we know now it may have been the only camp of its type ever set up in the Peninsula.

Up to 1877 a settler's terms of purchase, as summarized later by an Acting Deputy Minister, were, on paper, simple and easy. One-fifth of the purchasing price was to be paid at the time of the sale and the remainder liquidated in four equal yearly instalments with interest at the rate of 6 per cent. The settler was required to meet two other conditions: (*a*) continuous occupation and residence for three years and the clearing and fencing of five acres per 100 of the quantity purchased; (*b*) no exportation or sale of timber until conditions of occupation and sale had been fully complied with, *except under licence.*

But the lot of the settler was not simple and easy; it was atrociously hard. His soil was either too scant or too patchy to assure him enough food for his table, let alone enough dollars to pay the annual instalments on his purchase. The trees growing on his acres were his whole substance—his food, his shelter, his oxen, his horses, even the promise of his ultimate title to his domain, as one of his fervent defenders passionately told the House of Commons. But the owner of the trees was not really their master; he was not free to do with them as he wished. Before completing the purchase of his land he could not lawfully fell any of his trees for gainful purposes unless he had paid for a licence to do so, and then, on top of that, had remitted heavy dues to the Indian Department for the timber he had removed. The net profit on his outlay of money, enterprise, and labour was generally zero—and often less. Conditions were such as to frighten away from certain parts many a person who thought seriously of taking up land in the Peninsula. For instance, after 1870 on many square miles of Lindsay and St. Edmunds big timber operators had first claim upon the pines within their limits. Most of the red and white pines cut here were made into square "sticks" for export to Britain. What prospective settler in his right mind was willing to take up a farm lot in a forest stripped of its most valuable form of natural wealth? Yet the day was to come when the purchaser of a lot which he intended to clear for cultivation suffered the extreme anguish of having to stand by utterly helpless while before his eyes his property was despoiled by others of what he needed most in setting up a homestead on the frontier.

But the colonists would not let their misery numb them into silence. Their unceasing protests fairly deafened the Indian Department at Ottawa. In 1869 Alex. Sproat, the member for North Bruce, in the plainest of language told the House of Commons the story of gross injustice. Made desperate by official indifference and inaction, in March of 1872 a company of representative men of the Peninsula met at Wiarton and drew up a petition containing many sound, practical suggestions for righting the major evils. A deputation took the document to Ottawa. The response to it was little more than merely formal—a promise to consider cases of exceptional hardship; a lukewarm attempt to "deflate" in slight measure the "inflated" values of the sale in 1856.[1] The petitioners' gain, if any at all came from their effort, was too minute for them to sense it.

Late in 1873 Alexander Mackenzie and his Government came into power at Ottawa. The new Minister of the Interior, David Laird, with the efficiency of a new broom, spent part of the summer of 1875 in the Bruce Peninsula. After seeing the lamentable conditions of the colonists he announced certain measures of relief before the year was out. Provision was made that each settler's case would be dealt with on its merits; that interest would be remitted up to that year; that the scale of timber dues would be lowered. For the first time the long-suffering settlers believed they saw the dawn of a brighter day. But their hope was deceptive.

During the first few years of cutting pine on their limits in the Peninsula the Cooks found themselves stalled here and there by a certain exasperating condition: as soon as a settler purchased a farm lot within the Cooks' limits the pine on the property was his and the big fellow could not touch it. Hiram Cook declared that this provision did not allow large-scale operators time enough to make any profit on their investment; their right to cut should be extended to five years from the date of the Department's sale to the settler. Upon conferring with other lumber operators on Indian lands in Manitoulin and Algoma Cook found them sharing his opinion but learned that they would be content with an extension of three years. This exchange of views took place in 1877; some of the correspondence still exists. Cook laid the case

1. In 1897 and 1898 the Government once more resorted to "deflation" in regard to these same lands. Does a country, one wonders, ever really recover from the ills of severe inflation?

before the Honourable David Laird, now Superintendent-General
of Indian Affairs in the Mackenzie Government, who promised
that he himself would introduce a bill to lengthen the term of
cutting rights to three years. But Laird deferred action so long
that the lumbermen became impatient. R. A. Lyon, whose chief
limits were on Manitoulin Island, wrote a letter to E. B. Borron,
Government member for Algoma, requesting him to write to the
Honourable David Mills, who had succeeded Laird as Superintendent-General, urging him to pass a measure granting relief
to the distressed lumbermen on former Indian lands. He bolstered
his plea by pointing out that such a step would ease the Government's concern over the sluggish growth of the capital fund
held in trust by the Crown for the Indians. The change would
enable the woodsmen to cut much more timber and thus increase
the total of dues paid and earmarked for the benefit of the
Indians. Besides, no real harm would be done to *bona fide* settlers,
he claimed, through the proposed reservation of pine on their
lands. The effort spent upon this correspondence in April and
May of 1877 produced positive results in November; on the
twentieth day of that month an Order-in-Council was signed
providing for the easement requested by Cook and others; it was
announced by Mr. Mills on December 1.

All pine trees [reads the Order], being or growing upon any Indian land
hereafter sold, and at the time of such sale, or previously, included in any
timber license, shall be considered as reserved from such sale, and such
land shall be subject to any timber license covering the same, which may be
in force at the time of such sale, or may be granted within three years from
the date of such sale; and all pine trees of larger growth than twelve inches
in diameter at the butt may be cut and removed from such land, under a
timber license lawfully in force;

But the purchaser of the land, or those claiming under the purchaser, may
cut and use such trees as may be necessary for the purpose of building,
fencing and fuel on the land so purchased; and may also cut and dispose of
(but the latter only under a settler's license, duly obtained from the local
Indian Superintendent or Agent) all trees required to be removed in
actually clearing the land for cultivation, but no pine trees, except for
necessary building, fencing and fuel, as aforesaid, shall be cut beyond the
limit of such actual clearing before the issue of the patent for such land; and
any pine trees so cut and disposed of, except for said necessary building,
fencing and fuel, as aforesaid, shall be subject to the payment of regular
dues, and 50 per cent added thereto for trespass fine.

All trees on the land when the patent issues, to become the property of
the patentee.

To the settlers rejoicing in the recent lightening of an old
anxiety the publication of the Order-in-Council was like a bolt

from the blue. It scared prospective settlers away as if the region
were the scene of a deadly plague. That the Cooks did not fail
to try to take the toll of the settler the law allowed them is proved
by a letter that lies before me. On one of its pages Robert
Lymburner states that in 1881 his father, Horace Lymburner,
purchased land near Gillies Lake within the limits held first by
Cook Brothers and later by their successors. One day he received
from the latter a bill for 29 pine trees. Lymburner, fully aware
of the new conditions, replied curtly, admitting that he had cut
exactly 29 pines but solely for the erection of buildings required
for permanent occupancy of his tract of land. That was the last
he ever heard of the matter.

In the months that followed neither settlers nor operators were
idle. New injustice heaped upon an old unhealed injury goaded
the settlers into fury. The lumbermen hastened to take stock of
their future. It soon became plain to them that the production of
square timber in the Peninsula and elsewhere in eastern Ontario
was nearing its end. Rereading the text of their licences (or, as it
turned out, *mis*reading it) the Cooks thought they saw a bright
spot ahead. The licence conferred the right to cut all descriptions
of timber. The abundance of white cedar on the Peninsula offered
a wonderful opportunity to fulfil the demands of the railways for
ties, posts, and poles. On balance promise prevailed over the
unpromising.

Through an agent the Cook Brothers took the promise to North
Britain. There, despite the notorious fiasco of British investments
in Grand Trunk Railway shares, they quickly found a number of
Scots ready to put money into a project for developing Canada's
forest wealth. These set up a company with headquarters, president, and directors in Edinburgh, to take over the 97 square
miles of the Cooks' limits in The Bruce; the Company was
adorned with a grandiose title—British-Canadian Timber and
Lumbering Company. Into the new firm the shareholders put
the sum of £102,000, a good half-million of dollars. Whether or
not the Cook Brothers had any stock is not known, though it is
certain that Hiram Henry Cook was appointed manager. The
assignment to the overseas company of the licences of Cook
Brothers and of Simon S. Cook was made known to the public
in November of 1880.

The prospect of legalized "denudation" of their lands spurred the
settlers to besiege the Indian Department at Ottawa. No official

in his senses could fail to see that such a demonstration was prompted by the fear of some unusual menace. At last the way was opened to Sir John Macdonald, who had returned to power in 1878. To a strong delegation of representative citizens of the Peninsula he granted an interview and out of this interview there soon arose a difference between the Company and the Government. The point in dispute was whether the Cooks' original licences, now held by the Scottish corporation, permitted the cutting of every kind of timber or of pine alone. An analysis made by Mr. Vankoughnet, the Deputy Superintendent-General, disclosed a fact which we have already noted in these pages: the Cook Brothers' licence though giving the right to cut "every description of timber" restricted the holder to sawlogs and the making of square timber. But who in that day wanted sawlogs and square timber of, say, poplar, balsam, or cedar? Only cedar posts, ties, and poles were what the British-Canadian Company sought for then. On the other hand, the Simon S. Cook licence limited cutting to pine exclusively. The reputed shrewdness of big business had slipped badly.

On May 24, 1882, Sir D. L. Macpherson, Minister of the Interior, instructed Vankoughnet to inform the British-Canadian Company of the Prime Minister's request that their cutting be restricted to pine. The notice was accepted under protest but with such ill grace that the Department refused to renew the licences without further instructions from Sir John. The Company went ahead without a licence and cut a quantity of timber other than pine. This was seized by the Department. Court action was instituted but was halted at the request of Sir John. In December of 1882 permission was given the Company to continue operations on the old basis until April 30, 1883. A survey of the whole region was then made by the Department. The outcome was that the land was divided into two categories—one suitable for settlement, the other only for lumbering. The Department declined to renew the former Cook licences but offered to grant permission to cut timber exclusively on lands of the second category. The only inference to be drawn is that the offer was not taken up by the Company, since on June 24, 1884, B. B. Miller, Indian Land Agent at Wiarton, reported that in his territory no timber licences were in effect.

INDEX